CONSECRATION
TO ST. JOSEPH

THE WONDERS OF
OUR SPIRITUAL FATHER

By Donald H. Calloway, MIC

Available from:
Marian Helpers Center
Stockbridge, MA 01263

Prayerline: 1-800-804-3823
Orderline: 1-800-462-7426
Websites: fathercalloway.com
consecrationtostjoseph.org

Publication Date:
January 1, 2020. Solemnity of Mary, Mother of God
In Honor of the 150th Anniversary of the Proclamation of St. Joseph
as Patron of the Universal Church (1870-2020)

† IMPRIMATUR †
Most Rev. Jeffrey Monforton, DD
Bishop of Steubenville, Ohio
October 22, 2019

Imprimi Potest
Very Rev. Kazimierz Chwalek, MIC
Provincial Superior
The Blessed Virgin Mary, Mother of Mercy Province
October 10, 2019

Nihil Obstat
Dr. Robert A. Stackpole, STD
Censor Deputatus
August 31, 2019

Note: The *Nihil Obstat* and corresponding *Imprimatur* and/or *Imprimi Potest* is
not a certification that those granting it agree with the contents, opinions, or
statements expressed in the work; instead, it merely confirms that it contains
nothing contrary to faith or morals.

Library of Congress Catalog Number: 2019953316
ISBN: 978-1-59614-431-6

Cover Image: The artist of the cover image is unknown. All attempts have been made
by Marian Press to locate and give credit to the artist. In the event that the identity of
the artist becomes known, all due recognition will be given in future editions.

Acknowledgments: Mr. and Mrs. Donald & LaChita Calloway,
Matthew T. Calloway, Ileana E. Salazar, Teresa de Jesus Macias,
Milanka Lachman, Bethany Price, Fr. Richard Heilman, Colleen Faley

Printed in the United States of America

Dedication

*To the many people who prayed that
this book would come to fruition.
Your prayers and sacrifices made it happen!*

Thank you!

Table of Contents

INTRODUCTION

I did not understand him [St. Joseph] well enough, but that will change [1]

— St. John of the Cross

In the 16th century, St. John of the Cross, one of the greatest mystics of the Church, humbly acknowledged that he lacked a proper understanding of the greatness of St. Joseph. Inspired by the tremendous love that his friend, St. Teresa of Avila, had for St. Joseph, St. John of the Cross made a firm resolution to get to know and love St. Joseph better.

What about you? Do you know St. Joseph? Do you feel you understand his greatness and love for you? Well, my friends, get ready! *Consecration to St. Joseph* is going to unveil the wonders of St. Joseph like never before!

Now is the time of St. Joseph!

It's a bold claim, I admit. Yet I truly believe that in our day the Lord wants to direct our hearts, families, parishes, dioceses, and Church to St. Joseph in a major way. This action of the Holy Spirit in the life of the Church has been gaining momentum for a very long time.

Don't get me wrong: Saint Joseph has always held a special place in Christians' hearts. Across the centuries, saints, popes, mystics, scholars, and laity alike have praised and extolled the greatness of St. Joseph. In the 16th century, the Holy Spirit used St. Teresa of Avila to bring about a greater awareness of St. Joseph in the Church. Even before St. Teresa, saints such as St. Bernard of Clairvaux, St. Bernardine of Siena, and St. Lawrence of Brindisi strongly emphasized the greatness of St. Joseph.

In more recent times, Blessed William Joseph Chaminade, St. Peter Julian Eymard, Blessed Petra of St. Joseph, and St. André Bessette have kept devotion to St. Joseph prominent in the lives of God's people. Indeed, St. André Bessette initiated construction on what has become the world's largest church dedicated to St. Joseph — St. Joseph's Oratory in Montreal, Canada. Saint José Manyanet, a priest in 19th-century Spain, fervently promoted devotion to St. Joseph and the Holy Family. He prophesied that a "time of St. Joseph" would soon arrive in the life of the Church. He wrote:

> I believe that the true time of Saint Joseph has not arrived yet: after two thousand years we started only now to glimpse something of the mystery in which he is immersed.[2]

Well, my friends, guess what? Now is the time of St. Joseph! How can I state this with such conviction? Simple: God has given us clear indications that he wants his people to pay more attention to St. Joseph — clearer indications than in any previous era in Church history. In 1961, St. Pope John XXIII put it very bluntly. He wrote:

> In the Holy Church's worship, right from the beginning, Jesus, the Word of God made man, has enjoyed the adoration that belongs to him, incommunicable as the splendor of the substance of his Father, a splendor reflected in the glory of his saints. From the earliest times, Mary, his mother, was close behind him, in the pictures in the catacombs and the basilicas, where she was devoutly venerated as "Holy Mother of God." But Joseph, except for some slight sprinkling of references to him here and there in the writings of the Fathers [of the Church], for long centuries remained in the background, in his characteristic concealment, almost as a decorative figure in the overall picture of the Savior's life. It took time for devotion to him to go beyond those passing glances and take root in the hearts of the faithful, and then surge forth in the form of special prayers and of a profound sense of trusting abandonment. The fervent joy of pouring forth these deepest feelings of the heart in so many impressive ways has been saved for modern times![3]

What the Vicar of Christ clearly stated is that *now* is the time of St. Joseph. We are living in modern times, the time in which the Church is witnessing an unprecedented era of devotion to St. Joseph. According to St. Pope John XXIII, God desires devotion to St. Joseph to surge forth in our day in the form of special prayers of "trusting abandonment." This means one thing in particular: *It's time for total consecration to St. Joseph!*

Let me explain further about how God has been leading the Church to this moment.

In 2018, I published a daily devotional to St. Joseph entitled *St. Joseph Gems: Daily Wisdom on Our Spiritual Father*. In the introduction, I present a list of remarkable events — divine indicators, if you will — that have taken place over the past 150 years that show St. Joseph's increasing importance in the life of the Church. They clearly indicate that we are living in an unprecedented time of St. Joseph. Here's the list:

1868 — Blessed Jean-Joseph Lataste, OP, writes a letter to Blessed
Pope Pius IX asking him to declare St. Joseph the "Patron
of the Universal Church."

1870 Blessed Pope Pius IX declares St. Joseph the "Patron of the
Universal Church."

1871 — Founding of the Josephites by Cardinal Herbert A. Vaughan

1873 — Founding of the Congregation of St. Joseph by St.
Leonardo Murialdo

1878 — Founding of the Oblates of St. Joseph by St. Joseph Marello

1879 — Apparitions at Knock, Ireland. Saint Joseph appears with
the Blessed Virgin Mary, St. John the Apostle, and Jesus
(appearing as the Lamb of God).

1889 — Pope Leo XIII writes *Quamquam Pluries*, an encyclical
letter on St. Joseph.

1895 — Blessed Petra of St. Joseph begins construction on a shrine
to St. Joseph in Barcelona, Spain. It is consecrated in 1901.
At her beatification in 1994, St. John Paul II calls Blessed
Petra the "apostle of St. Joseph of the 19th century."

1904 — Saint André Bessette constructs an oratory dedicated to St.
Joseph in Montreal, Canada. It expands, is declared a minor
basilica, and finally is completed in 1967. Today, it is known
as St. Joseph's Oratory and is considered by many to be the
preeminent international center of devotion to St. Joseph.

1908 — Saint Luigi Guanella begins constructing a church dedicated
to St. Joseph in Rome. It is completed and consecrated as a
basilica in 1912.

1909 — Saint Pope Pius X officially approves the Litany of St. Joseph.

1914 — Saint Luigi Guanella founds the Pious Union of St. Joseph
for the Salvation of the Dying.

1917 — Apparitions at Fatima, Portugal. During the last apparition
on October 13, St. Joseph appears holding the Child Jesus
and blessing the world.

1921 — Pope Benedict XV inserts the phrase "Blessed be St. Joseph,
her most chaste spouse" into the Divine Praises.

1947 — Spanish Discalced Carmelites found *Estudios Josefinos*, the
first theological journal devoted to St. Joseph.

1950s — The alleged apparitions of Our Lady of America given to Sr.
Mary Ephrem emphasize a renewed devotion to St. Joseph,
and St. Joseph himself speaks to the visionary about this
devotion.

1955 — Venerable Pope Pius XII establishes the Feast of St. Joseph
the Worker, to be celebrated on May 1.

1962 — Saint Pope John XXIII inserts St. Joseph's name into the
Canon of the Mass (Eucharistic Prayer I).

1989 — Saint Pope John Paul II writes *Redemptoris Custos*, an
apostolic exhortation on St. Joseph.

2013 — Pope Francis, echoing and fulfilling the intentions of Pope Emeritus Benedict XVI, inserts the name of St. Joseph into all Eucharistic Prayers. He also consecrates Vatican City State to St. Joseph.

Whoa! Did you know all that? Most people are unaware of these remarkable events. Without exaggeration, the Church has done more to promote St. Joseph in the last 150 years than in the previous 1,800 years of Christianity! But why now? Why St. Joseph?

There are many reasons, but I believe there are two that are especially important.

First, we need the spiritual fatherhood of St. Joseph to help us protect marriage and the family. Marriage and the family have always been under attack, but in modern times, the threats have reached extraordinary heights. Many people no longer know what it means to be a man or a woman, let alone what constitutes a marriage and a family. Many countries even claim to have redefined marriage and the family. There is great confusion on these matters, greater confusion than in any previous era of human history. The Servant of God Sr. Lucia dos Santos, the longest-lived visionary of the Fatima apparitions, knew the seriousness of the times and made a powerful statement about this issue. She wrote:

> The final battle between the Lord and the kingdom of Satan will be about marriage and the family.[4]

To combat and overcome Satan's deceptions, the Church needs St. Joseph. His example and protection are the only way out of the confusing mess we are in. Who else can we turn to who can help us understand what marriage and the family are all about if not to the Head of the Holy Family and the Terror of Demons?

Second, the entire world needs to be re-evangelized, including the vast majority of baptized Christians. Saint Joseph was the first missionary. Today, he desires again to bring Jesus to the nations. Many nations and cultures that were previously Christian have fallen away from their Christian roots and are on a path of self-destruction. Countries once established on Judeo-Christian principles have become overrun by ideologies and organizations that seek to strip society of all that is sacred. Without a major turnaround, civilization itself is going to self-destruct.

In an apostolic exhortation on St. Joseph in 1989, St. John Paul II reminded us of the necessity of invoking St. Joseph in the work of re-evangelizing the world. He wrote:

> This patronage [of St. Joseph] must be invoked as ever necessary for the Church, not only as a defense against all dangers, but also, and indeed primarily, as an impetus for her renewed commitment to evangelization in the world and to re-evangelization in those lands and nations where religion and the Christian life were formerly flourishing and are now put to a hard test.[5]

Now is the time to consecrate yourself to St. Joseph! God is telling his Church that, in order to defend marriage and the family, elevate morals, recover lost ground, and win souls for Jesus Christ, we need to bring St. Joseph onto the battlefield. He is the Terror of Demons! With his powerful spiritual fatherhood, incredible love for his spiritual children, and constant intercession, the Church can be renewed as a light to the nations, a beautiful city on a hill (see Mt 5:14-16)!

What exactly is consecration to St. Joseph? In other words, what does it mean for a person to be consecrated to St. Joseph? Well, it basically means that you acknowledge that he is your spiritual father, and you want to be like him. To show it, you entrust yourself entirely to his paternal care so that he can lovingly help you acquire his virtues and become holy. Total consecration to St. Joseph means you make a formal act of filial entrustment to your spiritual father so that he can take care of your spiritual well-being and lead you to God. The person who consecrates himself to St. Joseph wants to be as close to their spiritual father as possible, to the point of resembling him in virtue and holiness. Saint Joseph, in turn, will give those consecrated to him his loving attention, protection, and guidance.

Perhaps someone reading this has already consecrated themselves entirely to the Blessed Virgin Mary, and is wondering if they can consecrate themselves to St. Joseph and entrust everything to him, as well. The answer is a resounding *"Yes!"* God desires that all children be committed to the love and care of a mother and a father. You are not a member of a single-parent spiritual family. Mary is your spiritual mother, and St. Joseph is your spiritual father. The spiritual fatherhood of St. Joseph is extremely important for your spiritual growth. Total consecration to Mary is not diminished by total consecration to St. Joseph. Mary wants you to consecrate yourself to St. Joseph! Everything you have given to Jesus and Mary can also be given to St. Joseph. Be at peace. The Hearts of Jesus, Mary, and St. Joseph are one.

"How is consecration to St. Joseph done?" you ask. To be honest, there are an endless number of ways. A simple prayer of entrustment is sufficient. However, if you truly want to understand the greatness of your spiritual father, it is best to follow a thorough program of preparation and consecration. Such a program should cover St. Joseph's person, privileges, titles, and virtues, especially his paternal love for God the Son and the rest of humanity. *Consecration to St. Joseph* offers a comprehensive program of preparation and consecration to St. Joseph for individuals, families, parishes, and dioceses. Through this program, I hope to spark the first worldwide movement of consecration to St. Joseph!

So what's the program? What's the method? Well, as I prayed about how to organize this preparation for consecration to St. Joseph, I thought it best to emulate the tried-and-true 33-day preparation method employed by St. Louis de Montfort in his Marian consecration. Why re-invent the wheel, right? The method of 33-day preparation is simple, straightforward, and allows a person to cover the subject matter quite well. Saint Louis de Montfort's method of preparation also requires a very important element: prayer.

Like St. Louis de Montfort's program of Marian consecration, *Consecration to St. Joseph* has three parts.

PART I
33-Day Preparation

Before you start the 33-day preparation, you need to pick a consecration date (Day 33), which will then guide you to a beginning date. You are free to begin and end on any day you like, but I have provided a chart on page 10 that lists the liturgical feasts associated with St. Joseph. Personally, I think it is best to choose a date for your consecration that coincides with a liturgical feast of St. Joseph. It is very important for you to remember that the consecration date is Day 33.

As for the content of the 33-day preparation, the Litany of St. Joseph serves as the template for the program. The Litany of St. Joseph is a powerful prayer and will help you come to know and love your spiritual father. The Litany of St. Joseph highlights many of St. Joseph's titles, privileges, and heroic virtues. On each day of the 33-day preparation (Day 1 and Day 2 are the only exceptions), a short exposition on one of the invocations in the Litany of St. Joseph is presented (in Part I), followed by a reading on St. Joseph (a section

Litany of St. Joseph

of Part II), concluding with the recitation of the Litany of St. Joseph (found in Part III). Following this method, you will come to know and love St. Joseph in a deeper way, and be prepared for total consecration to your spiritual father. The 33-day preparation requires about 20 to 30 minutes a day. Oh, and if you miss a day, don't panic. Just make it up and continue your preparation. You can do this!

PART II
The Wonders of Our Spiritual Father

Part II contains the material for the readings assigned on each day of the 33-day preparation. The majority of the readings are short. Ten of them are a little longer, but don't worry. None of them are burdensome. Trust me: You are going to fall in love with St. Joseph as a result of these readings.

I have designed Part II to be a book within a book. What this means is that Part II is to be used for each day of the 33-day preparation, but it can also be read as its own book, apart from the 33-day preparation.

Let me explain why I set it up this way.

Most likely, the majority of people who acquire *Consecration to St. Joseph* are going to go straight into the 33-day preparation. However, there might be some people who get the book but are not quite ready for consecration to St. Joseph. Some people might feel that they want to get to know St. Joseph better before committing to a month-long preparation for consecration to a saint they don't know much about. Those folks can skip Part I (the 33-day preparation) and simply read Part II as its own book. You should know, though, that if you choose to read Part II without doing the 33-day preparation, you will need to re-read the assigned sections from Part II if you decide to do the 33-day preparation. (The designated daily reading from Part II follows a different order when you do it with the 33-day preparation in Part I.)

So why is Part II called *The Wonders of Our Spiritual Father?* I could give you a long answer, but I'll let St. Josemaría Escrivá give you a hint. He states:

St. Josemaría Escrivá

> Saint Joseph, more than anyone else before or since, learned from Jesus to be alert to recognize God's wonders.[6]

Our God is a God of wonders! One of his greatest wonders is St. Joseph. The wonders of your spiritual father are about to be revealed to you like never before. Naturally, there are a lot of wonders associated with St. Joseph, but in researching and writing this book, I discovered that there are 10 wonders of St. Joseph that really stand out. In focusing your attention on these 10 wonders, you will acquire a fuller picture of who St. Joseph is and why you should deeply love him.

PART III
Prayers to St. Joseph

Part III of your preparation for consecration to St. Joseph is extremely important. It involves prayer. Your preparation for consecration to St. Joseph *must* include prayer. Daily prayer. Without daily prayer, your preparation for consecration to St. Joseph would only impart information about St. Joseph and not help you to acquire a filial relationship with St. Joseph. You definitely need to know many things about St. Joseph, but it is very important that you also fall in love with him. Daily prayer to St. Joseph will help you develop a loving relationship with your spiritual father. For this reason, the book not only unpacks the Litany of St. Joseph for its theological richness, but also leads you to pray the Litany on a daily basis. By the end of the 33 days, you might just find that you have the Litany of St. Joseph memorized!

Part III includes several acts of consecration to St. Joseph, as well as many other prayers to your spiritual father. On the day of your consecration, feel free to use whichever act of consecration you like best; you can also make up your own, if you like. If you are doing the preparation and consecration as a group, it is recommended that you all recite the same consecration prayer together as a group. You will also find the *Veni, Sancte Spiritus* prayer in this section.

At the end of the book, you will find the instructions on "How to Make the 33-Day Preparation and Consecration as a Group" (see page 249). Everything you need to do for the weekly group meetings is provided, as well as discussion questions for each meeting. The group preparation and consecration is perfect for parishes and prayer groups. Everything your group needs to do the preparation and consecration is contained in one book. (Each person does need to have their own book, though.)

Consecration to St. Joseph concludes with a meditation for the Solemnity of St. Joseph by Blessed William Joseph Chaminade; an incredible article by Fr. Reginald Garrigou-Lagrange, OP; a brief list of churches and shrines dedicated to St. Joseph around the world; and beautiful artwork that has been exclusively commissioned for this book.

My dear friend, you are about to embark on a journey that is going to change your life. To be close to St. Joseph is a special grace from God. By making this 33-day preparation and consecration to St. Joseph, you will be truly blessed. In his day, St. Maximilian Kolbe asked the question, "Who are you, O Immaculate Conception?" He sought to provide an answer to that question through his preaching, writing, and an apostolate of Marian consecration. Today, many people are asking a similar question about St. Joseph: "Who are you, St. Joseph?" *Consecration to St. Joseph* will answer that question and offer to the Church a renewed understanding and appreciation of the great St. Joseph.

Now is the time for consecration to St. Joseph!

Very Rev. Donald H. Calloway, MIC, STL
Vicar Provincial — Marian Fathers of the Immaculate Conception
Blessed Virgin Mary, Mother of Mercy Province

← Veni, Sancte, Spiritus

← Solemnity of St Joseph

Consecration Chart

START OF THE 33 DAYS	FEAST DAY	CONSECRATION DAY
December 22	Feast of the Holy Spouses*	January 23
January 1	Presentation of the Lord	February 2
February 15**	Solemnity of St. Joseph	March 19
March 30	St. Joseph the Worker	May 1
April 11	Our Lady of Fatima	May 13
July 20	Our Lady of Knock	August 21
September 30	All Saints	November 1
November 8	Our Lady of Loreto	December 10
November***	Holy Family	December

* For more on this feast, see pg. 125.

** During a leap year, when February has 29 days, the starting date is February 16.

*** The Solemnity of the Holy Family generally falls on the First Sunday after Christmas. If Christmas itself is on a Sunday, be sure to check what day the bishops designate as the Solemnity of the Holy Family and begin your consecration 32 days before the consecration date (Day 33).

PART I
33-Day Preparation

DAY 1

Why Consecration to St. Joseph?

When God wishes to raise a soul to greater heights, he unites it to St. Joseph by giving it a strong love for the good saint.[1]

— St. Peter Julian Eymard

Do you want to ascend to greater heights in the spiritual life? Consecration to St. Joseph will take you there.

Many Christians have consecrated themselves to the Virgin Mary so as to be more closely united to Jesus. Without a doubt, consecration to Mary is one of the best things you can do for your spiritual life. The essence of Marian consecration is to help you become "another Mary" for Jesus, a faithful, loving, and trusting companion of the Savior. Consecration to St. Joseph does something similar.

CONSECRATION TO ST. JOSEPH WILL HELP YOU BECOME "ANOTHER JOSEPH" FOR JESUS AND MARY. That is, entrusting yourself entirely to St. Joseph helps you become a faithful, loving, and trusting companion of Jesus and Mary!

In the New Testament, we read that Jesus "increased in wisdom and in stature, and in favor with God and man" (Lk 2:52) under the watchful care of his parents. Such an "increase" can happen to you, too, if you entrust yourself to the paternal care of St. Joseph. Saint Bernard of Clairvaux explains how it works. He writes:

> Who and what manner of man this blessed Joseph was, you may conjecture from the name by which, a dispensation being allowed, he deserved to be so honored as to be believed and to be called the father of God. You may conjecture it from his very name, which, being interpreted, means "Increase."[2]

Saint Joseph is "The Increaser." He has paternal love for you and the power to increase the presence of God in your life and take you to greater heights in the spiritual life. For centuries, this "secret" of St. Joseph lay hidden. Saints, mystics, and a handful of popes knew of it. Now it is your turn to discover it.

NOW IS THE TIME OF ST. JOSEPH! The Church and the world greatly need St. Joseph. We need him to help us return to the love of Jesus and to living lives of virtue. We desperately need St. Joseph's protection

13

as well. The family — the foundation of society — is under attack. The family of God — the Catholic Church — is also undergoing vicious assaults from the world, the flesh, the devil, and some of her own children. We need St. Joseph to protect us. He is our loving and merciful spiritual father, holy, strong, and ready to help. He is forever linked to Jesus, Mary, and the Church. He protected the Holy Family; he will protect us, too, if we entrust ourselves to his paternal heart and his spiritual care.

SAINT JOSEPH IS YOUR SPIRITUAL FATHER. All children resemble their parents. You are a child of St. Joseph. You need to resemble him, especially by imitating his virtues and faithfulness to Jesus and Mary. Saint Joseph plays a vital (life-giving) role in your spiritual growth and well-being. This is the heart of consecration to St. Joseph. Blessed William Joseph Chaminade explains it well. He states:

> He [St. Joseph] was not a passive instrument in the great work of our salvation; he played a very active role, and that is why he was included in the merciful counsels of the incarnate Wisdom.[3]

The merciful love of God has given St. Joseph to you as a spiritual father. Are you ready to ascend to greater heights in the spiritual life? Are you ready to draw nearer to Jesus and Mary, and experience an increase in virtue? Let's go to Joseph!

> We are going to consecrate ourselves to St. Joseph. We shall place at his feet all that we are and all that we have.[4]
>
> — St. Peter Julian Eymard

Pray the *Veni, Sancte Spiritus* (page 247)*
Pray the Litany of St. Joseph (page 233)

* If the 33-day preparation is being done by a group, the *Veni, Sancte Spiritus* has already been prayed.

DAY 2

The Litany of St. Joseph

Knowing by experience St. Joseph's astonishing influence with God, I would wish to persuade everyone to honor him with particular devotion. I have always seen those who honored him in a special manner make progress in virtue, for this heavenly protector favors in a striking manner the spiritual advancement of souls who commend themselves to him.[1]

— St. Teresa of Avila

You have probably heard of St. Maximilian Kolbe, the heroic priest who gave his life for another prisoner in the concentration camp at Auschwitz. Saint Maximilian was a zealous promoter of Our Lady and Marian consecration. He founded the Militia Immaculatae in 1917 to spread devotion to Our Lady around the world. But have you heard of Fr. Joseph Kentenich, another great promoter of devotion to Our Lady?

In 1941, Fr. Kentenich was arrested by the Gestapo and put in prison in Germany. For medical reasons, the Nazis did not intend to send him to a concentration camp. Zealous for Our Lady, however, Fr. Kentenich requested he be sent to the concentration camp at Dachau. He wanted to offer his suffering for the Marian movement he had initiated in 1914, called Schoenstatt. He founded the Schoenstatt Movement in order to teach Our Lady's virtues to people and transform the world through Marian consecration. Father Kentenich spent three years in Dachau.

Father Kentenich's method of Marian consecration is known as the "covenant of love." He believed that a covenant of love with Mary would transform the world by turning the members of Schoenstatt into "apparitions of Mary." Not literal apparitions, of course; rather, by imitating Mary's virtues, the members of Schoenstatt would become reflections of Mary, "apparitions" of Our Lady, in the world. The Church and the world need such apparitions!

The Church and the world also need "apparitions" of St. Joseph: men and women who radiate the virtues of St. Joseph, especially his faithful love as a husband and father. In a world plagued with gender ideology and confusion about marriage and the family, reflections of Mary and St. Joseph are very much needed. Consecration to St. Joseph and imitation of his virtues will make this happen.

15

The Litany of St. Joseph will prepare you for total consecration to your spiritual father and teach you how to resemble his virtues. The litany dates back to at least the 16th century and has been prayed by countless saints. The version you will pray was approved and indulgenced by St. Pope Pius X in 1909. Through the Litany of St. Joseph, you will learn the virtues and wonders of your spiritual father and become an "apparition of St. Joseph" in the world.

> I take refuge in thy arms [St. Joseph], so that thou mayest lead me in the path of virtue.[2]
>
> — St. Clement Mary Hofbauer

Saint Joseph is your model for loving Jesus, Mary, and souls. Models are meant to be replicated. Through imitation of St. Joseph's virtues, you will become like your model and have a tremendous impact on the world. Saint Joseph's virtues will become your virtues. You are to become "another Joseph."

> His [St. Joseph's] eminent virtues constitute his merit and he becomes our model.[3]
>
> — Blessed William Joseph Chaminade

> St. Joseph is our guide and our model. Because our vocation is like his, we must live his life, practice his virtues, and assimilate his spirit.[4]
>
> — St. Peter Julian Eymard

> Let us love Jesus above all, let us love Mary as our mother; but then, how could we keep from loving Joseph, who was so intimately united to both Jesus and Mary? And how can we honor him better than by imitating his virtues? Now, what else did he do in all his life but contemplate, study, and adore Jesus, even in the midst of his daily labors? Behold, therefore, our model.[5]
>
> — St. Madeleine Sophie Barat

Pray the Litany of St. Joseph (page 233)
Pray the *Memorare* to St. Joseph (page 240)

DAY 3

God, the Father of Heaven,
Have Mercy on Us

Our heavenly Father has had only one saint to represent him on earth. Hence he bestowed everything he could on that favored saint, and equipped him with all that he needed to be his worthy representative.[1]

— St. Peter Julian Eymard

God the Father loves you. He loves you so much that he sent his Son into the world to save you. But saving you is not all the Father sent his Son to do for you. He sent his Son to save you *and* make you a child of God. Through Jesus, you are able to have a filial relationship with God the Father. Through Jesus, you can cry out, "Abba, Father!"

(1) Save us (2) make us His children

To be a child of God is why you were created; it's the very purpose for which you exist. And there is only one way to the Father: Jesus Christ (see Jn 14:6). Only Jesus has the power to take you to the Father. Yet, in God's merciful love, St. Joseph plays a very important role in your spiritual growth and journey to the Father.

CONSECRATION TO ST. JOSEPH WILL INCREASE THE PRESENCE OF THE FATHER IN YOUR LIFE. We learn this truth from the life of Jesus himself. When the Heavenly Father sent his Son into the world to save us and make us his children, he selected one saint to represent him on earth: St. Joseph. Jesus, in living under the roof of St. Joseph and being his Son, gave us a personal example of total entrustment to St. Joseph. Jesus loved, obeyed, and imitated his earthly father. Saint Joseph is the only man that Jesus ever called father; Jesus delighted in being known as the "son of Joseph" (see Jn 6:42). We, too, should consider it an honor to be his children. If, according to the plans of the Father, Jesus needed St. Joseph, how much more do we need him, too!

THE FATHERHOOD OF ST. JOSEPH INCREASED THE PRESENCE OF THE HEAVENLY FATHER IN THE LIFE OF JESUS. Now, to be clear, St. Joseph is not God. He cannot add anything to the divine and eternal communion existing between God the Father and God the Son.

17

Nor can St. Joseph improve the ability of Jesus, as a Divine Person, to perpetually behold the presence of his Heavenly Father. Rather, St. Joseph was chosen to stand in the place of the Heavenly Father *according to the demands of Jesus' human nature.*

God the Father doesn't have a human nature. Every time Jesus saw St. Joseph, heard him speak, watched him work, or witnessed his chaste love for Mary, the humanity of Jesus witnessed a perfect reflection of the Heavenly Father.

> God chose to make Joseph his most tangible image on earth, the depository of all the rights of his divine paternity, the husband of that noble Virgin who is Mistress of angels and men.[2]
>
> — Blessed William Joseph Chaminade

WHAT THE HEAVENLY FATHER DID FOR JESUS, HE WANTS TO DO FOR YOU. God the Father wants you to entrust yourself to the loving paternal care of St. Joseph in a manner similar to God's entrustment of the human nature of Jesus to St. Joseph. God planned these entrustments, both of Jesus to St. Joseph and of the members of the Church to St. Joseph, from all eternity; they were not done haphazardly. Saint Joseph is the shadow of the Heavenly Father. He was the image and reflection of the Father for Jesus. God the Father wants you to accept St. Joseph as your spiritual father as well. Jesus is the one in whom we see most perfectly the image of the mercy and love of his heavenly Father (as he said: "He who has seen me has seen the Father" [Jn 14:9]), but Jesus also wants to share with us the one who was for him the earthly image of his heavenly Father.

> This holy man [St. Joseph] had such towering dignity and glory that the Eternal Father most generously bestowed on him a likeness of his own primacy.[3]
>
> — St. Bernardine of Siena

Read "Our Spiritual Father" (page 100)
Pray the Litany of St. Joseph (page 233)

DAY 4

God, the Son, Redeemer of the World,
I have Mercy on Us

The holy example of Jesus Christ who, while upon earth, honored St. Joseph so highly and was obedient to him during his life
should be sufficient to inflame the hearts of all with devotion to
this saint.[1]

— St. Alphonsus Liguori

Are you familiar with the phrase *"To Jesus through Mary"*? It's a
wonderful expression of devotion coined in the early 18th century
by St. Louis de Montfort. In his book *True Devotion to Mary*, St.
Louis taught that Mary is the surest, easiest, and fastest way of going
to Jesus. To instill this message in people's hearts, St. Louis fervently
promoted the rosary and Marian consecration. What is interesting,
though, is that in all of St. Louis' writings, he only mentions St. Joseph
a few times. Why is that? Didn't he love St. Joseph? Oh yes, St. Louis
de Montfort loved St. Joseph very much. Every saint loves St. Joseph.
The reason he didn't offer any significant teaching on St. Joseph is
because the Church had not yet developed a theology of St. Joseph.

An understanding of the greatness of St. Joseph did not begin to
flourish in the devotional life of the Church until the mid-19th century,
100 years after St. Louis de Montfort lived. Were St. Louis de Montfort preaching in the streets of France today, he would most likely
be heard extolling the wonders of St. Joseph. He might even add
St. Joseph to his famous phrase, and say, *"To Jesus through Mary and
Joseph!"* Jesus wants you to know and love his mother *and* his father.

Mary and Joseph form the most faithful image of Jesus; and for
this reason I can formulate the shortest path to holiness: "For
me, to live is Jesus, it is Mary and Joseph."[2]

— Venerable Francis Xavier Nguyễn Văn Thuận

The two greatest saints in Christianity are Mary and St. Joseph.
Consecration to St. Joseph flows naturally from baptismal consecration
to Jesus Christ and filial consecration to Mary. Indeed, consecration
to St. Joseph, your spiritual father, allows you to be consecrated to
each person of the Holy Family!

In our day, marriage and family are under attack. Jesus and Mary want you to be consecrated to St. Joseph because there is no father or husband who knows more about the sacredness of marriage and the family or the self-sacrificing love required of fathers and husbands than St. Joseph. His paternal mission continues from heaven. He is our guardian, loving protector, and fearless defender. He is the model of saintly fatherhood. After Christ, St. Joseph is the model of heroic manhood and the defender of marriage, chastity, and life itself. Consecration to St. Joseph is the key to overcoming the anthropological confusion so prevalent in our times. Under the watchful, steadfast love and care of St. Joseph, all ideologies and idols will crumble and fall before Jesus Christ!

> How thou [St. Joseph] didst rejoice to have always near you God himself, and to see the idols of the Egyptians fall prostrate to the ground before him.[3]
>
> — Blessed Januarius Maria Sarnelli

CONSECRATION TO ST. JOSEPH WILL INCREASE YOUR LOVE FOR JESUS! The entire life and mission of St. Joseph points to Jesus. Saint Joseph never points to himself. His role is to lead everyone to Jesus, just as Mary does. Mary was predestined to be the Immaculate Mother of the Savior; St. Joseph was predestined to be the earthly father of the Savior and your spiritual father. Your spiritual father has been given all the graces necessary to complete his mission, a mission that includes increasing your relationship with Jesus.

> Joseph carried Jesus Christ first to Egypt, then to Judea, and so traced for us the path of the apostles who preached his name to the Jews and to the Gentiles.[4]
>
> — St. Hilary of Poitiers

> Saint Joseph was the guardian of Jesus and Mary. He was naturally also the one who introduced those souls eager to approach them more closely.[5]
>
> — Blessed Jean Joseph Lataste

Read "Privileges of Devotion to St. Joseph" (page 226)
Pray the Litany of St. Joseph (page 233)

DAY 5

Prayer

God, the Holy Spirit,
Have Mercy on Us

How great his [St. Joseph's] union with God, how sublime his gift of prayer, how wonderful the direction of the Holy Spirit![1]

— Blessed William Joseph Chaminade

The Holy Spirit wants you to know and love St. Joseph. With the exception of Our Lady's life, the Holy Spirit was more active in the life of St. Joseph than in any other saint. The earthly father of Jesus never did anything without seeking the direction of the Holy Spirit. Saint Joseph's docility to the Holy Spirit made it possible for him to communicate with God even while he slept! *Definition of Holiness*

SAINT JOSEPH WANTS YOU TO BE DOCILE TO THE DIRECTION OF THE HOLY SPIRIT SO THAT YOU CAN BE LED IN THE WAYS OF HOLINESS. What is holiness, anyway? Is it some unattainable spiritual summit you can never hope to reach? No, it is not. Holiness is living in intimate, loving communion with God. More specifically, holiness is observing the two great commandments of love of God and neighbor, avoiding sin, leading a life of virtue, and abiding in sanctifying grace. None of this is possible without the Holy Spirit in your life.

Wherever St. Joseph is present, the Holy Spirit is present. And St. Joseph would tell you that if you want to be filled with the Holy Spirit there is one absolutely necessary thing: prayer. Without prayer, you will never be able to have intimacy with God. Without prayer, you will not be able to follow the direction of the Holy Spirit.

To be holy, you need to imitate St. Joseph. You need to maintain a heart aflame with love of God and neighbor through committing to a devout interior life. Don't panic after reading this. You don't have to become a monk or a nun. Holiness is for everyone. Yet, no matter what your vocation in life, holiness is only attained by those who pray and have an active interior life, ignited and sustained by the Sacraments, fueled by prayer and a life of charity. *Holiness*

SAINT JOSEPH IS A MODEL OF THE INTERIOR LIFE FOR ALL HIS CHILDREN. Saint Joseph was not a priest, yet he is holier than all priests, including the patron saint of parish priests, St. John Vianney. After

21

Jesus and Mary, St. Joseph is the holiest, most prayerful, and most virtuous person who has ever lived. He avoided anything and everything that displeased the Holy Spirit. How did he do it? Prayer. Through prayer, St. Joseph perfectly exercised the virtues of faith, hope, and charity, as well as the moral virtues of prudence, temperance, justice, and fortitude.

> Consider that the entire life of Saint Joseph was interior and hidden in God; so little known to the world that but a few holy writers mention him in a few places; and of his death give no information. His was a life of prayer, quiet work, and constant sacrifice, and at the same time, a life shining with the splendor of all virtues.[2]
>
> — St. Joseph Sebastian Pelczar

There has never been another quite like St. Joseph, and there never will be. Yet you can become "another Joseph" in the world. You can become an "apparition" of Joseph for others. If you imitate St. Joseph's dedication to prayer and the interior life, you can resemble your spiritual father.

CONSECRATION TO ST. JOSEPH WILL INCREASE THE HOLY SPIRIT IN YOUR LIFE. Through consecration to St. Joseph, the Holy Spirit will recognize St. Joseph in you and pour extraordinary graces into your heart, mind, and soul. You can be a saint! Ask the Holy Spirit to make you into "another Joseph." Ask the Holy Spirit to fill you with graces similar to those he gave to the paternal heart of St. Joseph.

> Those souls most sensitive to the impulses of divine love have rightly seen in Joseph a brilliant example of the interior life.[3]
>
> — St. John Paul II

Read "Gifts of the Holy Spirit" (page 153)
Pray the Litany of St. Joseph (page 233)

DAY 6

Holy Trinity, One God,
Have Mercy on Us

He [St. Joseph] is head of the Holy Family, father of the trinity
on earth which resembles so closely the Holy Trinity on high.[1]

— St. Peter Julian Eymard

The Holy Trinity is a family, a Holy Family. They want you to
be a member of their family. To make this happen, they have
established a trinitarian replica on earth — an earthly trinity. The
trinity on earth consists of Jesus, Mary, and St. Joseph. In a sense,
they are the first church. Membership in this family will prepare you
for membership in God's eternal family in heaven.

SAINT JOSEPH IS THE FATHER OF THE TRINITY ON EARTH. **Many saints**
have compared the earthly trinity (Jesus, Mary, and Joseph) to the
heavenly Trinity (Father, Son, and Holy Spirit). The comparison
has its limitations, of course. Mary and St. Joseph are not divine,
and the Holy Spirit is not a mother. Nonetheless, the comparison is
important because it teaches us something about God's Trinitarian
family. Saint Francis de Sales offers us a great insight on this subject.
He writes:

> There is no doubt at all that St. Joseph was endowed with all
> gifts and graces required by the charge which the Eternal Father
> willed to commit to him, over all the domestic and temporal
> concerns of our Lord, and the guidance of his family, which was
> composed of three persons only, representing to us the mystery
> of the Most Holy and Adorable Trinity. Not that there is any real
> comparison in this matter excepting as regards our Lord, who
> is one of the persons of the Most Blessed Trinity, for the others
> were but creatures; yet still we may say that it was a trinity on
> earth representing in some sort the Most Holy Trinity.[2]

Saint Francis de Sales teaches us a very important truth in this
statement. He beautifully articulates that the trinity of Nazareth
(Jesus, Mary, and St. Joseph) represents the heavenly Trinity (Father,
Son, and Holy Spirit) and, therefore, consists only of three persons.
In other words, Jesus did not have any biological brothers and sisters.
This is what the Catholic Church has always taught. But the Church

has also always taught that the Trinity in heaven and the trinity on earth want you to be a member of their family through adoption!

Let's be clear, though: You are never going to become a divine person. You and I are not God, and we never will be. God does, however, want to bring us into the familial life of his Triune Godhead through spiritual adoption. This happens when we are baptized. As members of the Mystical Body of Christ, the Church, we are made members of God's family on earth, the Holy Family. Membership in the Holy Family on earth prepares us to enter the Holy Family in heaven.

IF YOU WANT TO BE A MEMBER OF THE TRINITARIAN FAMILY IN HEAVEN, YOU NEED TO BE A CHILD OF ST. JOSEPH ON EARTH. Saint Joseph, your spiritual father, will help you become a true child of the Heavenly Father. Saint Joseph will teach you how to love, pray, sacrifice, and work. He will teach you how to do the will of God. The pathway to heaven is paved with virtues, and St. Joseph will give you a father's example of holiness. With his holy assistance, your transition to the Trinity in heaven will be an easy one. Membership in the family of Nazareth — accepting St. Joseph as your father, Mary as your mother, and Jesus as your brother — is the surest, easiest, and quickest way of becoming a member of the Trinitarian family in heaven.

> What an honor it was [for St. Joseph] to enter into an alliance with the family of the heavenly Father, to become the third person of the created Trinity.[3]
>
> — Blessed William Joseph Chaminade

Read "St. Joseph's Oratory" (page 83)
Pray the Litany of St. Joseph (page 233)

DAY 7

Holy Mary, *Pray for Us*

All Christians belong to St. Joseph because Jesus and Mary belonged to him.[1]

— St. Leonard of Port Maurice

You belong to Jesus. He wants you to grow in virtue and holiness — that is, in true love of God and neighbor. To make this happen, you must imitate Jesus. In particular, the best way is to imitate his total entrustment to Mary and St. Joseph.

Jesus is not offended when people entrust themselves to Mary and Joseph. How could he be? He is the first one to have entrusted himself to them! He, more than anyone else, wants you to love Mary and St. Joseph. He wants you to love them and resemble them.

What brother would be offended if his younger siblings expressed reverence toward their mother and father? What man would be upset if another person wrote a song about his mother or placed roses at her feet? Likewise, what son would be disturbed if someone praised the virtues of his father? A person who honored a father would not receive condemnation from the father's son. On the contrary, such a person would receive praise and tremendous favors from the son. Well, this is exactly what Jesus stands ready to do for those who honor Mary and St. Joseph. Jesus will give them everything. Jesus stands ready to give you everything!

Now, if a son is willing to give gifts to the person who honors his mother and father, what kind of gifts would a husband give to the person who honors his wife? All we have to do is look to St. Joseph to find out. Saint Joseph will empty the treasure of heaven for those who honor Mary, his wife!

SAINT JOSEPH WILL GREATLY BLESS THOSE WHO LOVE AND HONOR MARY. The Virgin Mary is St. Joseph's wife, his queen, and the delight of his heart. She was the only woman who could ever satisfy his chaste heart. As Adam was not fulfilled until he rested in a creature similar to himself (Eve), Joseph only found rest when he found Mary. When he took Mary's hand in marriage, he consecrated himself to her and made a promise to treasure her femininity, especially her blessed virginity. He was her beloved provider, protector, and servant. Saint Joseph earnestly desires for her to be honored and loved by everyone.

SAINT JOSEPH WILL INCREASE YOUR LOVE FOR THE VIRGIN MARY. Saint Joseph is so in love with Mary that he wants everyone to acknowledge her beauty. What husband would not want this for his wife? Doesn't every husband desire for his wife to be loved and honored by others? What husband would not do everything in his power to increase the reverence shown to his bride? If you allow St. Joseph to increase your love for his queen, he will empty the treasures of heaven for you. He has access to all the treasures of heaven!

CONSECRATION TO ST. JOSEPH WILL MAKE YOU A KNIGHT OF THE HOLY QUEEN! Saint Joseph knows that Mary is worth living for, fighting for, and dying for. She is the Queen of the Kingdom of Heaven. To fight for her is to fight for the King. Saint Joseph, the most valiant of knights, knows that the surest, easiest, and fastest way to the King is through the Queen. His mission is to reveal this truth to souls.

For her part, Mary has full confidence in the chivalrous love of St. Joseph, her knight. She completely trusts him. Saint Joseph will teach you how to be a knight of the Holy Queen as well, making you capable of conquering hearts for the Kingdom of Heaven.

> A servant of Mary will have a tender devotion to St. Joseph, and by his pious homage of respect and love, will endeavor to merit the protection of this great saint.[2]
>
> — Blessed William Joseph Chaminade

> O my dear father St. Joseph, I want to love you with the love that Mary has for you.[3]
>
> — Blessed Bartolo Longo

Read "The Consecrated Knight" (page 121)
Pray the Litany of St. Joseph (page 233)

DAY 8

Saint Joseph, *Pray for Us*

We see that at the beginning of the New Testament, as at the beginning of the Old, there is a married couple. But whereas Adam and Eve were the source of evil which was unleashed on the world, Joseph and Mary are the summit from which holiness spreads all over the earth. The Savior began the work of salvation by this virginal and holy union.[1]

— St. Pope Paul VI

Marriage - heart of Creation and Redemption

Marriage is at the heart of creation and redemption. As St. Pope Paul VI states, Adam and Eve were present at the beginning of creation (Old Testament), and Joseph and Mary are present at the beginning of God's re-creation (New Testament). Jesus himself speaks of the Kingdom of Heaven as a wedding feast (see Mt 22:2).

Saint Pope Paul VI's statement at the beginning of this section is incredibly profound. On some level, he is presenting the idea that St. Joseph is the head of the new covenant family, as Adam was head of the first covenant family. This is a fascinating idea, one that has rarely been explored in theological studies. Usually, when we think of the new head of the human family (the new Adam) we think of Jesus (see 1 Cor 15:45), and rightly so. Jesus is God; he alone regenerates humanity. Nonetheless, as Head of the Holy Family, St. Joseph was the head of our Head. He is the father of our Savior, the Patron of the Universal Church, and our spiritual father.

SAINT JOSEPH IS A NEW ADAM. Saint Joseph is, after Christ, the new head of the human family. As such, we are obliged to obey the Fourth Commandment in his regard: "Honor your father and your mother" (Ex 20:12). Failure to love and honor St. Joseph is an offense against God. In fact, the fatherhood of St. Joseph is so important for us that our spiritual growth depends on it. If Jesus himself increased in wisdom and knowledge through the fatherhood of St. Joseph, we need St. Joseph's fatherhood to help us acquire the "proper attire" needed for entrance into the wedding feast of heaven (see Mt 22:12).

SAINT JOSEPH WILL HELP YOU GET TO THE WEDDING FEAST OF HEAVEN. Since we know that St. Joseph loves us and so we love and honor him in return, we can trust that he will help us get to heaven.

The greatest thing any father can do for his children is help them get to heaven. Our first father (Adam) ruined this possibility for all his children. Our first father's disobedience caused the downfall of all creation and kept us from entering heaven. Saint Joseph's fatherhood, on the other hand, elevates us and helps us to enter heaven. He loves us, helps us become saints, and brings us to the only path that leads to heaven: Jesus.

SAINT JOSEPH IS THE DELIGHT OF SAINTS. Every saint loves St. Joseph. It is impossible to find a single saint who did not love St. Joseph. While devotion to St. Joseph developed slowly over time, no saint ever disliked St. Joseph. It is impossible to truly have love of God and neighbor in your heart — that is, be holy — if you disdain the husband of Mary and the earthly father of Jesus Christ. To enter heaven, you need to resemble your spiritual father in his steadfast love. He will help you acquire the correct attire — virtues and holiness — needed to enter the wedding feast of heaven!

> It is written, "The first man, Adam, became a living being," the last Adam a life-giving spirit. But the spiritual was not first; rather the natural and then the spiritual. The first man was from the earth, earthly; the second man, from heaven. As was the earthly one, so also the earthly, and as is the heavenly one, so also are the heavenly. Just as we have borne the image of the earthly one, we shall also bear the image of the heavenly one.
>
> — 1 Cor 15:45-49

Read "Delight of Saints" (page 85)
Pray the Litany of St. Joseph (page 233)

DAY 9

Noble Offspring of David,
Pray for Us

He [God] saw to it that Joseph be born of the royal family; He wanted him to be noble even with earthly nobility. The blood of David, of Solomon, and of all the kings of Judah flows in his veins.[1]

— St. Peter Julian Eymard

In the Gospels of Matthew and Luke, we learn that St. Joseph is of the lineage of the Davidic kings. The Old Testament prophets always taught that the Messiah would come from the Davidic line. Mary, our spiritual mother, was most likely a descendant of King David as well, but her ancestry is not given in the New Testament. Matthew and Luke present the lineage of Joseph because the Davidic ancestry of the Messiah needed to be shown through the father's line. Therefore, Matthew and Luke made a point of emphasizing that even though Jesus is not the biological son of Joseph, he is the Son of Joseph by law. As such, Jesus has a legal right to be called a descendant of King David.

> The espousals between Joseph and Mary are an episode of great importance. Joseph was of the royal line of David and, in virtue of his marriage to Mary, would confer on the Son of the Virgin — on God's Son — the legal title of "Son of David," thus fulfilling the prophecies.[2]

— Pope Benedict XVI

SAINT JOSEPH WAS KING OF THE HOLY FAMILY. He was not the king of Nazareth, Israel, or anything like that. Since every man is the king of his home, St. Joseph was the king of his house. In the home of Nazareth, St. Joseph was king, Mary was queen, and Jesus was the prince awaiting the kingdom prepared for him by his Heavenly Father. Jesus is King of Kings and Lord of Lords, of course, but God's providential love desires that we acknowledge the kingship of St. Joseph in the Holy Family. Jesus himself gave us an example of the filial love and reverence we owe to St. Joseph, our spiritual father.

29

SAINT JOSEPH IS A NOBLE LORD. Many saints have often lovingly referred to St. Joseph as their "lord." Saint Teresa of Avila was particularly fond of referring to St. Joseph as her lord. In using this term, no saint intends to claim that St. Joseph is God. Saint Joseph is not God. Saints sometimes use the term "Lord" when addressing St. Joseph out of respect, as is done when addressing dignitaries and rulers. Saints are pious and love to express their filial relationship to Mary and St. Joseph in devotional language. Mary, for example, is called Madonna. ("Madonna" derives from the Latin *mea domina,* that is, "My Lady," and is the feminine form of "lord.")

> Since God has wanted to obey you [St. Joseph], allow me to be in your service, to honor you and love you as my Lord and Master.[3]
>
> — St. Alphonsus Liguori

> The whole Church recognizes St. Joseph as a patron and guardian. For centuries many different features of his life have caught the attention of believers. That is why, for many years now, I have liked to address him affectionately as "our father and lord."[4]
>
> — St. Josemaría Escrivá

Referring to St. Joseph as "lord" has biblical foundations as well. Remember Joseph in the Old Testament, the one sold into slavery by his brothers? Well, Joseph's brothers end up calling him their "lord" (see Gen 44) when they encounter him again and he saves their family from famine. For us, St. Joseph is more than a brother; he is our noble spiritual father. He is our loving spiritual father and lord.

> Noble St. Joseph, I rejoice that God found you worthy of holding this eminent position whereby, established as the father of Jesus, you saw the one whose orders heaven and earth obey subjecting himself to your authority.[5]
>
> — St. Alphonsus Liguori

Read "Son of David" (page 139)
Pray the Litany of St. Joseph (page 233)

DAY 10
Light of Patriarchs,
Pray for Us

How I love to call St. Joseph the Patriarch of Christians and of God's elect! How could we not give him this venerable title ... he, above all, who played such a large part in the mysteries of our spiritual regeneration?[1]

— Blessed William Joseph Chaminade

The word "patriarch" means father. What all the patriarchs of the Old Testament foreshadowed, and all Christian fathers are called to reflect, is the paternal light of God shining through the fatherhood of St. Joseph. After Christ, St. Joseph is the greatest of all the patriarchs; he is the greatest of all fathers!

Picture to yourself the sanctity of all the patriarchs of old, that long line of successive generations which is the mysterious ladder of Jacob, culminating in the person of the Son of God. See how great was the faith of Abraham, the obedience of Isaac, the courage of David, the wisdom of Solomon. After you have formed the highest opinion of these saints, remember that Joseph is at the top of the ladder, at the head of the saints, the kings, the prophets, the patriarchs, that he is more faithful than Abraham, more obedient than Isaac, more generous than David, wiser than Solomon, in a word, as superior in grace as he is close to the source, Jesus sleeping in his arms.[2]

— Blessed William Joseph Chaminade

SAINT JOSEPH IS A REFLECTION OF THE FATHER OF LIGHTS. In the Letter of James, we read:

Every good and perfect gift is from above, coming down from the Father of lights, with whom there is no alteration or shadow caused by change.

— Jas 1:17

In the beginning, God created the great luminaries in the heavens: the sun, the moon, and the stars. Without light, creation would be in darkness. In the New Testament, the Father establishes a new creation in Christ. Through Christ, the Father places his divine life, love, and light within our hearts. Saint Joseph and his fatherhood play a very important role in God's wonderful plan. Saint Joseph is the perfect reflection of the Father of Lights, and he helps us to receive the light of Christ. Saint Joseph is a bearer of light. He brings Jesus, the true Light of the World, to us.

SAINT JOSEPH WILL HELP YOU LIVE IN THE LIGHT OF GOD. You are a child of the light. As a Christian, Jesus gives you a share in his light. He makes you the light of the world (see Mt 5:14-16).

> All of you are children of the light and children of the day. We are not of the night or of darkness.
>
> — 1 Thess 5:5

> For you were once darkness, but now you are light in the Lord. Live as children of light, for light produces every kind of good-ness and righteousness and truth.
>
> — Eph 5:8-9

THE "LUMEN PATRIARCHARUM" TERRIFIES SATAN. In the Latin version of the Litany of St. Joseph, the title "Light of Patriarchs" appears as "*Lumen Patriarcharum.*" The Devil hates St. Joseph and his light. Satan's other name is *Lucifer*, which means "light bearer." Lucifer lost the light because of his pride and disobedience to God. Now, Satan lives in perpetual darkness and abhors the light. Satan fears your spiritual father because St. Joseph is a humble creature of flesh and blood, the perfect reflection of the Father of Lights. Saint Joseph is a true and everlasting light bearer, an icon of God the Father. After Jesus and Mary, there is no person that Satan detests more than St. Joseph. Stay close to St. Joseph and walk in the light!

> I wish to extend a particular word of encouragement to fathers so that they may take St. Joseph as their model. He who kept watch over the Son of Man is able to teach them the deepest meaning of their own fatherhood.[3]
>
> — Pope Benedict XVI

Read "*Ite ad Ioseph!*" (page 108)
Pray the Litany of St. Joseph (page 233)

DAY 11
Spouse of the Mother of God, *Pray for Us*

How hard he [St. Joseph] must have prayed to come to know and ever increase in love toward his immaculate wife.[1]

— Blessed Gabriele Allegra

There has never been a man more in love with a woman than St. Joseph was in love with Mary. What dignity and holiness were required of St. Joseph to be the husband of Mary! In her feminine Heart, Mary knew that she was secure in the manhood of St. Joseph. He was her knight and warrior. Every wife desires such a husband — a gentleman, a protector, and a good father.

Women deserve men who are strong and protective, yet gentle, loving, and trustworthy. Every woman wants to find security in the arms of a man who is willing to lay down his life for her. The Church and the world need men like St. Joseph. He is the model husband.

Saint Joseph was the spouse of Mary. In the same way, each father sees himself entrusted with the mystery of womanhood through his own wife. Dear fathers, like St. Joseph, respect and love your spouse; and by your love and your wise presence, lead your children to God.[2]

— Pope Benedict XVI

Every Catholic heart wants shepherds like St. Joseph as well, priests and bishops — spiritual fathers — who are gentlemen, chivalrous warriors, protectors, and defenders. Catholics expect their priests and bishops to be prayerful, trustworthy, gentle, compassionate, and virtuous. The bride of Christ, the Church, deserves to have leaders who are willing to fight off the wolves for love of the flock, slay spiritual dragons, and preach the truth with passion, Christian charity, and zeal. Saint Joseph is the model of all fatherhood. Without looking to the model of St. Joseph, no husband, father, or priest will ever fully understand what it means to be a sacrificial man, a loving husband and father, and a truly masculine saint.

SAINT JOSEPH IS THE MODEL HUSBAND AND FATHER. The vocation of all men is to be at the service of those entrusted to their love and care. Many men have forgotten this today, but St. Joseph will help them remember. He will help men be holy and chivalrous again. All men discover in St. Joseph a model of strength, fidelity, heroism, and virtue. If men — husbands, fathers, priests, and bishops — follow the example of St. Joseph, families will be loving and secure, husbands will be holy, priests will be dragon-slayers, and bishops will again be shepherds of souls and pillars of truth.

SAINT JOSEPH IS A MODEL FOR ALL MEN. Real men are true gentlemen, at the service of others. Real men love. Real men protect women and children against any and all threats. Real men are willing to die for their wives and children. Holy priests and bishops are willing to suffer and die for the souls entrusted to their care. Priests and bishops of this caliber are not afraid of ridicule, slander, poverty, or imprisonment. Men like St. Joseph are willing to fight for what they love, what is good, true, and beautiful. May the Church and families once again be filled with such men!

> To you, O Blessed Joseph, we come in our trials, and having asked the help of your most holy spouse, we confidently ask your patronage, also.[3]

> — Pope Leo XIII

Blessed be St. Joseph, her most chaste spouse!

Read "Young Husband of Mary" (page 115)
Pray the Litany of St. Joseph (page 233)

DAY 12

Chaste Guardian of the Virgin, Pray for Us

It was necessary that divine Providence should commit her [Mary] to the charge and guardianship of a man absolutely pure.[1]

— St. Francis de Sales

Chastity is a virtue. A very important virtue.

To be chaste is to have self-mastery, to be in control of your passions and sexuality. Contrary to what many people think, a person who exercises chastity is not repressing or rejecting the beauty of human sexuality. On the contrary, chastity preserves the human heart and body for authentic self-giving. All people, no matter their vocation in life, are called to chastity. Chastity is the virtue that prevents us from being slaves to our passions and acting like irrational animals.

Celibacy, on the other hand, is a special form of chastity. God calls some men and women to celibacy for the sake of the Kingdom of Heaven. Saint Joseph was both chaste and celibate. He was called by God to espouse a virgin consecrated to God in her mind, body, and soul. Saint Joseph was the Chaste Guardian of the Virgin.

Saint Joseph and Mary lived in what is often called a "Josephite marriage." They were truly husband and wife, but they never engaged in sexual relations. Their vocation was to be united in heart, mind, and soul, but never in body. They were both consecrated to God and sacrificed a natural good for a greater good: the salvation of souls.

SAINT JOSEPH IS PURE OF HEART. To be chaste is to be pure of heart. If a person's heart is not pure, they are incapable of seeing God. Saint Joseph's heart is exceptionally pure. Saint Joseph gazed on the countenance of God in the Person of his Son for decades. Poets have often stated that the eyes are the window to the soul. If this is true, St. Joseph must have had the most chaste and pure eyes of any husband who ever lived. His eyes and heart were pure-intentioned, chaste, and afire with love for Jesus and Mary.

Modern man has become blinded by impurity. The world encourages premarital relations, cohabitation, contraception, and many other immoral practices. Chastity is a forgotten virtue today. Even married couples live with the idea that they are free to do whatever they desire with the body of their spouse. However, this is not true. Chastity is required in marriage as well, in order for couples to truly love one another, to retain their dignity and respect for each other.

YOUR SPIRITUAL FATHER IS A GENTLEMAN. Saint Joseph is the first Christian gentleman; next to Jesus, he is the greatest example of masculine chastity. He was married to the most beautiful woman in the world, and he treated her with respect, dignity, and reverence. If men today were more like St. Joseph — protectors and defenders of beauty, instead of users and abusers of the feminine mystery — what a different world this would be.

God wants all men to be like St. Joseph. He is the *first* Chaste Guardian of the Virgin. Most men will be called to marriage, while some are called to consecrated celibacy. Both vocations are necessary. Without marriage, there are no children. Without priests, there are no Sacraments. Married men need to be chaste in marriage; priests and bishops need to be like St. Joseph in their chaste love for the virginal Church — guardians, defenders, and protectors of the beauty entrusted to them, not users and abusers of the sacred mysteries.

> Joseph, the just man, is appointed to be the steward of the mysteries of God, the *paterfamilias* and guardian of the sanctuary, which is Mary the bride and the Logos in her. He [Joseph] thus becomes the icon of the bishop, to whom the bride is betrothed; she is not at his disposal but under his protection.[2]
>
> — Pope Benedict XVI

Read "Feast of the Holy Spouses" (page 125)
Pray the Litany of St. Joseph (page 233)

DAY 13

Foster Father of the Son of God, *Pray for Us*

> The position of St. Joseph as husband and foster father gives witness to the dignity of fatherhood.[1]
>
> — Venerable Joseph Mindszenty

Christians use many terms to describe the fatherhood of St. Joseph. He is called the legal, putative, spiritual, virginal, and foster father of Jesus. While none of these titles is found in the New Testament, they are all legitimate ways of describing St. Joseph's fatherhood. Of these titles, foster father is the most common. The reason it is the most common title is that the naming of a child in ancient Jewish custom was the legal responsibility of the father.

> Although you [St. Joseph] are not necessary for the [child's] conception and birth, nevertheless you will be necessary for [his] sustenance; and your first care will concern his name.[2]
>
> — St. Albert the Great

Saint Joseph's legal responsibility of naming the Christ Child was given by God when the angel revealed to St. Joseph that he was not to be afraid to take Mary — and the Child in her womb — into his home and under his care. Saint Joseph's role of naming the Savior is an extremely important one. It is meant to signify to the world that St. Joseph is the legal father of Jesus.

> Saint Joseph's dignity springs from his privilege of being the legal father of the Incarnate Son of God. Here, then, is a man whom the Son of God calls father, one whom he [Jesus] serves and obeys and before whom he kneels for a paternal blessing.[3]
>
> — St. Peter Julian Eymard

Saint Joseph's role as the "Foster Father" of Jesus might come across as something merely contractual, but the Latin provides us with a deeper insight into St. Joseph's role. In Latin, the title given to St. Joseph to signify his role as foster father is *Filii Dei Nutricie*. Literally, it means "Nurturer of the Son of God." As you can see, the title foster father is a very poor translation from the Latin original.

Calling St. Joseph the foster father of Jesus is valid, of course, but it needs to be emphasized that St. Joseph's fatherhood was more than a legal fatherhood; St. Joseph's fatherhood was an authoritative, affectionate, faithful, and everlasting fatherhood.

SAINT JOSEPH'S SPIRITUAL FATHERHOOD IS FOREVER. The loving relationship between a spiritual father and child endures forever. In other words, Jesus continues to be the Son of Joseph in heaven. In paradise, St. Joseph no longer exercises a "legal" fatherhood over Jesus, but his relationship of love, affection, and faithfulness toward Jesus, as well as the Mystical Body of Jesus, remains. Unlike marriage, where the relationship does not remain into eternity (see Mt 22:30), St. Joseph's spiritual fatherhood over Christ and his Mystical Body endures forever.

Spiritual fatherhood, like spiritual motherhood, endures forever. Were this not the case, the Church would need to cease invoking Jesus as the "Son of Joseph." The Church would also be required to cease invoking Mary, who is in heaven, as our spiritual mother.

SAINT JOSEPH WILL ALWAYS BE YOUR SPIRITUAL FATHER. What is valid for Jesus is valid for you. Saint Joseph is forever your spiritual father. As he took care of Jesus while on earth, St. Joseph will take care of you on your earthly pilgrimage. Saint Joseph is your loving provider, educator, and protector. When your life on earth is over, St. Joseph will continue to be your father, not on an earthly level, but on a spiritual level. In heaven, you will forever be known as a child of St. Joseph.

> No one will ever be able worthily to praise Joseph, whom thou,
> O true only-begotten Son of the Eternal Father, has deigned to
> have for thy foster father![4]
>
> — St. Ephrem the Syrian

Read "Virginal Father of Jesus" (page 127)
Pray the Litany of St. Joseph (page 233)

DAY 14
Zealous Defender of Christ,
Pray for Us

He [St. Joseph] protects those who revere him and accompanies them on their journey through this life — just as he protected and accompanied Jesus when he was growing up.[1]

— St. Josemaría Escrivá

From the moment the angel revealed to St. Joseph that he was to be the father of the Messiah to when he took his final breath in the arms of Jesus and Mary, St. Joseph zealously defended Jesus.

Saint Joseph always defended his Son from any threat against him. Saint Joseph was a dutiful watchman, guarding, defending, and sacrificing everything for Jesus and his safety. Saint Joseph offered the same protection for his wife, too. He protected his Son and his wife as a loving father and faithful husband.

In some translations of the Litany of St. Joseph, the title "Zealous Defender of Christ" (in Latin, *Christi Defensor Sedule*) is given as "Diligent Defender of Christ" or "Watchful Defender of Christ." Both are acceptable translations and have similar meanings — namely, St. Joseph defended Jesus. As a child of St. Joseph, you can have great confidence knowing that your spiritual father also desires to zealously defend you.

SAINT JOSEPH ZEALOUSLY DEFENDS YOU. The paternal mission of St. Joseph is not finished. A father's work is never finished until his children are safely home. In heaven, St. Joseph no longer needs to watch over and protect Jesus. You, however, are not yet in heaven. You need the protection of St. Joseph. Your spiritual father knows what is harmful to your soul, and he wants to watch over you and help you arrive safely home. Saint Joseph will never abandon you. Your role is to entrust yourself to his diligent care and never look back.

Our destiny is in the hands of Joseph. Joseph, the guardian of his Lord and the spouse of his Queen, Joseph, the foster father of Jesus and the head of the Holy Family, has in his kindness deigned to accept us as his children and permits us to call him father.[2]

— Blessed William Joseph Chaminade

You have nothing to fear with St. Joseph at your side. What is there to be afraid of with such a zealous defender as your father who loves you? Saint Joseph held the Maker of the Universe in his hands. Saint Joseph fed the Creator of the heavens. In his role as earthly father to Jesus, St. Joseph lovingly commanded the Son of God. Heaven and earth obeyed him. All hell trembles before him!

> Joseph's name will be a name of protection all during our lives.[3]

> — Blessed William Joseph Chaminade

SAINT JOSEPH WILL INCREASE YOUR ZEAL FOR CHRIST. As your father and model, St. Joseph will teach you how to defend Christ zealously. If you are a faithful disciple of Jesus Christ, you are going to be criticized, hated, ridiculed, and mocked by the world — oftentimes by your own family and friends. Your suffering will be great, but your witness to truth — your witness to Jesus — will be greater. Saint Joseph will help you be a zealous witness to the truth of Jesus Christ.

YOUR DEFENSE OF CHRIST MUST BE GREAT. You should always strive to defend the person and name of Jesus Christ against all blasphemy, insult, and sacrilege. You must defend the Church, as well as her teachings and Sacraments, from all attacks, heresies, and falsehoods. To defend the Church is to defend Christ. You must resemble your spiritual father, always willing to sacrifice yourself for love of truth. Like St. Joseph, you, too, can bring many souls to Jesus.

> How happy and blessed are they whom you [St. Joseph] love and whom you take under your protection![4]

> — Blessed William Joseph Chaminade

Read "Savior of the Savior" (page 159)
Pray the Litany of St. Joseph (page 233)

DAY 15

Head of the Holy Family,
Pray for Us

Jesus and Mary not only bent their wills to Joseph's, for he was head of the Holy Family, but they lovingly surrendered their hearts to him as well.[1]

— St. Peter Julian Eymard

Today, calling a man the "head" of the family is frowned upon. God is not worried about political correctness, however. He established the family and designated that fathers be the heads of their families. Now, this doesn't mean that men are better than women. The greatest human person who ever lived was not a man, but a woman — Mary, the Mother of God. (Jesus is a divine Person.) Jesus and Mary both delighted in the headship of St. Joseph in their home.

Why are many people offended by such terminology today? Sadly, it often stems from having been emotionally, physical, or sexually abused by a father figure. Such abuse breaks the heart of God. Yet the crisis in manhood can be corrected if men begin to imitate St. Joseph. His fatherly example shows that strength, authority, and headship are meant to be at the service of others.

In Joseph, heads of the household are blessed with the unsurpassed model of fatherly watchfulness and care.[2]

— Pope Leo XIII

HUSBANDS AND FATHERS NEED TO IMITATE ST. JOSEPH. **Families** around the world will experience a revolution of holiness if husbands imitate St. Joseph. Important passages in the New Testament will no longer be seen as offensive but life-giving.

Be subordinate to one another out of reverence for Christ. Wives should be subordinate to their husbands as to the Lord. For the husband is head of his wife just as Christ is head of the church, he himself the savior of the body. As the church is subordinate to Christ, so wives should be subordinate to their husbands in everything. Husbands, love your wives, even as Christ loved the church and handed himself over for her to sanctify her, cleansing her by the bath of water with the word, that he might present to himself the church in splendor, without spot or wrinkle or any such thing, that she might be holy and without blemish. So [also] husbands should love their wives as their own bodies. He who loves his wife loves himself. For no one hates his own flesh but rather nourishes and cherishes it, even as Christ does the church, because we are members of his body. "For this reason a man shall leave [his] father and [his] mother and be joined to his wife, and the two shall become one flesh." This is a great mystery, but I speak in reference to Christ and the church. In any case, each one of you should love his wife as himself, and the wife should respect her husband.

— Eph 5:22-33

MAKE ST. JOSEPH THE SPIRITUAL HEAD OF YOUR FAMILY. Obtain a statue or a beautiful image of St. Joseph for your home. Place it in a prominent location and frequently invoke the intercession of St. Joseph as a family. You will see the difference St. Joseph makes.

Dear Brothers and Sisters, the sacrament which unites you to each other, unites you in Christ! It unites you with Christ! "This mystery is a profound one!" (Eph 5:32). He comes to you and is present in your midst and dwells in your souls. In your families! In your homes! Saint Joseph was well aware of this. For this reason he did not hesitate to entrust himself and his family to God. By virtue of this trust he completely fulfilled his mission, entrusted to him by God for the sake of Mary and his son. Supported by the example and protection of St. Joseph, offer a constant witness of devotion and generosity.[3]

— St. John Paul II

Read "The Holy House of Loreto" (page 180)
Pray the Litany of St. Joseph (page 233)

DAY 16
Joseph Most Just,
Pray for Us

He [St. Joseph] won for himself the title of "The Just Man," and thus serves as a living model of that Christian justice which should reign in social life.[1]

— Pope Pius XI

What does it mean to call St. Joseph a just man? Saint Josemaría Escrivá provides a great answer for us. He states:

Saint Joseph was an ordinary sort of man on whom God relied to do great things. He did exactly what the Lord wanted him to do, in each and every event that went to make up his life. That is why Scripture praises Joseph as "a just man." In Hebrew a just man means a good and faithful servant of God, someone who fulfils the divine will (cf. Gen 7:1; 18:23-32; Ezek 18:5ff; Prov 12:10), or who is honorable and charitable toward his neighbor (cf. Tob 7:6; 9:6). So a just man is someone who loves God and proves his love by keeping God's commandments and directing his whole life towards the service of his brothers, his fellow men.[2]

What about you? Are you just? Do you love God, keep his commandments, and act with honor and charity toward your neighbor?

SAINT JOSEPH WILL INCREASE IN YOU THE VIRTUE OF JUSTICE. Theologians define the virtue of justice as "giving to another his due." For example, in our relationship with God, we owe it to him to be grateful for our existence, and to praise him for his goodness. We act justly toward God, giving him his due, when we worship him, especially by our participation in Holy Mass on Sundays and Holy Days of Obligation. If we fail to do this, we are not loving God. We are not acting justly toward God; we are not giving him his due.

For St. Joseph, being a just man meant he observed the dictates of the Jewish religion. This required him to travel to Jerusalem three times a year — a long distance from Nazareth — and participate in various rituals and ceremonies. You, on the other hand, most likely live a short distance from a Catholic church. If you can't spend one hour a week thanking God and worshipping him, you are not loving God or giving God his due. You are not a just man.

Holy Mass is not about the priest, the people, or the choir. It's about returning love for love and giving God his due. Yes, priests should preach well, liturgical music should be sacred and inspiring, and it's always pleasant to see familiar faces at Mass. Yet even if you find the priest less than edifying, the music a distraction, and the congregation spiritually dead, you need to remember it's not about them — it's about you acting justly and lovingly toward God. There is no greater way to tell God "I love you," give thanks to God, and worship him than through the Holy Sacrifice of the Mass. "Eucharist" means "thanksgiving."

God is not the only one that we are to act justly towards out of love. You also need to give others their due. Do you? Do you love, venerate, and honor Mary, your spiritual mother? Do you love, venerate, and honor St. Joseph, your spiritual father? Do you treat members of your family with love, respect, and dignity? What about your neighbors, co-workers, and everyone else with whom you daily interact? If you are an employer, do you offer a just wage? Remember the Golden Rule: "Do unto others as you would have them do unto you" (Lk 6:31). Your spiritual father acted justly and lovingly toward everyone; you should, too.

> Do you wish to know why Joseph is called just? Because he possessed perfectly all the virtues.[3]
>
> — St. Maximus of Turin

> The Gospel describes St. Joseph as a Just Man. No greater praise of virtue and no higher tribute to merit could be applied to a man.[4]
>
> — St. Pope Paul VI

Read "Just and Reverent Man" (page 141)
Pray the Litany of St. Joseph (page 233)

DAY 17

Joseph Most Chaste,
Pray for Us

Who can ever understand how great he [St. Joseph] had to be in this virtue of virginity who was destined by the Eternal Father to be the guardian, or rather the companion, of Mary's virginity?[1]

— St. Francis de Sales

In the Litany of Loreto, Mary is called "Mother Most Chaste." In the Litany of St. Joseph, our spiritual father is called "Most Chaste" as well. No other saints can be invoked as the most chaste, just, prudent, courageous, obedient, faithful, or any other virtue. Mary and St. Joseph together share these superlative qualities, in part, because their hearts as husband and wife are one.

"Where your treasure is, there will your heart be also" (Lk 12:34). Saint Joseph has three treasures: Jesus, Mary, and you. Nothing consumes the heart of St. Joseph other than these three treasures. The heart of St. Joseph is the heart of a loving father, and you have access to his heart. The Chaste Heart of St. Joseph is your home.

In Catholicism, when we speak of devotion to the Hearts of Jesus and Mary, we are essentially referring to devotion to the personhood of Jesus and Mary. We love the Sacred and Immaculate Hearts — and often depict them in art — because we love the persons of Jesus and Mary. While devotion to the Hearts of Jesus and Mary is well established in the Church — each having liturgical feast days — devotion to the heart of St. Joseph has not fully developed in the Church. Perhaps there will one day be a liturgical feast honoring St. Joseph's heart, but only God knows the future. Whether it happens or not, all children desire a father whose heart (person) is strong, protective, and gentle. Saint Joseph has such a heart. He has the heart of a father, a king, a warrior, and a chaste gentleman. His chaste heart beats with love for you.

SAINT JOSEPH WILL HELP YOU HAVE A CHASTE HEART. Lust is the predominant vice at work in the hearts of men today. The world is filled with immoral and lust-filled actions. These actions greatly offend God, ruin families, and cry out to heaven for justice. Did not Our

Lady warn St. Jacinta of Fatima that many souls go to hell because of sins of the flesh?

In the battle for purity, everyone needs to go to St. Joseph. If a man — or a woman — struggles with lust, they must go to St. Joseph. If temptations against purity batter your mind, heart, and soul, run to your spiritual father. Cling to St. Joseph! Your spiritual father is capable of increasing the virtue of chastity in your heart and leading you to true, virtuous love of God and neighbor. You will be victorious against lust and triumphant over sin if you take refuge beneath the fatherly cloak of St. Joseph. Prayer is difficult when you are assailed with temptations against purity, but St. Joseph will fight for you if only you invoke his holy name.

Men, in particular, need to imitate the chaste heart of St. Joseph. The world needs men who love their wives as St. Joseph loved Mary. If men reverence their wives as holy temples, families will be renewed, dragons will be slain, and the evils of our age that attack the dignity of the human person will be overcome. The imitation of St. Joseph will spread a revolution of holiness over the earth.

> That God may be more favorable to our prayers, and that he may come with bounty and promptitude to the aid of his Church, we judge it of deep utility for the Christian people, continually to invoke with great piety and trust, together with the Virgin-Mother of God, her chaste spouse, the Blessed Joseph.[2]
>
> — Pope Leo XIII

Read "Santo Anello" (page 136)
Pray the Litany of St. Joseph (page 233)

DAY 18

Joseph Most Prudent,
Pray for Us

What prudence was required to educate a God become a child, who willed to obey him [St. Joseph] for thirty years![1]

— Blessed William Joseph Chaminade

What is prudence? In modern times, many people consider it to be a vice or a flaw. If a person is cautious or circumspect in moral matters, they are quite often called a prude. Prudence, however, is a virtue — an extremely important virtue.

The *Catechism of the Catholic Church* provides a concise definition of prudence. It states:

> Prudence is the virtue that disposes practical reason to discern our true good in every circumstance and to choose the right means of achieving it ... It is not to be confused with timidity or fear, nor with duplicity or dissimulation. It is called *auriga virtutum* (the charioteer of the virtues); it guides the other virtues by setting rule and measure.[2]

Saint Thomas Aquinas taught that prudence is the "principal of all the virtues." Its role is to govern the other cardinal (preeminent) virtues: temperance, justice, and fortitude. Without prudence, a person will be either too lenient or too harsh. Prudence serves as a guide and a "charioteer," helping the soul to avoid erroneous extremes.

PRUDENCE IS THE VIRTUE OF KINGS AND RULERS. Without prudence, no leader can exercise temperance, justice, and fortitude. Saint Joseph, king of the Holy Family and your spiritual father, is (after Jesus) the most prudent of all men. In every situation in life, he is a model of prudence. He prayed and waited on the Lord to reveal the mysteries of his wife's pregnancy to him. He educated the God-Man and, in every situation, allowed prudence to govern his actions.

The prudence of St. Joseph was a supernatural prudence.[3]

— Blessed William Joseph Chaminade

Supernatural prudence is different from human prudence. Human prudence guides a person to avoid difficulty, suffering, and

47

hardship. Supernatural prudence, on the other hand, does not seek to avoid suffering. Supernatural prudence embraces the cross out of love and always strives for the greater good. By God's grace, St. Joseph's prudence was supernatural and heroic. Before the wisdom of the cross was revealed to the world, St. Joseph willingly and voluntarily embraced suffering for the good of others. Before the mystery of co-redemptive suffering was unveiled to souls, St. Joseph lived it out of love.

SAINT JOSEPH WILL INCREASE IN YOU THE VIRTUE OF PRUDENCE. Saint Joseph will help you exercise supernatural prudence. In every situation, he will teach you to allow prudence to be your charioteer, guiding you to always do what is right for the sake of love of God and neighbor, no matter how much you have to suffer for it.

> Saint Joseph teaches us that prudence is correct knowledge about things to be done or, more broadly, the knowledge of things that ought to be done and of things that should be avoided.[4]
>
> — Servant of God John A. Hardon

A man of human prudence would never arise from sleep and flee to Egypt with his spouse and child in response to a dream. A man of human prudence would quickly rebuke any man who informed his wife that her heart would be pierced with a sword and his Son be a cause of division. But St. Joseph is no ordinary man. By the power of the Holy Spirit, he is a man of supernatural prudence. He ponders, prays, discerns, and acts. Prudence is his charioteer. With St. Joseph, the virtue of supernatural prudence will be your charioteer as well.

> Master that he [St. Joseph] is, he remains always the prudent and faithful servant. Saint Joseph, of the family of the kings of Judah, leads a poor and hidden life. Because he was destined to become, as it were, the governor and father of a weak and humble God, it was fitting that he should resemble him.[5]
>
> — Blessed William Joseph Chaminade

Read "Seven Sorrows and Seven Joys" (page 157)
Pray the Litany of St. Joseph (page 233)

DAY 19

Joseph Most Courageous,
Pray for Us

So perfectly was he [St. Joseph] dead to the world and the flesh,
that he desired nothing but the things of heaven.[1]

— St. Bridget of Sweden

Saint Joseph desired nothing but the things of heaven. He lived
entirely for love of Jesus Christ and, after Mary, is Jesus' most
faithful disciple. Saint Joseph is the father of Jesus, but he is also a
disciple of Jesus. It takes courage to be a faithful disciple of Jesus.
Many are willing to follow Jesus when it is pleasant, but not many are
willing to follow Jesus when it is difficult and filled with sorrow. Saint
Joseph was always faithful, always courageous.

In different translations of the Litany of St. Joseph, the title
"Most Courageous" is sometimes rendered as "Most Valiant" or
"Most Strong." The three titles have the same essential meaning:
Saint Joseph was courageous and fearless. He feared nothing other
than offending God and exercised tremendous fortitude in his protection of Jesus and Mary. Fortitude is a cardinal virtue that strengthens
the will and gives a person courage and a firm resolve to do God's
will, even in the midst of great suffering.

SAINT JOSEPH IS A MAN OF COURAGE. The root word of courage is
"*cour,*" meaning "heart." To be courageous is to love the good more
than you fear evil and suffering. The courageous man is stouthearted,
bold, and brave in the midst of trials. That St. Joseph was courageous,
no one can deny. It took courage for St. Joseph to take his family into
enemy territory (Egypt). He knew that he might need to defend his
wife and Child against physical assaults, and he was willing to do it.
No man who is easily intimidated would embark on such a journey.
Saint Joseph is intimidated by no one.

SAINT JOSEPH WILL HELP YOU TO BE COURAGEOUS. To be a saint, you
must be courageous. If you imitate St. Joseph, you will not hesitate to
enter enemy territory or undergo spiritual combat. Egypt was a land
notorious for thieves, pagan rituals, idols, and sorcerers. Saint Joseph
fears no man because God is with him. Your spiritual father is a man

on fire with love for God! "If God is for us, who can be against us?" (Rom 8:31).

SAINT JOSEPH WILL INCREASE THE VIRTUE OF FORTITUDE IN YOU. Do you remember the passage in Scripture when Jesus came walking on the water to his disciples? The disciples were terrified, and Jesus had to calm their spirits, saying: "Take courage! It is I. Do not be afraid" (Mt 14:27). What about you? What are you afraid of? Losing your job? Sacrificing your good name and worldly honors? Saint Joseph sacrificed everything for love of Jesus and Mary. Your spiritual father was a poor man and of no esteem in the world. Yet demons and the sorcerers of Egypt were terrified of the courageous heart of St. Joseph.

Jesus himself learned courage from the example of St. Joseph. Jesus witnessed his father's courage in Egypt, Nazareth, Jerusalem, and the many other places they traveled together. Saint Joseph gave his Son an example of manly love, courage, strength, and fortitude. With St. Joseph as your spiritual father, you also have nothing to be afraid of. Our Lord himself, immediately before his suffering and death, instructed his disciples to exercise manly courage, telling them, "In the world you will have trouble, but take courage, I have conquered the world" (Jn 16:33). Set your face toward the heavenly Jerusalem and never look back!

> O Joseph, virgin father of Jesus, most pure spouse of the Virgin Mary, pray for us daily to the Son of God, that, armed with the weapons of his grace, we may fight as we ought in life, and be crowned by him in death.[2]
>
> — St. Bernardine of Siena

Read "Old Men Don't Walk to Egypt" (page 113)
Pray the Litany of St. Joseph (page 233)

DAY 20

Joseph Most Obedient,
Pray for Us

If you want to know St. Joseph's obedience, look at how he rose at night at the angel's voice and, giving no care to hunger, hardships, or cold, went to Egypt where he led a hard life until the next command of God.[1]

— St. Joseph Sebastian Pelzcar

Obedience is a misunderstood virtue. Many people are of the opinion that obedience to authority limits their freedom, requiring them to hand over their rights to others. This is not the case. In fact, obedience to laws is a part of everyday human life. A road sign, for example, doesn't take away a person's freedom. Road signs and other legitimate laws are designed to give people true freedom and happiness. You are able to disobey stop signs while driving, but obedience to the stop sign is what allows you and others to reach your destinations in safety.

Natural law and divine law are not inhibitors to freedom. In God's plan, the purpose of these laws is to help us reach our ultimate destination: heaven. Those who fail to obey reason and the divine dictates will end up psychologically, anthropologically, and spiritually frustrated, and run the risk of never reaching heaven.

SAINT JOSEPH IS A MODEL OF OBEDIENCE. Obedience requires trust. Lack of trust on the part of our first parents (Adam and Eve) is what caused all mankind to fall into sin. In the Garden of Eden, our first parents were tricked into disobeying God by the serpent. The devil instilled in their minds doubts regarding God's trustworthiness. "Did God really say you would die?" (Gen 3:1). Our new parents, Mary and St. Joseph, trusted God and were willing to suffer for their obedience to God. Mary and Joseph were certain that God had their best interests in mind.

Why was St. Matthew so keen to note Joseph's trust in the words received from the messenger of God, if not to invite us to imitate this same loving trust?[2]

— Pope Benedict XVI

SAINT JOSEPH WILL INCREASE THE VIRTUE OF OBEDIENCE IN YOU. You are probably familiar with the heavenly visions given to St. Faustina containing the Divine Mercy message and devotion. Did you know that St. Faustina also had visions of St. Joseph? Saint Faustina loved St. Joseph very much and frequently turned to him for his powerful intercession, asking him to help her do the will of God and be faithful to her mission of spreading devotion to God's mercy. With the help of St. Joseph, St. Faustina was able to complete her mission and be obedient to her superiors, even when they sent her for a psychological evaluation!

The virtue of obedience is not only for nuns and priests, though. Everyone needs to be obedient to both natural and divine law. Obeying the 10 Commandments, the teachings of the Catholic Church, attending Mass faithfully on Sundays and Holy Days of Obligation, and going to Confession when you fall into sin are all ways of showing that you trust and obey God.

Everyone needs to trust God and obey the natural law as well. The person who defends marriage as an institution between one man and one woman is obeying the natural law. Protecting children in the womb by voting for candidates who are uncompromisingly pro-life is also a sign of being obedient to the natural law. Resisting the nonsense of gender ideology is another way of obeying the natural law. If you are mocked, ridiculed, and made to suffer for your trust and obedience to divine and natural law, you are not far from the Kingdom of Heaven.

> Joseph, in obedience to the Holy Spirit, found in the Holy Spirit the source of love.[3]
>
> — St. John Paul II

Read "Sleeping St. Joseph" (page 200)
Pray the Litany of St. Joseph (page 233)

DAY 21

Joseph Most Faithful,
Pray for Us

> The Church admires the simplicity and the depth of his [St. Joseph's] faith.[1]
>
> — St. John Paul II

Venerable Fulton J. Sheen spoke of three rings in marriage: the engagement ring, the wedding ring, and the suffering. Those who are married know this to be true. Marriage is not easy. It begins with a honeymoon and will be filled with many hardships, difficulties, and trials. For a marriage to work, mutual love, sacrifice, and faithfulness are necessary.

A Christian's relationship with God is a spiritual marriage. It, too, requires mutual love, sacrifice, and faithfulness. Those who are spiritually espoused to God need to be faithful in good times and in bad, in health and in sickness, in riches and in poverty. Saint Joseph was always faithful to his wife and to God.

SAINT JOSEPH IS A MODEL OF FAITH. Faith is one of the three theological virtues (faith, hope, and charity). But what exactly is faith? How is it defined? The Letter to the Hebrews gives us a good definition. It states: "Faith is the assurance of things hoped for, the conviction of things not seen" (Heb 11:1). Christian faith acknowledges who Jesus is, adheres to his teaching, and trusts in his promises.

> Joseph was deeply pious; he prayed much for the coming of the Messiah.[2]
>
> — Blessed Anne Catherine Emmerich

A Christian is called to have faith in Jesus *and* trust in him. Acknowledging who Jesus is just is not enough. Demons acknowledge who Jesus is (see Mt 8:29; Mk 5:7; Lk 8:28), but they don't love or trust him. Saint Joseph, on the other hand, is a model of faith *and* trust. He knows who Jesus is and trusts in him. Saint Joseph held fast to Jesus' words even when his mind and senses were unable to completely understand what Jesus meant. Saint Joseph exercised an active, trusting, and zealous faith.

Saint Joseph never doubted the divinity of Jesus or his power to conquer evil. To the world, Jesus looked like an ordinary child, but St. Joseph knew he was God. He adored our Lord in the cradle, in the home in Nazareth, in the Temple in Jerusalem, and as a grown man in his workshop. Saint Joseph was always aware that, in seeing Jesus, he was gazing upon God Almighty.

Saint Joseph was faithful to Jesus in good times and in bad (at the birth of Jesus in Bethlehem and when Jesus was lost in the Temple in Jerusalem). Saint Joseph was faithful to Jesus in health and in sickness (teaching Jesus to be a good carpenter and dying in the arms of Jesus). Saint Joseph was faithful to Jesus in riches and in poverty (when gold was given to Jesus by the Magi, and when the gold ran out and they lived in poverty in Egypt).

SAINT JOSEPH WILL INCREASE YOUR FAITH. Today, it is not easy to be faithful to Jesus. The world does not want you to trust Jesus, hope in his promises, or love him. If you live according to the teachings of Jesus, you will be ridiculed and mocked by the world, and maybe even by your family and friends. Should you endure exile and isolation out of love for Jesus, he is worth it. Should you suffer financial loss out of love for the truth, God will reward you. If you are belittled, spoken ill of, and calumniated because of your stance against abortion, homosexual "marriage," and contraception, your reward will be great in heaven.

Imitate the faith and loving trust of St. Joseph. Be steadfast, trusting, and intrepid in your faith.

> It is precisely the intrepid faith of St. Joseph that the Church needs today in order to courageously dedicate herself to the urgent task of the new evangelization.[3]
>
> — St. John Paul II

Read "Adorer of Christ" (page 172)
Pray the Litany of St. Joseph (page 233)

DAY 22

Mirror of Patience,
Pray for Us

This flower of Israel [St. Joseph] had the faith of Abraham, the piety of David his ancestor, the wisdom of the prophets, a patience more heroic than that of Job and of Tobias, and a zeal greater than that of Elijah for the glory of God.[1]

— Blessed Gabriele Allegra

Patience is a virtue that many people find hard to practice. Remaining peaceful and calm can be very challenging when you find yourself in a situation that is completely out of your control. Indeed, there are countless things in life that will test your patience.

In modern times, advances in technology have put almost everything in life at our fingertips. Our meals, entertainment, music, and contacts are instantly available to us. With this capability, it can be very difficult to wait and acquire the virtue of patience. If you want to be like St. Joseph, however, you must learn patience.

Blessed are all those who wait on the Lord.

— Is 30:18

SAINT JOSEPH IS A MODEL OF PATIENCE. Life was not easy for St. Joseph. His mission required a lot of waiting. If St. Joseph did not accompany Mary on her journey to Elizabeth's house, he had to wait three long months to see his wife again. When St. Joseph observed that his wife was pregnant, he had to wait for the Lord to reveal what he wanted him to do in response to the wondrous pregnancy. Such trials of patience must have been extremely challenging for St. Joseph. Saint Joseph used them as an opportunity to grow in patience and holiness. He mastered every opportunity.

Saint Joseph exhibited heroic patience in Egypt. Taking his wife and newborn Child to a country with a different language, culture, religion, and currency must have filled his heart with anxiety. Finding work in Egypt and providing food and shelter for his family could not have been easy. What husband and father would not be in a constant state of anxiety in such a situation? He had no idea how long he would have to stay in Egypt. Yet, in every situation, St. Joseph was always peaceful, kind, calm, and abandoned to Divine Providence.

Exercising patience does not mean that a person will be free of the anxieties of life. When Mary and Joseph lost Jesus for three days in Jerusalem, we are told that they searched for their beloved Son with great anxiety (see Lk 2:48). They were greatly concerned but had boundless confidence in Divine Providence.

SAINT JOSEPH WILL INCREASE YOUR PATIENCE. You, too, are going to experience many trials in life, trials that will test your love and your patience. Whether you like it or not, your patience is going to be tried. Hardly a day will go by in which you will not be given the opportunity to acquire patience. God allows such trials because he wants us to grow in virtue.

A concrete area in your life where you can exercise the virtue of patience is by being merciful to others, especially when you know their faults. Saint Joseph lived with two perfect people, but he must have frequently encountered unpleasant and difficult people: employers, co-workers, tax collectors, politicians, etc. You, too, will experience unpleasant people in life. In such instances, imitate the patience of St. Joseph. Ask God for the grace to love your neighbor. Be kind, peaceful, and merciful.

In the workplace, offer forgiveness for offenses. On the highway, be patient and courteous. With difficult family members and friends, be pleasant and merciful. Exercising patience and mercy always brings about good. The lovingly patient and merciful person is always victorious, in this life or the next!

> He [St. Joseph] was always imperturbable, even in adversities.
> Let us model ourselves after this sublime example and let us learn
> to remain peaceful and tranquil in all of life's circumstances.[2]
>
> — St. Joseph Marello

Read "The Roman Canon" (page 94)
Pray the Litany of St. Joseph (page 233)

DAY 23

Lover of Poverty,
Pray for Us

Truly, I doubt not that the angels, wondering and adoring, came
thronging in countless multitudes to that poor workshop to
admire the humility of him who guarded that dear and divine
child, and labored at his carpenter's trade to support the son and
the mother who were committed to his care.[1]

— St. Francis de Sales

Saint Joseph was unpretentious in the eyes of the world. He had no
worldly ambition or desire for recognition.

Throughout the centuries, people have often wondered what
the financial status of the Holy Family was, or what their living conditions were. To answer this question, we need look no further than
the New Testament. The Holy Family was poor. Very poor.

Saint Joseph was so lowly and poor in the sight of the world
that the Wise Men who entered the stable in Bethlehem did not even
acknowledge his presence (see Mt 2:11). When the Holy Family
journeyed to the Temple in Jerusalem to participate in the Jewish
ritual of purification for a new mother, Joseph couldn't even afford
to purchase a lamb for a burnt offering (see Lev 12:6-7). Lambs were
expensive. Saint Joseph could only offer a poor man's gift, that is, two
turtledoves or two young pigeons (see Lev 12:8).

The Holy Family lived on Divine Providence. Had Baby Jesus
not been given gold, frankincense, and myrrh by the Wise Men in
Bethlehem (see Mt 2:11), it is likely that St. Joseph would not have
had money to purchase food and other necessities for his family
when they traveled to Egypt. When they had left from Nazareth for
Jerusalem to fulfil the census, they had not brought many things
with them because they expected to return to Nazareth. The gifts
of the Wise Men were God's providential way of taking care of the
Holy Family. Years later, after returning to Nazareth from Egypt, the
Holy Family lived for almost 30 years in a house in Nazareth that
was simple and small.

"Blessed are the poor in spirit, for theirs is the kingdom
of heaven" (Mt 5:3). Have you ever wondered what that actually
means? Is Jesus saying that poverty is wonderful? No, that's not what

he is saying. What he is saying is that those who are detached from the things of this world are not far from the Kingdom of Heaven. When a person is detached from the things of this world, poverty is understood to be a virtue. The person who is detached from material things is truly blessed in spirit and rich in the sight of God. This explains why St. Joseph is called "Lover of Poverty." He relied on Divine Providence for all of his needs.

SAINT JOSEPH WILL HELP YOU BE POOR IN SPIRIT. Saint Joseph will teach you how to be detached from material things and abandoned to Divine Providence. You will never find true happiness in material goods. Those who allow their relationship to God to depend on whether they have worldly things are destined for unhappiness. The person who is poor in spirit, on the other hand, is able to proclaim, "The Lord gave and the Lord has taken away; blessed be the name of the Lord" (Job 1:21).

The silence of St. Joseph proves his greatness and poverty of spirit. Everyone likes to boast of their achievements and have others acknowledge their work. Saint Joseph, however, never saw the results of his hard work and sacrifice. He trusted that God would bring good fruit from his labor and years of service to Jesus and Mary. And God did — more than St. Joseph could have ever imagined. He was poor in the world, but rich in the Kingdom of Heaven.

He [St. Joseph] lived content in his poverty.[2]

— St. Bonaventure

Read "Perpetual Adoration" (page 171)
Pray the Litany of St. Joseph (page 233)

DAY 24
Model of Workmen,
Pray for Us

At the workbench where he [St. Joseph] plied his trade together
with Jesus, Joseph brought human work closer to the mystery of
the Redemption.[1]

— St. John Paul II

The devil hates an honest and diligent worker. At the beginning
of human history, the wicked serpent initiated his attack on the
human family in the workplace — that is, the garden God gave Adam
and Eve to tend and keep. Lucifer hates work. He particularly dis-
dains the fact that because of love, God humbled himself and became
a man, making himself capable of manual labor. Jesus spent many
years in St. Joseph's workshop diligently working. It was preparation
for his re-entering man's original workshop — a garden; the Garden
of Gethsemane, specifically — and accomplishing the work of our
redemption.

Jesus is God. Together with the Father and the Holy Spirit,
he made the heavens and the earth. Our Lord's ability to create far
exceeds anything we can possibly imagine. When he became flesh,
Jesus sanctified human work and elevated it to a level of greatness that
did not exist prior to his Incarnation. Though divine, God humbled
himself, became a man, and worked like a man. In his humanity, he
learned how to work as a man by imitating the example of his earthly
father, St. Joseph.

SAINT JOSEPH IS THE MODEL WORKMAN. If St. Joseph taught the
God-Man how to work, he is more than capable of serving as our
model as well. Hard work benefits the person, the family, and society.

He [St. Joseph] belongs to the working-class, and he bore the
burdens of poverty for himself and the Holy Family, whose
tender and vigilant head he was.[2]

— Pope Pius XI

Work is not always easy and pleasant. Putting in a hard day's work
can be taxing on the mind, body, and soul. Sometimes work can be

downright burdensome. As a carpenter, Jesus knew this firsthand. He offers comfort to all who make their living by the sweat of their brow.

> Come to me, all who labor and are burdened, and I will give you rest. Take my yoke upon you, and learn from me, for I am meek and humble of heart, and you will find rest for your souls. For my yoke is easy, and my burden is light.
>
> — Mt 11:28-30

SAINT JOSEPH WILL TEACH YOU HOW TO BE A DILIGENT WORKER. Our Lord desired to do manual labor for many years before initiating his public ministry. Why did he do it? He did it because he wanted to sanctify work and teach us that work is honorable and pleasing to God. However, neither Jesus nor St. Joseph were workaholics. Workaholics are of no benefit to themselves, the family, or society. God does not delight in a workaholic.

Jesus learned the proper place of work in his life through the loving example of St. Joseph. Saint Joseph made time for God, family, recreation, and rest. Saint Joseph modeled these aspects of human life for Jesus. Saint Joseph will teach you these important lessons as well.

Saint Joseph also serves as the model workman for the imitation of those who work for the salvation of souls, especially deacons, priests, bishops, and religious. Consecrated souls are to work diligently and faithfully in God's vineyard. This work, too, can be difficult and burdensome. Priests, deacons, and consecrated religious are human; they need rest and recreation like everyone else. On rare occasions, God gives extraordinary graces for a person to perform heroic penances, fasts, and mortifications. However, God never desires for his workers to burn out from sheer exhaustion. He wants them to take delight in mountain streams, forests, and sunsets. He wants priests and nuns who are like St. Joseph: loving, prayerful, hard-working, and not afraid to rest.

> Let us ask St. Joseph to foster staunch vocations for our Lord.[3]
>
> — St. Peter Julian Eymard

Read "Saint Joseph the Worker" (page 217)
Pray the Litany of St. Joseph (page 233)

DAY 25
Glory of Domestic Life,
Pray for Us

Joseph loved Jesus as a father loves his son and showed his love
by giving him the best he had.[1]

— St. Josemaría Escrivá

In the 16th century, St. Teresa of Avila helped reform the female
branch of the Carmelite Order. She had a tremendous devotion
to St. Joseph and named the majority of her reformed convents after
him. To protect the convents (and the nuns in them), she buried
medals of St. Joseph around the convents as a sign that they belonged
to God and St. Joseph. In the 20th century, St. André Bessette did
something similar.

Saint André wanted to erect a shrine dedicated to St. Joseph in
Montreal, Canada. He found the perfect location and placed medals
of St. Joseph around the property as a way of asking St. Joseph to
bless and obtain the property. Needless to say, he got it!

SAINT JOSEPH WANTS TO BLESS YOUR HOME. If you lovingly welcome
St. Joseph into your home, invoke his intercession, and honor him in
pious devotions, he will greatly bless your domestic life. Wherever St.
Joseph is present, Jesus and Mary are present as well.

Saint Joseph wants to be in your home and present in your
family life. Even if you move, he wants to go with you. Speaking of
moving, let me quickly say something about a practice that concerns
me: There is no need for you to bury a statue of St. Joseph to sell
your house. Burying a statue of St. Joseph in an effort to sell a home
is a modern phenomenon. Saint Teresa of Avila and St. André Bessette never buried statues of St. Joseph. Statues, unlike medals, are
not made to be buried. Statues represent a person, and are meant to
be venerated *above ground*, not buried in the ground. Place a statue
of St. Joseph inside your home and pray to St. Joseph frequently for
your domestic needs, including the selling of your home. Do not
bury a statue of St. Joseph in your yard.

You are the light of the world. A city set on a mountain cannot
be hidden. Nor do they light a lamp and then put it under a

bushel basket; it is set on a lampstand, where it gives light to all
in the house.

— Mt 5:14-15

Whatever you do, never bury a statue of St. Joseph upside
down. People sometimes do this bizarre practice as a form of spiritual
bribery, promising to turn the statue of St. Joseph right side up only
if their home is sold. Such a practice is akin to treating a statue of
St. Joseph as a talisman or a good luck charm. Saint Joseph is your
spiritual father, not a trinket. There's no need to bury a statue of him.
Talk to him; he hears you.

SAINT JOSEPH LOVES DOMESTIC LIFE. Saint Joseph is the saint of the
hidden years of Jesus. This reality is incredible to ponder. Consider
your own memories of living at home: family outings, birthdays,
religious celebrations, playing together, singing, etc. Most likely,
you only lived in the house of your parents for 20 years or so. Our
Lord, however, lived with Mary and St. Joseph for 30 years. The
love, intimacy, and familiarity Jesus, Mary, and St. Joseph shared is
amazing! Saint Joseph knew what Jesus' walk sounded like. He knew
the sound of Jesus' sneeze, laughter, and voice raised in song. He
knew Jesus' mannerisms, morning routine, posture, smile, yawn, and
favorite food and drink. These are treasured memories that reside
deep in the heart and mind of St. Joseph.

> Jesus and Mary themselves obey and offer their homage to
> Joseph, for they reverence what the hand of God has established
> in him, namely, the authority of spouse and the authority of
> father.[2]

— Pope Pius XI

Read "Saint Joseph's Workshop" (page 169)
Pray the Litany of St. Joseph (page 233)

DAY 26
Guardian of Virgins,
Pray for Us

I prayed to St. Joseph to watch over me. From my childhood, my devotion to him was mingled with my love for the Blessed Virgin. Each day I recited the prayer, "O Saint Joseph, father and protector of virgins." It seemed to me that I was well protected and completely sheltered from every danger.[1]

— St. Thérèse of Lisieux

Saint Joseph has a special love for those consecrated to God through religious vows. Saint Joseph loves everyone, of course, but he has a special place in his heart for virgins. A virgin himself, St. Joseph knows firsthand the intimacy that a virgin is capable of having with God. Saint Joseph lived for 30 years with the two greatest virgins to ever grace this planet: Jesus and Mary. Virginity is a treasure. It is a treasure that St. Joseph guards and wants others to know about.

REMEMBER ST. JOSEPH! **Many people know the *Memorare* prayer to the Virgin Mary. What many people don't know about is the *Memorare* to St. Joseph. It's almost identical to the Marian *Memorare*. The *Memorare* to St. Joseph goes like this:**

> Remember, O most chaste spouse of the Virgin Mary, that never was it known that anyone who fled to thy protection, implored thy help, or sought thy intercession was left unaided. Inspired by this confidence, I fly unto you, my spiritual father, and beg your protection. O foster father of the Redeemer, despise not my petitions, but in your goodness hear and answer me. Amen.

Saint Faustina's religious community, the Sisters of Our Lady of Mercy, recite the *Memorare* to St. Joseph every day. Saint Faustina herself had a tremendous devotion to St. Joseph and daily asked his intercession for her vocation and mission. She wrote:

> Saint Joseph urged me to have a constant devotion to him. He himself told me to recite three prayers [the Our Father, Hail Mary, and Glory Be] and the *Memorare* [to St. Joseph] once every day. He looked at me with great kindness and gave me to know how much he is supporting this work [of mercy]. He

has promised me this special help and protection. I recite the requested prayers every day and feel his special protection.[2]

SAINT JOSEPH WILL HELP YOU BE A GUARDIAN OF VIRGINITY AND PURITY. If you maintain a daily loving relationship with St. Joseph, your eyes, intentions, heart, and relationships can be pleasing to God and free of anything that goes against purity. If you walk with St. Joseph, you will find less and less pleasure in filthy and perverse films. Such "entertainment" will repulse your soul. Music that is foul, degrading to women, and offensive to God will not appeal to you either. This doesn't mean you must only listen to Christian music or watch Christian movies, but it does mean that you will know light from darkness.

Everyone is going to be tempted to sin against purity — some more than others. In St. Joseph, everyone has a guardian and a protector. Turn to him in times of temptation and you will grow in innocence and purity. Frequently ask his intercession to keep your heart pure and chaste.

I have taken for my advocate and protector, the glorious St. Joseph, to whom I have recommended myself with all the fervor of my heart, and by whom I have been visibly aided. This tender father of my soul, this loving protector hastened to snatch me from the wretched state in which my body languished, as he had delivered me from greater dangers of another nature, which threatened my honor and my eternal salvation.[3]

— St. Teresa of Avila

I beg the great St. Joseph, in whom I have a very great confidence, to come to my aid.[4]

— St. Elizabeth of the Trinity

Read "A Miraculous Staircase in New Mexico" (page 189)
Pray the Litany of St. Joseph (page 233)

DAY 27
Pillar of Families,
Pray for Us

Those who are devoted to prayer should, in a special manner, cherish devotion to St. Joseph. I know not how anyone can ponder on the sufferings, trials, and tribulations the Queen of Angels endured whilst caring for Jesus in his childhood, without at the same time thanking St. Joseph for the services he rendered the Divine Child and his Blessed Mother.[1]

— St. Teresa of Avila

Jesus, Mary, and Joseph love families. Their three hearts are very concerned about what is happening to families today. Families are falling apart.

Modern man has distanced himself from God and attempted to redefine what it means to be a family. As a result, divorce rates are at an all-time high; the majority of married couples use contraception; abortion is legal; and it is socially acceptable for children to be raised by two dads and/or two moms. The family stands on the edge of a great precipice.

Various programs backed by very powerful resources nowadays seem to aim at the breakdown of the family. At times it appears that concerted efforts are being made to present as "normal" and attractive, and even to glamourize, situations which are in fact "irregular." Indeed, they contradict "the truth and love" which should inspire and guide relationships between men and women, thus causing tensions and divisions in families, with grave consequences particularly for children. The moral conscience becomes darkened; what is true, good, and beautiful is deformed; and freedom is replaced by what is actually enslavement.[2]

— St. John Paul II

Saint John Paul II is absolutely correct. God established the family to be a school of love, something beautiful, delightful, and life-giving, and the devil and his agents want to destroy it. How are we ever going to turn the situation around? How can we return to order? The only way is to elevate the Holy Family as the model and blueprint of the family. When the Holy Family is celebrated in society, we will again know the sanctity of motherhood, the heroism of fatherhood, and the blessing of children.

SAINT JOSEPH WANTS TO BE THE PILLAR OF YOUR FAMILY. A pillar is a foundation. In order for your home to stand on a firm foundation and be unshakable, your family needs St. Joseph. He will teach your family the importance of prayer, mutual respect, purity, honesty, forgiveness, love, and, most importantly, placing God above all things.

SAINT JOSEPH LOVES THE FAMILY! Saint Joseph, the pillar of the family, teaches us the importance of motherhood, fatherhood, and children. He is the saint of the childhood and hidden years of Jesus. He teaches modern man that the only true definition of a family is that it consists of a mother, a father, and children. The notion of a "modern family" is a deception from the devil. The redefinition of marriage and the family causes the breakdown of society, culture, morals, and true family values.

In the person of St. Joseph, men can learn what it means to be a husband and a father. They must be self-sacrificing for women, children, and the common good. It is honorable for men to sacrifice themselves for others. Manhood and fatherhood are perfected through love, sacrifice, and faithfulness to those entrusted to their care. The exercise of such manhood is how husbands and fathers become pillars of civilization, and indeed, become holy. A world filled with men like St. Joseph will experience a renewal of social and moral order.

> I saw Jesus assisting his parents in every possible way, and also on the street and wherever opportunity offered, cheerfully, eagerly, and obligingly helping everyone. He assisted his foster-father in his trade, and devoted himself to prayer and contemplation. He was a model for all the children of Nazareth.[3]
>
> — Blessed Anne Catherine Emmerich

Read "Silent Witness" (page 191)
Pray the Litany of St. Joseph (page 233)

DAY 28
Comfort of the Afflicted,
Pray for Us

Nothing will be refused him [St. Joseph], neither by Our Lady nor by his glorious Son.[1]

— St. Francis de Sales

Comforting the afflicted is a work of mercy. The Church has seven Spiritual Works of Mercy and seven Corporal Works of Mercy. The works of mercy help us to be devout followers of Jesus Christ by serving others; they help us to be like St. Joseph.

SEVEN CORPORAL WORKS OF MERCY	SEVEN SPIRITUAL WORKS OF MERCY
Feed the Hungry	Teach the Ignorant
Give Drink to the Thirsty	Pray for the Living and the Dead
Clothe the Naked	Correct Sinners
Shelter the Homeless	Counsel Those in Doubt
Visit the Prisoners	Console the Sorrowful
Comfort the Sick	Bear Wrongs Patiently
Bury the Dead	Forgive Wrongs Willingly

The Latin title *Solatium Miserorum* is generally translated as "Comfort of the Afflicted," but it can also be rendered "Solace of the Miserable" or "Solace of Those in Misery." Experiencing misery or feeling miserable is not pleasant. Yet the reality is that we are all going to have miserable moments in life. This world is a valley of tears, and everyone is going to suffer. There is no way around it. Whether it's financial problems, marital hardships, psychological struggles, difficulties in relationships, the death of loved ones, or a thousand other woes, we will all experience misery in life. It's good to have someone we can turn to for comfort and solace in such times.

SAINT JOSEPH WILL COMFORT YOU IN DIFFICULT TIMES. Life is filled with many sorrows. Loved ones will die, children sometimes rebel, and gravity will eventually take away your youthfulness, making you old and immobile. No matter what life brings, however, St. Joseph will always be your consolation, comfort, and solace. He knows well the hardships of life. He is a kind and loving father. He comforts everyone who comes to him in times of affliction. His fatherhood is unlike any other.

> Let us commend ourselves to our good father, St. Joseph, who is the Patriarch of troubled people, since he himself went through so much trouble.[2]

> — St. Joseph Marello

A loving father provides comfort to his children, especially when they are going through difficulties. A father's wisdom and presence are reassuring and life-giving. Knowing you can always go to your father in difficult times reassures you that everything will be okay, even when your world seems to be falling apart. Regrettably, many people have never experienced this kind of love from a father. Many people today have grown up with emotionally abusive, distant, and less-than-virtuous fathers. This has led many people to experience great anxieties and fears in life, as well as a tremendous sense of insecurity.

God wants you to rest in St. Joseph's fatherhood. Saint Joseph will never abandon you. No matter what your experience of fatherhood has been, St. Joseph will always be there for you. He is your spiritual dad, and he loves you. He will never hurt you. He would give his life for you a million times over.

When life has you down, run to your spiritual father. Pour out your heart to him. Tell him your troubles. He is the most loving of fathers. He is always available for you, always attentive, always understanding.

> If discouragement overwhelms you, think of the faith of Joseph; if anxiety has its grip on you, think of the hope of Joseph; if exasperation or hatred seizes you, think of the love of Joseph, who was the first man to set eyes on the human face of God in the person of the Infant conceived by the Holy Spirit in the womb of the Virgin Mary. Let us praise and thank Christ for having drawn so close to us, and for giving us Joseph as an example and model of love.[3]

> — Pope Benedict XVI

Read "Pious Union of St. Joseph" (page 215)
Pray the Litany of St. Joseph (page 233)

DAY 29

Hope of the Sick,
Pray for Us

As the Church's Liturgy teaches, he [St. Joseph] "cooperated in the fullness of time in the great mystery of salvation" and is truly a "minister of salvation."[1]

— St. John Paul II

God has healed many people through the intercession of St. Joseph, such as St. Teresa of Avila. She often told people how she was so terribly ill that she considered herself half-dead, but after praying to St. Joseph, she experienced a miraculous cure.

Saint Thérèse of Lisieux would have died in infancy were it not for the intercession of St. Joseph. Saints Louis and Zélie Martin, Thérèse's parents, were very devoted to St. Joseph. They named two of their children after St. Joseph but, sadly, both of the children died in childbirth. When Zélie was again pregnant, she believed the child in her womb was a boy, and she planned to name the child Joseph. After childbirth, however, the baby was discovered to be a girl, and it was decided that her name would be Thérèse.

Shortly after Thérèse was born, she became deathly ill. No one knew the cause of the illness. Her mother, having already experienced the death of several other children, was greatly saddened but resigned to God's holy will. Fearing that little Thérèse was going to die, Zélie knelt before a statue of St. Joseph in her bedroom and asked the saint to heal her daughter. Miraculously, Thérèse was healed! Thérèse's mother wrote down an account of what had happened to her little Thérèse. She wrote:

> I went up to my room [little Thérèse was on the first floor with a wet nurse], I knelt at the feet of St. Joseph, and I asked him for the grace of healing for the little one, while resigning myself to God's will. I do not often cry, but I was crying as I prayed. I didn't know if I should go downstairs. In the end, I decided to go down, and what did I see? The baby was nursing vigorously. She did not let go until 1 p.m. She spit up a bit and fell back as though dead on her wet nurse. There were five of us around her. Everyone was stunned. There was a worker who was crying; I felt my blood run cold. The baby had no visible breath. It did no

good for us to lean over to try and discover a sign of life because we could see nothing. But she was so calm, so peaceful, that I thanked God for having her die so gently. Then a quarter of an hour went by, and my little Thérèse opened her eyes and started to smile.[2]

SAINT JOSEPH OFFERS HOPE IN TIMES OF SICKNESS. If you or someone you know is sick, go to St. Joseph. Jesus wants you to go to your spiritual father and ask him for help and healing. It's up to God whether or not a physical healing will be given, but it doesn't hurt to ask, as St. Zélie did for her little Thérèse.

If you or a loved one receive a healing, don't forget that you are still going to suffer in life. Saint Thérèse was healed as an infant, but she suffered many other ailments in life, and eventually succumbed to death. Even Lazarus, whom Jesus raised from the dead, died again. Thus, whether you experience a physical healing or not, St. Joseph always offers hope for an illness-free life in heaven. Saint Joseph will help you be abandoned to Divine Providence.

> Like St. Joseph, let us live each day according to the dispositions of providence, doing whatever God suggests.[3]
>
> — St. Joseph Marello

Read "Votive Masses" (page 203)
Pray the Litany of St. Joseph (page 233)

DAY 30

Patron of the Dying,
Pray for Us

The name of Joseph will be our protection during all the days of our life, but above all at the moment of death.[1]

— Blessed William Joseph Chaminade

Saint Joseph died a holy and happy death. He died gazing upon Jesus and resting in the arms of Mary. What greater death could a person experience? God has designated St. Joseph as the Patron of the Dying because he wants us to experience a death similar to that of St. Joseph, a holy and happy death.

Death is a part of life, but it is not an easy part of life. Letting go and saying goodbye to family and friends is not easy. In many monasteries, there are signs that read *"Memento Mori"* ("Remember You Will Die"). The sign is not meant to be morbid, but rather to serve as a reminder that our life on earth will come to an end, and we need to be prepared for death.

We need to be prepared for death because Satan always tries to get a soul to despair and turn away from our loving God at the hour of death. Ask any priest; he will tell you that a spiritual battle takes place over a soul at the hour of death. For this reason, we need the intercession of our spiritual father to fortify us, protect us, and fill us with trust in God's love and mercy.

Jesus granted to him [St. Joseph] the special privilege of safeguarding the dying against the snares of Lucifer, just as he had also saved him [Jesus] from the schemes of Herod.[2]

St. Alphonsus Liguori

SAINT JOSEPH IS YOUR PERSONAL PATRON. Saint Joseph is everyone's personal patron because everyone is going to die. None of us is going to be here forever. You have a loving spiritual father who can help you prepare for death. On his deathbed, St. Joseph himself must have been concerned about the future of his wife and Son. Would they suffer? Would they be treated cruelly by others? Would their future be a happy one? Yet St. Joseph had boundless confidence in God's love and mercy. He died trusting in Divine Providence, full of confidence that God would take care of his wife and Son. With St. Joseph in your life, you do not have to be fearful of death either. When your time comes, St. Joseph will help you experience a happy and holy death.

> The Church encourages us to prepare ourselves for the hour of our death. In the litany of the saints, for instance, she has us pray: "From a sudden and unforeseen death, deliver us, O Lord," to ask the Mother of God to intercede for us "at the hour of our death" in the Hail Mary; and to entrust ourselves to St. Joseph, the patron of a happy death.[3]
>
> — *Catechism of the Catholic Church*

The *Catechism* tells us that, in order to prepare for death, we should "entrust ourselves to St. Joseph." In other words, consecrate yourself to St. Joseph! To prevent an unhappy death — a death that catches us unprepared, without the last Sacraments — prepare for it now by consecrating yourself to St. Joseph and living a holy life. In giving everything to St. Joseph, death will not catch you unprepared. Today, many people are not prepared for death. They do not consider their mortality, living as if they are immortal and immune to the grave. The finality of death will be a torture for such people.

As for you, live a pious life in union with the Church. Remain in a state of sanctifying grace. Go to Confession and Holy Communion frequently. Give everything to St. Joseph!

> He [a servant of St. Joseph] will beg of him the grace of dying as he himself did, with the kiss of Jesus and in the arms of Mary.[4]
>
> — Blessed William Joseph Chaminade

> Happy are you if your death has the assistance of St. Joseph. Then, no matter if flames devour you, or waters overwhelm you, or disease slays you, the prayers of St. Joseph will throw around you an all protecting mantle of defense.[5]
>
> — Venerable Nelson Baker

Read "Patron of a Happy Death" (page 206)
Pray the Litany of St. Joseph (page 233)

DAY 31
Terror of Demons,
Pray for Us

Jesus, Mary, and Joseph pursued their way through many towns of Egypt, driving out the demons not only from the idols, but out of many bodies possessed by them, curing many that were grievously and dangerously ill.[1]

— Venerable Mary of Ágreda

Demons fear Jesus. Demons fear Mary. Did you know that demons fear St. Joseph as well? It's true. Demons are absolutely terrified of St. Joseph.

Evil spirits are terrified of St. Joseph because he alone is the spouse of the Immaculata and the father of Jesus Christ. Saint Joseph is the gateway to Jesus and Mary. Everything that touches him becomes a relic. He saved the Savior from Herod, spent decades in adoration, exercised paternal authority over Jesus, and made it possible for Jesus and Mary to offer their sacrifice on Calvary. Demons have plenty to be afraid of in the person of St. Joseph. He is mighty!

SAINT JOSEPH IS A DRAGON SLAYER! The title "Terror of Demons" is the most unique title of St. Joseph. It is a fearsome and commanding title. It is the title of a warrior. The lily St. Joseph holds in his hand is a mighty spiritual weapon, a sword of purity. It has the power to pierce fire-breathing dragons (demons) and conquer every form of filth and darkness. The lily he wields is a threat to all the filthy forces of Satan.

Demons are terrified at the mere mention of St. Joseph's name. They fear everything about St. Joseph. "How terrified are they?" you ask. Well, terrified enough that they fear when he sleeps! When St. Joseph slumbers, he speaks to God! It doesn't matter if his mind and body are at rest. Saint Joseph's spirit is always at attention and ready to protect, defend, and fight for Jesus, Mary, and souls. When St. Joseph rises from sleep, demons know he will promptly do the will of God and block their evil intentions. Whether St. Joseph is awake or asleep, all hell trembles before the father and king of the Holy Family.

Saint Joseph is a quiet man, but he is not a timid man. One glance of his eyes sends all hell into flight. One word from his mouth routs the forces of darkness as an axe levels a field of trees! Who can stand against you if the Terror of Demons protects you?

SAINT JOSEPH WILL PROTECT YOU AGAINST SATAN AND HIS DEMONS. Satan is not a myth; neither are evil spirits and demons. The world considers these creatures to be fairytales and legends, but they are real. We are in a spiritual battle. Satan and his demons are out to get you.   .

Saint Peter offered the following description of the devil and the hellish threat he poses:

> Be sober and vigilant. Your opponent the devil is prowling around like a roaring lion looking for someone to devour. Resist him, steadfast in your faith, knowing that your fellow believers throughout the world undergo the same sufferings.
>
> — 1 Pet 5:8-9

To defeat the devil, you need Jesus, Mary, St. Joseph, and the teachings and Sacraments of the Catholic Church. Every Christian needs truth and the strong spiritual fatherhood of St. Joseph.

You are a child of St. Joseph. It doesn't matter if you are 6 years old or 60 years old. Jesus himself referred to grown men on the shores of Galilee as children (see Jn 21:5). Jesus is God, and he has appointed St. Joseph to be your loving spiritual father. In times of fear, oppression, mortal danger, and extreme temptation, run to your spiritual father. He will fight for you. The Terror of Demons is ready to slay dragons for you!

> Saint Joseph, may you and your immaculate spouse assist me in the final struggle.[2]
>
> — St. John Neumann

Read "Terror of Demons" (page 219)
Pray the Litany of St. Joseph (page 233)

DAY 32

Protector of the Holy Church,
Pray for Us

The Church invokes St. Joseph as her Patron and Protector through her unshakable trust that he to whom Christ willed to confide the care and protection of his own frail human childhood, will continue from heaven to perform his protective task in order to guide and defend the Mystical Body of Christ himself, which is always weak, always under attack, always in a state of peril.[1]

— St. Pope Paul VI

The Church needs the protection of St. Joseph. According to the designs of Providence, the Church has always needed his protection, but today it needs it more than ever. The Church is being assaulted by those outside it (Satan and the world) and by those inside it (many of her own children). Sadly, the Church also has to be protected from heterodox and spiritually weak priests and bishops.

Don't believe me? Well, on June 29, 1972, St. Pope Paul VI made the claim that "the smoke of Satan has entered the Church." He was right. The Church is in a mess. The smoke of Satan has infiltrated even the highest levels of the Church. The only way to clear away the smoke and make the Church beautiful again is to repent and return to order. There is no other way.

Jesus never promised that everyone in the Church would be holy. The weeds and the wheat grow together. The Church in her essence is holy because she is the bride of Christ, but there are many individual members of the Church who are not holy, marring the beauty of the bride of Christ by their sinful and criminal actions. In God's time, the weeds and the wheat will be separated. Our role is to stay close to St. Joseph. In this way, we will be wheat, not weeds.

To be faithful as humble collaborators with the divine plan over our lives, we need, along with the protection of the Virgin Mary, that of St. Joseph, a most powerful intercessor.[2]

— St. Pope John XXIII

SAINT JOSEPH PROTECTS THE CHURCH. The days in which we live are filled with scandal, confusion, and division. It is not easy to remain faithful, zealous, and hopeful. Yet, we have reason for hope. God

75

will never abandon us. Saint Joseph will never abandon us either. He knows what is going on in the Church, and he wants to correct it.

> Saint Joseph is always the choir director who intones the songs, but he sometimes allows a few sour notes.[3]

> — St. Joseph Marello

There are many sour notes in the Church today. Don't jump ship, though! In his time, the Heavenly Father will put his foot down. We will see the glory of the Church again. All is in the hands of Divine Providence. Trust.

At a time of persecution of the Church in Mexico, Blessed Miguel Pro turned to St. Joseph for help. His first Mass had been said at an altar of St. Joseph. He would later give his life as a martyr before a firing squad, crucifix in one hand, rosary in the other, and St. Joseph in his heart. Blessed Miguel offers words of comfort for the difficult times in which we live. He states:

> The splendor of the Resurrection [of the Church] is already on its way because now the gloom of the passion [of the Church] is at its height.[4]

Hold fast to Jesus, Mary, and St. Joseph. They are with us. Trust in Divine Providence.

> Lamb of God, who takes away the sins of the world,
> *spare us, O Lord.*

> Lamb of God, who takes away the sins of the world,
> *graciously hear us, O Lord.*

> Lamb of God, who takes away the sins of the world,
> *have mercy on us.*

Read "Patron of the Universal Church" (page 97)
Pray the Litany of St. Joseph (page 233)

DAY 33

He Made Him the Lord of His Household, *and Prince Over All His Possessions*

As Almighty God appointed Joseph, son of the patriarch Jacob, over all the land of Egypt to save grain for the people, so when the fullness of time was come and he was about to send on earth his only-begotten Son, the Savior of the world, he chose another Joseph of whom the first had been a type, and he made him the lord and chief of his household and possessions, the guardian of his choicest treasures.[1]

— Blessed Pope Pius IX

Our spiritual father St. Joseph is lord, chief, and guardian of the treasures of heaven! Many saints believe that Jesus referred to the greatness of St. Joseph in his preaching. It occurred when the mother of James and John asked Jesus if her sons could sit next to him in his kingdom. The text reads as follows:

Then the mother of the sons of Zebedee approached him with her sons and did him homage, wishing to ask him for something. He said to her, "What do you wish?" She answered him, "Command that these two sons of mine sit, one at your right and the other at your left, in your kingdom." Jesus said in reply, "You do not know what you are asking. Can you drink the cup that I am going to drink?" They said to him, "We can." He replied, "My cup you will indeed drink, but to sit at my right and at my left, this is not mine to give but is for those for whom it has been prepared by my Father." When the ten heard this, they became indignant at the two brothers. But Jesus summoned them and said, "You know that the rulers of the Gentiles lord it over them, and the great ones make their authority over them felt. But it shall not be so among you. Rather, whoever wishes to be great among you shall be your servant; whoever wishes to be first among you shall be your slave. Just so, the Son of Man did not come to be served but to serve and to give his life as a ransom for many."

— Mt 20:20-28

What are we to make of Jesus' statement? What persons has the Father prepared to sit next to Jesus in heaven? Obviously, Mary, the mother of Jesus, sits on Jesus' right side. She is the Queen Mother in

God's kingdom. What about the other side? Who is that seat reserved for? It makes sense that it is reserved for St. Joseph. It is fitting that God would place St. Joseph on the left side of Jesus because no saint is greater than the father of Jesus Christ!

> It is a monstrous crime for a father to be poor while the son lives in abundance. Who could imagine that the son of God, who is master of all virtues, would forget Joseph whom he loved and cherished as his father? He [Jesus] must have spared no effort to enrich him.[2]
>
> — Blessed William Joseph Chaminade

Seated on the left of Jesus in the Kingdom of Heaven, St. Joseph dispenses all the treasures of heaven.

> Devotion to St. Joseph is one of the choicest graces that God can give to a soul, for it is tantamount to revealing the entire treasury of Our Lord's graces.[3]
>
> — St. Peter Julian Eymard

SAINT JOSEPH IS YOUR INCREASER. Let him increase your intimacy with Jesus and Mary.

> Joseph is an all-powerful intercessor. We must, then, be devoted to him; we must honor him and consecrate ourselves to him. In that way we shall greatly please Jesus and Mary, who consider as done for themselves what is done for Joseph.[4]
>
> — St. Peter Julian Eymard

Pray the Litany of St. Joseph (page 233)
Read "Consecration Day" (page 79)

Consecration Day

O God, who, in your loving providence, chose Blessed Joseph to be the spouse of your most Holy Mother, grant us the favor of having him for our intercessor in heaven whom on earth we venerate as our protector. You, who live and reign forever and ever. Amen.

You've made it! Today, you are going to consecrate yourself entirely to St. Joseph.

A comprehensive program of consecration to St. Joseph has been long in the making. It has taken centuries for the secret weapon of consecration to St. Joseph to develop. It is now revealed, and you have been chosen by God to be the recipient of a tremendous blessing in the spiritual life. You have been selected at this time in history to be a part of *Consecration to St. Joseph*. Do you know how blessed you are?

In days of old, saints would have been delighted by a comprehensive method of preparation and consecration to St. Joseph. Their saintly instincts knew of the greatness and wonders of St. Joseph and each one, in their own way, sought to honor him and love him with a filial devotion. But it is you who will be ranked among the very first in the history of the Church to live in a tremendous era of devotion to St. Joseph. The era of St. Joseph!

The Holy Trinity wants St. Joseph to be more known and loved. You have been invited to imitate the virtues and holiness of St. Joseph's pure heart. With St. Joseph at your side, virtue and holiness will increase in your life. With St. Joseph's paternal cloak over you, you will be protected from spiritual harm. Fear nothing, my friend. Your spiritual father is the father of Jesus, the husband of the Mother of God, and the Terror of Demons!

Those who honor their father atone for sins ... In word and deed honor your father, that all blessings may come to you.

— Sir 3:3, 8

For the rest of your life, love, trust, and honor St. Joseph. Go to him in times of plenty, in times of poverty, in good times and in bad. He will be your guardian, your strength, and your certainty of not being lost. If you become weary, go to Joseph. If you become anxious, go to Joseph. When you are alone, mourning, or tempted, run to St. Joseph! He will never be far from you. He will hear your voice and be your quick defense. A fearless warrior, your spiritual father will rush to your side and protect you.

> God demands much from you, but he will favor you generously on this earth, and will exalt you, if you will but imitate St. Joseph in his virtues.[1]

> — St. Joseph Sebastian Pelczar

Never forget what you have learned in these days of preparation. Renew your consecration frequently. Strive to please the loving heart of your spiritual father. Avoid sin and live as a faithful member of the Church. Should scandals persist, keep your eyes fixed on Jesus, Mary, and St. Joseph. They will never disappoint you. They will never abandon you. They will always love you and be with you.

> I have prayed to our Lord that he might give me St. Joseph for a father, as he had given me Mary for a mother; that he might put in my heart that devotion, that confidence, that filial love of a client, of a devotee of St. Joseph. I trust the good Master has heard my prayers, for I now feel greater devotion to this great saint, and I am full of confidence and hope.[2]

> — St. Peter Julian Eymard

Pray an Act of Consecration to St. Joseph (page 235)

PART 11
The Wonders of
Our Spiritual Father

WONDER 1

DELIGHT OF SAINTS

I saw heaven opened and St. Joseph sitting upon a magnificent throne. I felt myself wonderfully affected when, each time his name was mentioned, all the saints made a profound inclination toward him, showing by the serenity and sweetness of their looks that they rejoiced with him on account of his exalted dignity.

— St. Gertrude the Great

Saint Joseph's Oratory

I have only my great devotion to St. Joseph. This it is that guides me and gives me full confidence.[1]

— St. André Bessette

Saints are heroes. Every hero deserves a place of honor. This is especially true of St. Joseph. He is the greatest saint, the greatest hero. He deserves a basilica in his honor!

The reality is that there are many shrines around the world dedicated to St. Joseph (see page 283 for a brief list). There is one, however, that stands out above all the rest: St. Joseph's Oratory in Montréal, Canada. Saint Joseph's Oratory is a basilica and is widely acclaimed as the preeminent international center of devotion to St. Joseph.

Saint Joseph's Oratory was founded by St. André Bessette. This incredible saint was born near Montréal in 1845. His birth name was Alfred, and his parents were devout Catholics; he was number eight of 12 children. Years later, when he entered religious life, he took the name André.

Alfred's father was a lumberjack by trade. Tragically, his father died after a tree fell on him when little Alfred was only 9 years old. Two years later, Alfred's mother died from tuberculosis, so Alfred became an orphan at age 12. Losing both his father and mother at such an early age, Alfred developed a strong devotion to St. Joseph and entrusted his life entirely to him. Alfred never had good health and never received much of an education either. As a young man, he moved to the United States for work and spent time in Connecticut working in several textile mills.

After a period of time, Alfred entered the Congregation of the Holy Cross and became a lay brother; he never became a priest. Due to his lack of education, Brother André was given the menial task of porter (doorman) of a college run by his religious community in Quebec. He remained in that role for more than 40 years. He was such a humble man that he often referred to himself as "St. Joseph's little dog." God had big plans for him though.

Though a humble doorkeeper, Brother André quickly became known all throughout Canada as a very holy and pious man. He spent countless hours praying with the people who came to the door to see him. He offered everyone devotional oil that he collected from the lamp beside a statue of St. Joseph and recommended that they take all their needs to St. Joseph. Countless miracles were worked through Brother André's intercession, but he always attributed the miracles to the loving intercession of St. Joseph.

Brother André was frequently mocked and ridiculed for his simple love of St. Joseph, piety, and devotion. Sadly, even members of the Church expressed their dislike of him, especially the attention he gave to every sick person who came to see him. Many members of the Church became jealous of Brother André because many people considered him a saint. On average, Brother André received more than 80,000 letters a year from people asking him for prayers. The letters were so numerous that he required four helpers to assist him with all the mail. The wisdom contained in his correspondence was always simple and straightforward: Go to Joseph!

> When you invoke St. Joseph, you don't have to speak much. You know your Father in heaven knows what you need; well, so does his friend St. Joseph. Tell him, "If you were in my place, St. Joseph, what would you do?"[2]
>
> — St. André Bessette

In thanksgiving for all the wonders taking place through the intercession of St. Joseph, Brother André desired to establish a shrine in honor of St. Joseph. He was given permission by his religious superiors for the project and, with the help of others, a small chapel dedicated to St. Joseph was erected in 1904. In 1924, construction of a basilica began on the site where he had built his small chapel in 1904. The basilica would be completed in 1967 and come to be known throughout the world as St. Joseph's Oratory, the largest shrine in the world dedicated to St. Joseph.

Unfortunately, St. André did not live to see the completion of the basilica. He died in 1937 at the age of 91. However, for his efforts to spread devotion to St. Joseph, he is known throughout the world as the greatest "Apostle of St. Joseph" of the 20th century. He was so loved and respected that more than 1 million people passed by his open coffin before his funeral Mass took place. He was beatified by St. John Paul II in 1982 and canonized by Pope Benedict XVI in 2010. On the universal liturgical calendar, St. André's feast day is celebrated on January 6, the day he died. In Canada, his feast is celebrated on January 7 because the Solemnity of the Epiphany is always celebrated on January 6, and solemnities take precedence.

Today, more than 2 million people visit St. Joseph's Oratory annually. People travel on pilgrimage to St. Joseph's Oratory from all over the world, asking for special graces through the intercession of St. Joseph and St. André Bessette. Whether they pray for health, assistance with difficult marriages, the conversion of wayward children, or other matters that weigh on the human heart, all who visit the basilica find peace, hope, and consolation in St. Joseph.

The earthly remains of St. André are reserved in the basilica, and a special reliquary contains his heart. In 1984, St. John Paul II journeyed to St. Joseph's Oratory as a pilgrim while on a papal visit to Canada. Before the tomb of St. André, the saintly pope poured out his heart to St. André and St. Joseph. Below is a section from St. John Paul II's beautiful prayer offered on that occasion:

> Blessed [Saint] Brother André Bessette, porter of the college, and custodian of the Oratory of St. Joseph, give hope to all those who continue to seek your help. Teach them confidence in the virtue of prayer, and with it, the path of conversion and the Sacraments. Through you, and through St. Joseph, may God continue to pour out his blessings. Amen.[3]

Delight of Saints

With the exception of our loving Mother, St. Joseph stands above all the saints.[1]

— St. Maximilian Kolbe

Saint Joseph is a unique saint. He is honored and loved as the man closest to Christ. His virtues and holiness are extraordinary.

Many Fathers of the Church — for example, St. Jerome and St. Augustine — praised St. Joseph as an example of love, humility, and dedication to Jesus and Mary. Saint Gregory Nazianzen considered St. Joseph to be so holy that he called him the most luminous of all the saints. He wrote:

> The Almighty has concentrated in St. Joseph, as in a Sun of unrivalled luster, the combined light and splendor of all the other saints.[2]

Saint Gregory Nazianzen's statement is a bold one. As a Doctor of the Church, his teaching has perennial value. Is he claiming that St. Joseph's holiness exceeds even that of Our Lady? No, that's not what he is saying. There is, however, something very important to be learned from St. Gregory's exalted praise of St. Joseph.

Let me explain.

From the beginning of Christianity, all of Jesus' followers acknowledged the superlative holiness of Mary, the mother of Jesus. It was rare, however, for anyone in the early Church to refer to Mary as a saint. "Why is that?" you wonder. Well, the early Christians considered Mary to be so holy that they gave her a unique category of holiness. Her person and privileges are so great that she was given the title "All-Holy Mother of God." Even today, it is extremely rare for a Catholic to refer to the Virgin Mary as "St." Mary. When that title is used by Catholics, it is generally used for a building or an institution that has been named in honor of the Virgin Mary. For example, many churches, schools, and hospitals are named "St. Mary's." In everyday conversation, however, it is almost unheard of for a Catholic to refer to the Virgin Mary as "St. Mary." If a Catholic does call her "St. Mary," it is very likely that the person is a convert to Catholicism from one of the many Protestant denominations.

This helps us to understand why saints throughout history refer to St. Joseph as the greatest of all the saints; namely, the Virgin Mary is in a different category altogether. In the Kingdom of God, Mary is the most elevated of all creatures, but St. Joseph outranks all the other saints. Please keep this distinction in mind as you make your way through the rest of the book. At times, it will seem as though saints, blesseds, and popes are claiming that St. Joseph is holier than Mary in their statements. Just remember — he isn't.

Okay. So the early Church understood St. Joseph to be the holiest human person after Mary, but what about the statement

Jesus himself made regarding the greatness of St. John the Baptist? Remember that? In the Gospel of Luke, Jesus says: "I tell you, among those born of women, no one is greater than John [the Baptist] ... " (Lk 7:28). Isn't Jesus saying that St. John the Baptist is greater than St. Joseph?

Actually, that's not what Jesus is saying at all. In the 16th century, St. Lawrence of Brindisi offered an articulate and well-thought-out response to this exact question. He wrote:

> Though not his [Jesus'] father by generation, he [St. Joseph] was his father in his upbringing, his care, and the affection of his heart. It seems to me, therefore, that Joseph is clearly the holiest of all the saints, holier than the patriarchs, than the prophets, than the apostles, than all the other saints. The objection cannot be raised that the Lord said of John the Baptist: *Among those born of women there has been none greater than John the Baptist* [Lk 7:28; see also Mt 11:11]. Just as this cannot be understood to mean that John is even holier than Christ or the Blessed Virgin, so it can't be understood in reference to blessed Joseph, the spouse of the Virgin Mary and the father of Christ, for just as husband and wife are one flesh, so too Joseph and Mary were one heart, one soul, one spirit. And as in that first marriage God created Eve to be like Adam, so in this second marriage he made Joseph to be like the Blessed Virgin in holiness and justice.[3]

Saint Lawrence's reasoning is theologically brilliant and flawless. After all, Jesus and Mary themselves were born of women. Jesus can't possibly be stating that St. John the Baptist is greater than the Son of God and his Immaculate Mother!

To better understand why Jesus is not saying that John the Baptist is greater than St. Joseph, it is important to examine the entire statement made by Jesus in the Gospel of Luke. It reads: "I tell you, among those born of women, no one is greater than John [the Baptist]; *yet the least in the kingdom of God is greater than he*" (Lk 7:28, emphasis added). When you read the entire passage, you realize that Jesus is making this statement *before the new covenant is established*.

Saint John the Baptist is the greatest Old Testament figure because he is the friend of the Bridegroom. He is the greatest man, not because he is the holiest man who ever lived, but because he is the "best man" at the wedding of the Messiah (see Jn 3:29). He is the greatest man of the old covenant, not the new covenant.

Who is the more important person at a wedding, the best man or the bride? The answer is obvious. The bride is the greatest. What

Jesus is saying, therefore, is that everyone, even the least person in the Kingdom of Heaven (that is, those who celebrate the wedding of the Lamb), is espoused to God and, therefore, greater than the best man at the wedding. In heaven, even the least person is greater than John the Baptist was held to be on earth because they are eternally espoused to God.

Another way of understanding the preeminence of St. Joseph over all the saints, including St. John the Baptist, is by acknowledging the supreme dignity of the fatherhood of St. Joseph. As great as John the Baptist is, he was not the father of Jesus Christ. Fatherhood has rights and privileges to accompany its duties and responsibilities, and the fatherly mission of St. Joseph required greater graces than any other saint has ever received.

> In any kingdom not only the king and queen, who shine forth in the kingdom like the sun and the moon, but also the kingdom's princes, dukes, governors, etc., and especially the parents and blood relatives of the king, who shine like the stars in the sky, are held in honor by the king's good and faithful subjects. So, my friends, reason certainly demands that in the kingdom of Christ not only Christ and the Blessed Virgin be worthy of high esteem, but also all the saints and especially this blessed man, Joseph, the father of Christ and spouse of the most holy Virgin, be held in highest honor by Christ himself as his father and by the most holy Virgin as her husband.[4]
>
> — St. Lawrence of Brindisi

Saint Lawrence is a remarkable apologist for St. Joseph! By the way, St. Lawrence is also a Doctor of the Church.

In the same sermon, St. Lawrence offers yet another reason why St. Joseph's exalted place in the Kingdom of Heaven is greater than that of any other saint:

> If Christ sits at the right hand of his Father in the glory of paradise above all the choirs of angels, because he is the first of all the predestined and was the holiest of the holiest in this world, and if the Blessed Virgin, by reason of her own holiness, holds the second place after Christ because she is also second by reason of predestination from eternity and grace in time, it seems to me that because Joseph holds the third place after Christ in eternal predestination and grace in time, so by the same reasoning he also holds the third place in the glory of paradise.[5]

Saint Joseph is the greatest saint in the Kingdom of Heaven because God predestined him for that position. This reality should make our hearts extremely joyful!

> Rejoice, devout servants of St. Joseph, for you are close to para-dise; the ladder leading up to it has but three rungs, Jesus, Mary, Joseph.[6]
>
> — St. Leonard of Port Maurice

> Who is not aware that, after the Blessed Mother, St. Joseph is, of all the saints, the one who is the dearest to God?[7]
>
> — St. Alphonsus Liguori

The exalted status given to St. Joseph by Doctors of the Church has led to a particular way of describing the love and reverence due to St. Joseph. The following distinctions were created by theologians and are very helpful for understanding the reverence due to God and his saints.

latria (adoration) ➙ God
hyperdulia (highest reverence) ➙ Mary
protodulia (first revered) ➙ St. Joseph
dulia (revered) ➙ All other saints

In a unique place, over all others, is God. He alone is worthy of adoration. In Greek, the word for adoration is *latria*. Only God is worthy of *latria* (adoration). The Virgin Mary, below God but above everyone else (including the highest choirs of angels), is given a special form of veneration whose Greek name is *hyperdulia*, which means "highest reverence." Saint Joseph, below Mary but above all the other saints, is accorded a form of veneration whose Greek name is *protodulia*, which means "first revered" among all the other saints. Last but not least are the saints. We acknowledge their holiness and honor them with a type of veneration whose Greek name is *dulia*, which means "reverence."

One saint who loved and revered St. Joseph in an extraordinary manner is St. Teresa of Avila, another Doctor of the Church. In her autobiography, St. Teresa tells the story of how she was healed from a serious illness through the intercession of St. Joseph. Her miraculous healing led her to zealously spread devotion to St. Joseph. She was so convinced of the power and efficacy of St. Joseph's intercession that she challenged people to put devotion to St. Joseph to the test.

Saint Teresa of Avila was a bold woman! This is what she wrote in her autobiography:

> I wish I could persuade everyone to be devoted to the glorious St. Joseph, for I have great experience of the blessings which he can obtain from God. I do not remember that I have ever asked anything of him which he has failed to grant. I am astonished at the great favors which God has bestowed on me through this blessed saint, and at the perils from which he has delivered me, both in body and in soul. To other saints, the Lord seems to have given grace to help us in some of our necessities. But my experience is that St. Joseph helps us in them all; also that the Lord wishes to teach us that, as he was himself subject on earth to St. Joseph, so in heaven he now does all that Joseph asks. This has also been the experience of other persons whom I have advised to commend themselves to the saint. I only request, for the love of God, whoever will not believe me will test the truth of what I say, for he will see by experience how great a blessing it is to recommend oneself to this glorious patriarch and to be devoted to him.[8]

Many people have taken St. Teresa up on her devotional challenge. Saint Teresa's confidence in St. Joseph rests on firm theological foundations, too. Several centuries before St. Teresa, St. Thomas Aquinas, another Doctor of the Church and universally acclaimed as the greatest theologian in the history of the Church, called the powerful intercession of St. Joseph unlimited! He wrote:

> There are many saints to whom God has given the power to assist us in the necessities of life, but the power given to St. Joseph is unlimited: It extends to all our needs, and all those who invoke him with confidence are sure to be heard.[9]

Truth be told, there are an endless number of holy men and women who have extolled the greatness of St. Joseph. All saints delight in him. To list all of the saints who loved and were devoted to him would be impossible, but there are a select few who really stand out:

St. Bernardine of Siena
St. Lawrence of Brindisi
St. Teresa of Avila
St. Francis de Sales
Venerable Mary of Ágreda
St. Alphonsus Liguori
Blessed William Joseph Chaminade
Blessed Maria Repetto

St. Peter Julian Eymard
Blessed Jean-Joseph Lataste
St. Leonardo Murialdo
St. Luigi Guanella
Blessed Anne Catherine Emmerich
St. Joseph Marello
Blessed Maria Teresa of St. Joseph
Blessed Petra of St. Joseph
St. André Bessette
Venerable Fulton J. Sheen
St. Josemaría Escrivá
Blessed Gabriele Allegra

You might be familiar with some of the names on the list, but I bet there are some you have never heard of. Don't worry: You will find out more about many of them in this book. They are the champions of St. Joseph!

Saints, blesseds, and mystics are not the only ones who have loved and delighted in St. Joseph. Many popes have also praised the greatness of St. Joseph.

Blessed Pope Pius IX
Pope Leo XIII
Pope Benedict XV
Venerable Pope Pius XII
St. Pope John XXIII
St. John Paul II

The list of popes is considerably shorter than the list of saints, isn't it? The reason is because papal promotion of St. Joseph, while not entirely new, took centuries to develop. It took Church leaders a very long time to fully recognize the greatness of St. Joseph and proclaim that greatness in official documents. Nonetheless, once the papacy started to promote St. Joseph, it really took off! After Blessed Pope Pius IX, there hasn't been a single pope who has not praised the greatness and unique holiness of St. Joseph. (See page 318 for commissioned art depicting the above-mentioned 26 champions of St. Joseph.)

Did you know that Pope Leo XIII taught that the dignity of St. Joseph is so great that it can be considered higher than that of the angels, even the highest choirs of angels? He wrote:

The dignity of the Mother of God is so elevated that there can be no higher created one. But since St. Joseph was united to the Blessed Virgin by the conjugal bond, there is no doubt that he approached nearer than any other to that super-eminent dignity of hers by which the Mother of God surpasses all created natures. Conjugal union is the greatest of all; by its very nature it is accompanied by a reciprocal communication of the goods of the spouses. If then God gave St. Joseph to Mary to be her spouse he certainly did not give him merely as a companion in life, a witness of her virginity, a guardian of her honor, but he made him also participate by the conjugal bond in the eminent dignity which was hers.[10]

Whoa! Pope Leo XIII's theological statement is one of the most powerful ever made about St. Joseph. Your spiritual father is higher than the angels!

In Catholic theology, it has always been taught that the Virgin Mary's love of God, and therefore her dignity and closeness to God, surpass those of all other created beings, including the angels. Her cooperation with God is unique because she collaborated materially (physically) in the Incarnation of the Second Person of the Holy Trinity. For centuries, it was thought that, after Mary's great dignity, the nine choirs of angels were nearer to God than all other creatures because of their role and mission as servants and ministers of God's holy will. However, as the theology of St. Joseph has developed and become more prominent in the life of the Church, it has become clear that there is another human person who is above all the choirs of angels: St. Joseph.

> O God, the glory of Joseph is known only by you and your angels. Men are not worthy to know it. This admirable saint is higher than the heavenly spirits.[11]
>
> — Blessed Bartolo Longo

> The dignity of St. Joseph is so great that none can be greater.[12]
>
> — St. George Preca

Saint Joseph has a dignity and closeness to God that surpasses that of all the holy angels. Angels are close to God because they are servants of his will; St. Joseph is close to God because he is the father of Jesus! Saint Joseph's cooperative role in the redemption required greater graces than any angel has ever received. Though not the biological father of Jesus (and therefore not someone who cooperated in the same way as Mary did in the Incarnation), St. Joseph nonetheless cooperated morally in the Incarnation by raising the God-Man with perfect paternal love. Mary was not an unwed mother when she conceived the Savior of the world in her womb. She was married to St. Joseph. The Incarnation took place within the context of St. Joseph's marriage to Mary. Saint Joseph's role was planned from all eternity, even before the creation of the angels.

Furthermore, Jesus never called any angel "father." No angel, no matter how exalted, ever educated the God-Man. God does not obey angels. Saint Joseph, on the other hand, not only educated Jesus, but was privileged to command the God-Man in his role as father of the Messiah. This fatherly love, dignity, and authority is reserved for St. Joseph. It is such a wondrous dignity that God made St. Joseph the spiritual father of all humanity, as well as the Patron of the Universal Church. No angel, regardless of their ranking in the heavenly choirs, has such dignity.

The surpassing dignity of the fatherhood of St. Joseph is the reason Pope Pius XI stated that the intercession of St. Joseph is "all-powerful" before God. He wrote:

> The intercession of St. Joseph is that of the husband, the putative father, the head of the family of Nazareth which was composed of himself, Mary, and Jesus. And as St. Joseph was truly the head or the master of that house, his intercession cannot be but all-powerful. For what could Jesus and Mary refuse to St. Joseph, he who was entirely consecrated to them all his life, and to whom they truly owed the means of their earthly existence?[13]
>
> — Pope Pius XI

Saint Joseph is the delight of saints and popes. He should be your delight as well.

> All the saints in glory assuredly merit honor and particular respect, but it is evident that, next to the Blessed Mother, St. Joseph possesses a just title to a more sweet, more intimate and penetrating place in our hearts, belonging to him alone.[14]
>
> — St. Pope John XXIII

> Saint Joseph, after Mary, is the greatest saint and the most dear to Jesus.[15]
>
> — Blessed Bartolo Longo

The Roman Canon

[Saint] Pope John XXIII, who had a great devotion to St. Joseph, directed that Joseph's name be inserted in the Roman Canon of Mass — which is the perpetual memorial of redemption — after the name of Mary and before the apostles, popes and martyrs.[1]

— St. John Paul II

Saint Joseph's name was inserted in the Roman Canon of Mass? What does that mean? Is St. Joseph a weapon?

Well, yes, St. Joseph is an extremely powerful weapon for Christianity, but what St. John Paul II is referring to is the Roman Canon, not a Roman cannon. "What's the Roman Canon?" you wonder. The Roman Canon is the ancient Eucharistic Prayer used by the priest at Mass. For centuries, there was only one Eucharistic Prayer in the Roman Rite. After the Second Vatican Council (1962-1965), the Church started to use four Eucharistic Prayers, with Eucharistic Prayer I retaining the name of "Roman Canon." It was into the Roman Canon (Eucharistic Prayer I) that St. Pope John XXIII inserted the name of St. Joseph.

To be honest, it's hard to believe that St. Joseph's name did not appear in the prayers of the Mass until the 20th century. Saint Joseph is, indeed, the Mirror of Patience! Nevertheless, the manner in which St. Joseph's name came to be included in the Mass is very inspiring.

Here's the story.

In 1958, a bishop with a great devotion to St. Joseph was elected to the papacy: Angelo Roncalli. He loved St. Joseph so much that he had contemplated taking the papal name Joseph (Pope Joseph). Out of respect for his earthly father, however, he decided to take the name John. Since there had already been many previous popes named John, he was known as John XXIII.

In 1962, Pope John XXIII opened the Second Vatican Council, entrusting the entire endeavor to St. Joseph. On November 10, 1962, at one of the sessions of the Council, a bishop named Petar Cule offered a presentation on St. Joseph to the other bishops. In his lengthy presentation, Bishop Cule requested that the name of Joseph be included in the Canon of the Mass (the Roman Canon). Unfortunately, Bishop Cule was not well-known, and due to his long, repetitious presentation, as well as his nervousness and inability to articulate things well, many of the cardinals and bishops at the

Bishop Cule

presentation began to murmur and ridicule him for his pious and lengthy speech. At one point, the moderator of the session requested that Bishop Cule end his "eloquent and holy sermon" about St. Joseph. The moderator's belittling words caused many of the cardinals and bishops to laugh, resulting in Bishop Cule shuffling his aged body back to his seat, seemingly defeated.

Listening in on the speech via closed circuit television was Pope John XXIII. He was not amused by the treatment given to Bishop Cule. Pope John XXIII knew Bishop Cule personally. He knew that Bishop Cule had suffered greatly under the Communists in Yugoslavia. Bishop Cule had been frequently interrogated by the Communists in cruel ways, eventually being sentenced to 11 years of hard labor in a concentration camp in Yugoslavia. The Communists even attempted to kill the bishop by placing him on a train that was deliberately wrecked in order to kill everyone on board. As a result of the wreck, the bishop's hips were shattered. After he was finally released from the concentration camp, the bishop suffered bouts of anxiety and nervousness, making it hard for him to speak without repeating himself. John XXIII knew that the bishop's presence at the Council had taken much effort, and that the good bishop wanted to be there to testify that he had been spared from death through the intercession of St. Joseph.

Bishop Cule's speech on St. Joseph nearly brought Pope John XXIII to tears, and caused the pope to act. On November 13, three days after Bishop Cule gave his presentation on St. Joseph, Pope John XXIII decreed that the name of St. Joseph would be included in the Roman Canon of the Mass! The decree went into effect on December 8, 1962.

Today, the name of St. Joseph appears in all four Eucharistic prayers. This came about during the pontificates of Benedict XVI and Francis. Pope Benedict XVI intended to insert St. Joseph's name into the three other Eucharistic Prayers, but was not able to accomplish it before his abdication of the papacy on February 28, 2013. Pope Francis, fulfilling the intentions of Pope Benedict XVI, officially placed the name of St. Joseph in all the Eucharistic Prayers on May 1, 2013.

The next time you attend Holy Mass, listen attentively to the priest as he prays the Eucharistic Prayer. Listen to hear the name of your spiritual father.

In communion with those whose memory we venerate,
especially the glorious ever-Virgin Mary,
Mother of our God and Lord, Jesus Christ,
and blessed Joseph, her Spouse ... .

— Eucharistic Prayer I (The Roman Canon)

Have mercy on us all, we pray,
that with the Blessed Virgin Mary, Mother of God,
with blessed Joseph, her Spouse ... .

— Eucharistic Prayer II

May he make of us
an eternal offering to you,
so that we may obtain an inheritance with your elect,
especially with the most Blessed Virgin Mary,
Mother of God,
with blessed Joseph, her Spouse ... .

— Eucharistic Prayer III

To all of us, your children,
grant, O merciful Father,
that we may enter into a heavenly inheritance
with the Blessed Virgin Mary, Mother of God,
with blessed Joseph, her Spouse ... .

— Eucharistic Prayer IV

When Pope John XXIII closed the first session of Vatican Council II and announced that the name of St. Joseph was going to be included in the canon of the Mass, a very important churchman telephoned me to say, "Congratulations! Listening to the pope's announcement, I thought immediately of you and how happy you'd be." And indeed I was happy, for in that conciliar gathering, which represented the whole Church brought together in the Holy Spirit, there was proclaimed the great supernatural value of St. Joseph's life.[2]

— St. Josemaría Escrivá

WONDER 2

OUR SPIRITUAL FATHER

Be in good spirits under the fatherly mantle of St. Joseph, a place
of safest refuge in trials and tribulations.

— St. Joseph Marello

Patron of the Universal Church

He [St. Joseph] was head of the divine household on earth with,
as it were, fatherly authority; he has the Church dedicated to his
loyalty and protection. Such a person possesses so surpassing a
dignity that no honor exists which should not be paid him.[1]

— Pope Leo XIII

Did you know that the root for the word "patron" is *pater*
("father")? Did you know that it was through the efforts of a
zealous Dominican priest that St. Joseph was proclaimed the Patron
of the Universal Church in 1870 by Blessed Pope Pius IX?

Here's the story:

The Dominican priest is Blessed Jean-Joseph Lataste (1832-
1869). Blessed Jean-Joseph was very devoted to St. Joseph. Prior to
entering the Dominicans, Jean-Joseph believed that his vocation was
to marriage. Engaged to be married, Jean-Joseph was not at peace
with his decision and discerned that God was instead calling him to
be a Dominican priest. After many years of study, he was ordained to
the sacred priesthood and quickly became known as a very pious priest
with a strong devotion to Our Lady of Lourdes, St. Mary Magdalene,
and St. Joseph. He loved the message of Lourdes so much that he
travelled to Lourdes to speak with St. Bernadette Soubirous personally.
He also had a great devotion to St. Mary Magdalene; as a result, he
conducted priestly ministry at a women's prison and later founded a
new Dominican community for women who had come out of prison,
the Dominican Sisters of Bethany. It was Blessed Jean-Joseph's great
love for St. Joseph, however, that inspired the Vicar of Christ to proclaim St. Joseph the Patron of the Universal Church.

The pope at the time was Blessed Pope Pius IX, the pope
responsible for declaring Mary's Immaculate Conception to be a

dogma of the faith. People from around the world, including many bishops, had written to the pope asking him to consider making this Marian doctrine a dogma. After much prayer, theological research, and inquiry, Blessed Pope Pius IX realized that such a dogma was both true and pleasing to God, and he agreed to their request. He made the declaration on December 8, 1854.

Blessed Pope Pius IX was also very devoted to St. Joseph, and for years had also been receiving letters from priests, bishops, and laity asking him to declare St. Joseph the Patron of the Universal Church. Blessed Pope Pius IX wanted St. Joseph to be more known and loved, and was very inspired by these requests, but he felt uncertain. Was it the right time for such a proclamation? Would it serve Christ and His Church well? That would all change when he received a letter from a zealous Dominican priest.

Like many others, Fr. Jean-Joseph Lataste had written a letter to the pope asking him to proclaim St. Joseph the Patron of the Universal Church. Blessed Jean-Joseph's letter was given to the pope in 1868. The Dominican was so convinced that God wanted this proclamation for the good of the Church that he told the pope that he had made a promise to God to offer his life as a sacrifice to bring about the patronage of St. Joseph for the entire Church. The pope was very moved by Jean-Joseph's petition and was convinced that God was speaking to him through the zealous Dominican.

> This good religious [Jean Joseph Lataste] is offering the sacrifice of his life to obtain that St. Joseph be declared Patron of the Universal Church. Father Lataste will shortly be granted his wish. We have received more than five hundred letters requesting that we declare St. Joseph patron of the Church, but Fr. Lataste is the only one who offered his life.[2]

> — Blessed Pope Pius IX

To fulfill his promise to God, Blessed Jean-Joseph took on many penitential practices and heroic mortifications, all for the intention of seeing the pope declare St. Joseph the Patron of the Universal Church. Blessed Jean-Joseph died in 1869 at the age of 36. Incredibly, one year later, on December 8, 1870 (the Solemnity of the Immaculate Conception), Blessed Pope Pius IX proclaimed St. Joseph the Patron of the Universal Church.

> On that December 8, 1870, it was this brief but lovely and admirable decree given *Urbi et Orbi* [to the city and to the world]

that has opened a store of rich and beautiful inspirations for the successors of Pius IX.[3]

— St. Pope John XXIII

The official decree proclaiming St. Joseph the Patron of the Universal Church reads:

As almighty God appointed Joseph, son of the patriarch Jacob, over all the land of Egypt to save grain for the people, so when the fullness of time had come and he was about to send to earth his only-begotten Son, the Savior of the world, he chose another Joseph, of whom the first had been the type, and He made him the lord and chief of his household and possessions, the guardian of his choicest treasures.

Indeed, he had as his spouse the Immaculate Virgin Mary, of whom was born by the Holy Spirit, Jesus Christ our Lord, who deigned to be reputed in the sight of men as the son of Joseph, and was subject to him.

Him whom countless kings and prophets had desired to see, Joseph not only saw but conversed with, and embraced in paternal affection, and kissed. He most diligently reared Him whom the faithful were to receive as the bread that came down from heaven whereby they might obtain eternal life.

Because of this sublime dignity which God conferred on his most faithful servant, the Church has always most highly honored and praised blessed Joseph next to his spouse, the Virgin Mother of God, and has besought his intercession in times of trouble.

And now therefore, when in these most troublesome times the Church is beset by enemies on every side, and is weighed down by calamities so heavy that ungodly men assert that the gates of hell have at length prevailed against her, the venerable prelates of the whole Catholic world have presented to the Sovereign Pontiff their own petitions and those of the faithful committed to their charge, praying that he would deign to constitute St. Joseph Patron of the Church. And this time their prayer and desire was renewed by them even more earnestly at the Sacred Ecumenical Council of the Vatican.

Accordingly, it has now pleased our Most Holy Sovereign, Pope Pius IX, in order to entrust himself and all the faithful to the Patriarch St. Joseph's most powerful patronage, has chosen to comply with the prelates' desire and has solemnly declared him [St. Joseph] Patron of the Catholic Church.

He arranged, moreover, that a declaration to this effect be promulgated through the present decree of the Sacred Congregation of Rites on this day sacred to the Immaculate Virgin Mother of God [December 8, 1870], the most chaste Joseph's Spouse.[4]

Our Spiritual Father

Inspired by the Gospel, the Fathers of the Church from the earliest centuries stressed that just as St. Joseph took loving care of Mary and gladly dedicated himself to Jesus Christ's upbringing, he likewise watches over and protects Christ's Mystical Body, that is, the Church.[1]

— St. John Paul II

Have you ever thought of St. Joseph in a fatherly way? Has it ever occurred to you that Jesus wants you to have St. Joseph as your loving spiritual father? The Church has always understood Mary's spiritual maternity of the Church, but it hasn't always understood St. Joseph's spiritual fatherhood in relation to the Church. To understand why, we have to take a look at what the Church has understood and taught about St. Joseph's fatherhood of Jesus.

In the first few centuries of Christianity, there were people in the Church, including Fathers of the Church, who were uncertain if St. Joseph could truly be called the father of Jesus. Regardless of the fact that Scripture clearly calls St. Joseph the father of Jesus (see Lk 2:33, 48), many early Christians were of the opinion that St. Joseph could not be called the father of Jesus in any way. They were cautious about such a title because they didn't want people to think that St. Joseph was the biological father of Jesus. Essentially, they didn't want to taint belief in the virginity of Mary in any way. It wasn't until St. Augustine's preaching in the fourth century that St. Joseph's fatherhood of Jesus was clearly explained by the Church. In one of his sermons, St. Augustine states that St. Joseph, though not the biological father of Jesus, is nonetheless a real father to Jesus because he exercised a fatherhood toward Jesus that was authoritative, affectionate, and faithful. After St. Augustine cleared up the matter of St. Joseph's fatherhood of Jesus, it was never questioned again. And because St. Joseph is truly the father of the Head of the Mystical Body of Christ, he is necessarily the father of the rest of the members of the Body of

Christ. This understanding of St. Joseph's patronage and fatherhood over the Church slowly begin to find its way into the writings of saints and mystics.

From Scripture, we know that St. Joseph watched over and protected Jesus as his father. From tradition, we know that St. Joseph watches over and protects Christ's Mystical Body, the Church, as the spiritual father of the Church. But what does this mean for you personally? Well, you are a member of the Church. Doesn't Jesus want St. Joseph to watch over you with the same paternal love, authority, affection, and fidelity that he exercised toward Jesus? The answer is "Yes!"

In the 19th century, Jesus himself explicitly commanded the Servant of God Sr. Mary Martha Chambon to call St. Joseph "father." This holy nun received extraordinary graces from Jesus, Mary, and St. Joseph, and is known as the "Mystic of the Holy Wounds." Jesus told Sr. Mary Martha the following:

> You must call St. Joseph your father, for I have given him the title and the goodness of a father.[2]

Through Baptism, you became a child of God and a member of God's family. Jesus is your Lord, Savior, and brother. The Son of God became your brother for a very specific reason: He wants you to share in his filial relationship with the Heavenly Father. This is a fundamental Christian truth. It is also a truth that helps us understand the spiritual fatherhood that St. Joseph exercises toward you.

Here's what I mean.

If Jesus is your brother, his parents become your parents. Not physically, of course, but spiritually. Specifically, Jesus' mother becomes your mother. Jesus' father becomes your father. If Mary is your mother, and Jesus is your brother, St. Joseph has to be your father. Any man married to your mother is your father. Again, the filial relationship you have with St. Joseph is not biological; it wasn't biological for Jesus, either. Yet this does not mean that St. Joseph's fatherhood is not real. Saint Joseph's spiritual fatherhood is very real. Were spiritual fatherhood not real, calling *Jesus'* Heavenly Father *your* Heavenly Father would be meaningless.

To gain a deeper appreciation of St. Joseph's spiritual fatherhood, let's turn to St. Josemaría Escrivá, who offers a candid observation:

> There is something I do not quite like in that title of foster father which is sometimes given to Joseph, because it might make us

think of the relationship between Joseph and Jesus as something cold and external. Certainly our faith tells us that he was not his father according to the flesh, but this is not the only kind of fatherhood.[3]

Now, there's nothing wrong with calling St. Joseph the foster father of Jesus. After all, "foster father" is one of the official titles used in the Litany of St. Joseph. Saint Josemaría knew that and accepted it. Nonetheless, St. Josemaría is absolutely correct that biological fatherhood is not the only kind of fatherhood.

With absolute certainty we can assert that the first time the Baby Jesus looked up to St. Joseph and spoke to him, Jesus did not exclaim: "Foster father!" No, the divine Infant would have joyfully cried out (in Aramaic) "Father!" or even "Daddy!" Again, there's nothing wrong with the term foster father, but it must be acknowledged that the New Testament never refers to St. Joseph as the "foster father" of Jesus.

Here's a concrete example: On one occasion, Mary and St. Joseph lost the Child Jesus for three days. Jesus' parents searched for him anxiously and, when they finally found him, his mother said to him, "Your father and I have been looking for you with great anxiety" (Lk 2:48). Mary did not say to Jesus: "Your foster father and I have been looking for you." Saint Joseph's fatherhood was more than a legal guardianship. His paternal relationship with Jesus was personal, authoritative, affectionate, moral, and loving. This is the kind of fatherhood that St. Joseph wants to have with you, too.

Saint Joseph is the best of fathers. His spiritual fatherhood was planned from all eternity.

> There is but one fatherhood, that of God the Father, the one Creator of the world, of all that is seen and unseen. Yet man, created in the image of God, has been granted a share in this one paternity of God (Eph 3:15). Saint Joseph is a striking case of this, since he is a father, without fatherhood according to the flesh. He is not the biological father of Jesus, whose Father is God alone, and yet he lives his fatherhood fully and completely. To be a father means above all to be at the service of life and growth. Saint Joseph, in this sense, gave proof of great devotion.[4]
>
> — Pope Benedict XVI

Perhaps you are wondering, "Why did Jesus need the fatherhood of St. Joseph at all since God is Jesus' Father?" It's a good question. Essentially, Jesus needed St. Joseph as a father because the human nature of Jesus required it. When the Son of God became incarnate, he placed himself under the anthropological (human) requirements of needing a human father to love, feed, educate, shelter, clothe, and protect him. Jesus, the Incarnate Word, is not a pure spiritual being. He is the God-Man. He has a divine nature and a human nature.

In his human nature, Jesus had physical, emotional, and psychological needs. God the Father doesn't have a body, emotions, or passions because he never became incarnate like his Son. The Heavenly Father can't physically touch, walk with, or embrace his Incarnate Son. Therefore, God the Father entrusts his Son to the watchful, loving care of a human father. Saint Joseph stands in the place of the Heavenly Father. He has been entrusted with taking care of the human nature, growth, and development of Jesus. Through the fatherhood of St. Joseph, Jesus grew into the fullness of his manhood.

> The growth of Jesus "in wisdom and in stature, and in favor with God and man" (Lk 2:52) took place within the Holy Family under the eyes of Joseph, who had the important task of "raising" Jesus, that is, feeding, clothing, and educating him in the Law and in a trade, in keeping with the duties of a father.[5]
>
> — St. John Paul II

The divine nature of Jesus did not need anything from St. Joseph, but the human nature of Jesus did require the fatherhood of St. Joseph. When the Son of God humbled himself and took on human nature, he placed himself under the laws of human growth and development. In order to grow into the fullness of his manhood, Jesus required a mother, a father, and time. All children require this.

Venerable Fulton Sheen provides an interesting statistic related to this topic. He states:

> Let those who think that the Church pays too much attention to Mary give heed to the fact that Our Blessed Lord himself gave ten times as much of his life to her as he gave to his apostles.[6]

In other words, the apostles spent three years with Jesus, but Mary spent more than 30 years with him! Why is this important? It's important because the human nature of Jesus needed to learn certain things from the maternal love and example of his mother. Our Savior is not a robot or an angel. In his human nature, he needed a mother to teach him about human life. But his mother was not the only one who taught him. As important as a mother is in the human development of a child, there is only so much a mother can teach a child, especially a boy.

Jesus is a male. As a male, he needed a father to teach him what it is to be a man. Jesus needed the fatherhood of St. Joseph as a model of masculinity for him to imitate. Only a father can do this for a son. How did Jesus learn to sacrifice as a man? He witnessed the daily example of his father. Where did Jesus learn to work as a man? He learned it in his father's carpentry shop. How did Jesus learn to pray and acquire the manners of a gentleman? Jesus learned all these things from his father, St. Joseph.

According to the divine plan, an earthly, human father was absolutely necessary in the life of Jesus. You've no doubt heard the adage, "Like father, like son." Well, it's true. In his preaching, Jesus himself spoke of the exemplary power of a good father. In the Gospel of John, Jesus says: "Amen, amen, I say to you, a son cannot do anything on his own, but only what he sees his father doing; for what he does, his son will do also" (Jn 5:19). Our Lord spoke these words in reference to his Heavenly Father, but they also apply to those aspects of Jesus' human nature that would be strengthened by the example of St. Joseph.

> Joseph fulfilled every aspect of his paternal role. He must certainly have taught Jesus to pray, together with Mary. In particular Joseph himself must have taken Jesus to the Synagogue for the rites of the Sabbath, as well as to Jerusalem for the great feasts of the people of Israel. Joseph, in accordance with the Jewish tradition, would have led the prayers at home both every day — in the morning, in the evening, at meals — and on the principal religious feasts. In the rhythm of the days he spent at Nazareth, in the simple home and in Joseph's workshop, Jesus learned to alternate prayer and work, as well as to offer God his labor in earning the bread the family needed.[7]
>
> — Pope Benedict XVI

Jesus spent decades learning the virtues of manhood from his father. Jesus wanted to be like his father, St. Joseph. Jesus thinks so highly of his earthly father that he wants you to be a child of St. Joseph, too. Jesus wants you to resemble St. Joseph.

But why do we need the fatherhood of St. Joseph if we already have a biological father who shares our nature and is supposed to take care of us? Allow me to provide the answer by asking you several other questions:

- Is your biological father the Spouse of the Mother of God and father of Jesus Christ?
- Does your biological father have the superlative of every virtue?
- Is your biological father the Head of the Holy Family, the Patron of the Universal Church, and the Terror of Demons?

Jesus wants you to have the spiritual fatherhood of St. Joseph because there is no man more capable of modeling true fatherhood for you than St. Joseph. His loving spiritual fatherhood has the power to draw you extremely close to the Hearts of Jesus and Mary, increase your virtue, protect you from Satan, and help you reach heaven.

Now, having stated that, I need to also make clear that the spiritual fatherhood of St. Joseph is not intended to take the place of the paternity of your biological father any more than the spiritual motherhood of Mary is meant to take the place of your biological mother. The spiritual parentage of St. Joseph and Mary is meant to supplement the witness and love of your earthly parents, helping you grow in the spiritual life, especially in virtue and holiness.

Hopefully, your biological parents have done their best at loving, educating, feeding, sheltering, clothing, protecting, and correcting you. If your parents have been virtuous and saintly, you should consider yourself extremely blessed. Today, sadly, many people have not had this experience. We live in a fallen world, and the majority of people have seen and experienced the flaws and imperfections of their parents. However, with St. Joseph and Mary as your spiritual parents, you are blessed with perfect parents and perfect models.

> We are undoubtedly children of Mary, and this is our glory and our consolation. But we are also adopted children of St. Joseph and this is no small reason for the confidence that we have in him.[8]
>
> — Blessed William Joseph Chaminade

Jesus wants you to accept St. Joseph as your spiritual father. This is true whether you have had a saintly or a sinful biological father. Saint Joseph is the greatest, most loving, and holiest of all fathers. He is the father of Christians and the perfect model of paternal love.

> He [St. Joseph] is the father of Christians, since he is the depository of the seed of grace which begot Christians. Now if St. Joseph is our father, let us imitate his deeds.[9]
>
> — Blessed William Joseph Chaminade

If the spiritual fatherhood of St. Joseph is so important, why didn't Jesus make us aware of St. Joseph's spiritual fatherhood 2,000 years ago? The simple answer is because it would have led to confusion. When Jesus spoke of the Father to his disciples, it would have been very confusing to them if he also spoke about the spiritual fatherhood of St. Joseph. This is most likely the reason why Jesus did not initiate his public ministry until after the death of St. Joseph. Jesus wants his disciples to know about the virtues, wonders, and spiritual fatherhood of St. Joseph, but for the sake of his mission, he had to leave the revealing of this mystery to the Holy Spirit and the Church.

That Jesus did not speak to his disciples about St. Joseph should in no way indicate to us that Jesus thought little of his father. On the contrary, the silence of Jesus regarding St. Joseph reveals the extreme holiness of St. Joseph. Jesus understood St. Joseph so well that he knew that his father would be more than willing to step aside so that Jesus could give priority to doing the Heavenly Father's will. For love of Jesus, St. Joseph was more than willing to step out of the picture and appear to be of no importance. Saint Joseph desires only one thing: that Jesus accomplish the mission that he was sent to do by his Heavenly Father. It doesn't matter to St. Joseph if he isn't center stage. Jesus loves this about St. Joseph. The humility of St. Joseph is a witness to his greatness!

Today, however, the time has come when, for the good of mankind, the Holy Spirit desires to fully reveal the virtues, wonders, and spiritual fatherhood of St. Joseph to the nations. This great mystery has been reserved for a time when the Church and the world would need it most.

Now is the time of St. Joseph!

In our day, Jesus wants the Church to know, love, honor, and seek refuge in the spiritual fatherhood of St. Joseph. There has never been a time in history when God's people have needed St. Joseph more. Why? Simply put, the majority of men no longer know or understand what it means to be a gentleman, let alone what it means to be a good father. Children have grown up with poor examples of fatherhood, if they have grown up with a father at all. Contraception, pornography, abortion, gender confusion, moral depravity, empty churches, morally corrupt clergy, and cultural chaos are only a few of the fruits of a society that lacks real men and fathers. Jesus wants to draw our attention to the spiritual fatherhood of St. Joseph in order to right these wrongs and bring order back to the Church and the world.

What, then, should we expect from the spiritual fatherhood of St. Joseph? What will he do for us? Saint Joseph loves us and so will joyfully do the exact same things that a biological father does for his children, only on a spiritual level. He will spiritually feed, shelter, clothe, educate, protect, and correct us. This is his role as father. With the exception of correction, St. Joseph did all these things for Jesus, our brother. Of course, St. Joseph also provided for all Jesus' physical needs for many years.

> If Joseph was so engaged, heart and soul, in protecting and providing for that little family at Nazareth, don't you think that now in heaven he is the same loving father and guardian of the whole Church, of all its members, as he was of its Head on earth?[10]
>
> — Venerable Pope Pius XII

> From the same fact that the most holy Virgin is the mother of Jesus Christ is she the mother of all Christians whom she bore on Mount Calvary amid the supreme throes of the Redemption: Jesus Christ is, in a manner, the first-born of Christians, who by the adoption and Redemption are his brothers. And for such reasons the Blessed Patriarch [St. Joseph] looks upon the multitude of Christians who make up the Church as confided especially to his trust.[11]
>
> — Pope Leo XIII

As the best and most loving of fathers, St. Joseph stands ready to shelter you in the safety of the Sacraments and teachings of the Catholic Church, clothe you with virtue, educate you in the interior life, protect you under his fatherly cloak, and correct you should you go astray.

> If anyone cannot find a master to teach him how to pray, let him take this glorious saint [Joseph] as his master, and he will not go astray.[12]
>
> — St. Bernadette Soubirous

Placing yourself under the fatherly cloak of St. Joseph is a great blessing in the spiritual life. In the Carmelite tradition, the cloak of St. Joseph is a very prominent theme in artistic depictions of St. Joseph. His cloak is a symbol of safety and fatherly protection. Similar to Mary shielding her children under her maternal mantle, St. Joseph lovingly protects his children under his fatherly cloak. In Catholic devotion, those who love St. Joseph will sometimes pray the Holy

Cloak Novena (see page 245). Novenas are normally nine days long, but the Holy Cloak Novena consists of 30 days of prayer in honor of the 30 years St. Joseph lived with Jesus. The Holy Cloak Novena is considered one of the most efficacious novenas in the treasury of the Church.

Place yourself under the paternal cloak of St. Joseph. Open your heart to the spiritual fatherhood of St. Joseph and experience the love of the best of fathers.

> It is natural and worthy that as the Blessed Joseph ministered to all the needs of the family of Nazareth and girt it about with his protection, he should now cover with the cloak of his heavenly patronage and defend the Church of Jesus Christ.[13]
>
> — Pope Leo XIII

> Glorious St. Joseph, spouse of the Virgin Mary, we beseech you through the heart of Jesus Christ, grant to us your fatherly protection.[14]
>
> — St. Francis de Sales

Ite ad Ioseph!

If you wish to be close to Christ, we again today repeat, "Go to Joseph."[1]

— Venerable Pope Pius XII

What is the closest possible union you can have with Jesus in this life? The answer is easy: your reception of Jesus in Holy Communion. There is no greater intimacy with Jesus possible in this life than when you receive the Eucharist at Holy Mass. The Blessed Sacrament is the Body, Blood, Soul, and Divinity of Jesus Christ.

Did you know that, without St. Joseph's earthly paternity of Jesus, you would not now be able to receive the Bread of Life? Saint Joseph was given the role of maintaining and protecting the sacred bread for you.

Let me explain.

You are probably familiar with the story in the Book of Genesis about the sons of Israel selling one of their brothers into slavery. The brother sold into slavery was named Joseph. Joseph ended up being taken by his owners to Egypt, far away from all his other kin. What the men did to their brother was horrible and shameful. But God had a plan.

Incredibly, Pharaoh, the king of Egypt, adopted Joseph into his own family so that Joseph was regarded as a son of Pharaoh. Joseph was given great authority; Pharaoh placed him in charge of all the granaries in Egypt. At that time, Egypt was considered the bread basket of the world, and Joseph did an incredible job of storing up grain.

> Joseph stored up huge quantities of grain, like the sand of the sea; it was so much that he stopped keeping records because it was beyond measure.
>
> — Gen 41:49

Though Joseph's brothers had sold him into slavery, God had wonderful plans for Joseph. After Joseph had stored up an immeasurable quantity of grain, a severe famine broke out in Egypt and the surrounding territories. As a result of the shortage of food, Pharaoh instructed everyone in Egypt: "Go to Joseph and do whatever he tells you!" (Gen 41:55). The famine became so extreme that Joseph's own brothers, the ones who had sold him into slavery, journeyed to Egypt in search of food.

When the brothers met the man in charge of the granaries in Egypt, so much time had elapsed that they did not realize that they were standing in the presence of their own brother, whom they had sold into slavery years ago. Like everyone else, they, too, considered Joseph to be Egyptian royalty, and they addressed him as their lord. Joseph, however, recognized them.

To make a long story short, Joseph hid his identity, but was filled with kindness and mercy toward his brothers. He provided grain for them, filling their sacks so they could take back plenty to their father, Israel. Eventually, Joseph revealed his identity to them and extended forgiveness to his brothers. Thanks to Joseph and his role as the keeper of the grain, countless lives were saved from famine and death.

The story related in the Old Testament is true and is a prefiguration of a much greater Joseph who would bring his Son, the Bread from Heaven, to safety in Egypt. Saint Joseph safeguarded a food capable of saving the entire world!

Saint Joseph, our spiritual father, is much greater than the Joseph of the Old Testament. Our Joseph was the keeper of the Bread from Heaven! His desire in heaven is that all of his children consume the Bread of Everlasting Life!

The former Joseph [of the Old Testament] was holy, righteous, pious, chaste; but this Joseph so far surpasses him in holiness and perfection as the sun outshines the moon.[2]

— St. Lawrence of Brindisi

God sent St. Joseph to Egypt so that, out of Egypt, St. Joseph could bring the Bread of Life to the nations. Saint Joseph saved our Bread from Herod; he protected and preserved him in Egypt; and he now desires that we receive the Bread of Life at Holy Mass. Unlike the Joseph of the Old Testament, St. Joseph's Heavenly Bread is more numerous than the sands of the sea. This Heavenly Bread is able to feed all the multitudes and satisfy every soul.

Pharaoh, the mighty king of Egypt, exalted Joseph and made him the highest prince in his kingdom, because he stored up the grain and bread and saved the people of his entire kingdom. So Joseph saved and protected Christ, who is the living bread and gives eternal life to the world.[3]

— St. Lawrence of Brindisi

He [St. Joseph] most diligently reared him whom the faithful were to receive as the bread that came down from heaven whereby they might obtain eternal life.[4]

— Blessed Pope Pius IX

If you want to form an idea of St. Joseph's greatness, consider that by a divine privilege he merited to bear the title "Father of Jesus." Reflect too that his own name "Joseph" means — an increase. Keeping in mind the great patriarch Joseph, sold by his brothers in Egypt, understand that our saint has inherited not only his name, but even more, his power, his innocence, and his sanctity. As the patriarch Joseph stored the wheat not for himself, but for the people in their time of need, so Joseph has received a heavenly commission to watch over the living Bread not for himself alone, but for the entire world.[5]

— St. Bernard of Clairvaux

Without Joseph, we would not have the Living Bread of the Eucharist. Mary "kneaded the dough" in her sacred womb; St. Joseph lovingly preserved the Bread in Egypt. He continues to guard and preserve the Bread of Life in every tabernacle in the world. Saint Joseph made it possible for all his children to receive the Bread of Everlasting Life.

[Saint] Joseph is still charged with guarding the Living Bread![6]

— Venerable Fulton J. Sheen

Today, there is a worldwide spiritual and moral famine on the earth. Souls are dying because of a lack of spiritual nourishment. Hearts are broken; marriages are ruined; lives are destroyed; children are murdered in the womb; and truth and common sense are in short supply. The spiritual and moral famine in the world is devastating every nation, laying waste to humanity. There is not a single country left that has not been affected by it. What are we to do? To whom can we go to find nourishment for our souls?

Go to Joseph and do whatever he tells you!

— Gen 41:55

WONDER 3

YOUNG HUSBAND OF MARY

I see him [St. Joseph] as a strong, young man, perhaps a few years older than Our Lady, but in the prime of his life and work.

— St. Josemaría Escrivá

Old Men Don't Walk to Egypt

We wonder why the Gospel makes so little mention of St. Joseph. But did it not say everything when it taught us that he was the husband of Mary?[1]

— Blessed William Joseph Chaminade

In 1981, Mother Angelica founded the Eternal Word Television Network (EWTN). Her blessed network is an extremely successful and fruitful Catholic media apostolate. Mother Angelica's common sense, simple wisdom, and unwavering orthodoxy have catechized the hearts and minds of millions of people around the world. Mother Angelica died in 2016, but EWTN continues to lead many people to Jesus Christ and the Catholic Church.

Mother Angelica loved St. Joseph. On one occasion, during a live telecast, a caller asked her a question about St. Joseph. The question went something like this: "Mother Angelica, do you think St. Joseph was old or young?" Mother Angelica answered with her classic wit, responding: "Well, my dear, that's a good question. There is no official Church teaching on whether or not St. Joseph was old or young, but I prefer a young Joseph. All I know, sweetie, is old men don't walk to Egypt!"

Mother Angelica's straightforward answer makes a lot of sense. Not only would an elderly man not be capable of walking to Egypt, but an old man wouldn't be able to walk from Nazareth to Bethlehem, either; Bethlehem is 80 miles from Nazareth, and the journey would have been across rough desert terrain.

Saint Joseph was required to walk a lot to support the Holy Family. After walking 80 miles from Nazareth to Bethlehem, St. Joseph was instructed by an angel to take the Child and his mother to Egypt. This required St. Joseph to take his family on another very long journey. The distance from Bethlehem to the border of Egypt is 40 miles. No historian believes that the Holy Family lived on the border. Rather, they went much farther into Egypt where there was the possibility of work, food, and some semblance of civilization. We don't know exactly where Jesus, Mary, and Joseph settled down in Egypt, but it did require them to walk farther than the border.

Have you ever been to the Holy Land or North Africa? If you have, you know that the terrain is rough, the heat intense, and the dangers many. Walking to Egypt, being there for years without knowing anyone, and trying to make a living are not things associated with elderly men.

And then, after many years of living in Egypt, St. Joseph learned from the angel that Herod was dead. Saint Joseph was now required to pack up his family and walk from Egypt all the way back to Nazareth. That's more than 120 miles! The distance from New York City to Philadelphia is 92 miles. Add another 30 miles, and that's what St. Joseph had to do. There was no Jersey Turnpike, with smooth roads and cozy rest stops along the way. It was uphill, downhill, and around hills.

The endless walking didn't stop once the Holy Family reached Nazareth either. As faithful Jews, the men of the household were required to travel to Jerusalem three times a year to fulfill the Law of the Lord. "Three times a year all your men shall appear before the Lord, the God of Israel" (Ex 34:23). Remember: That's 80 miles one way. That is a lot of walking!

Saint Joseph could not have been an old man when he espoused Mary. Old men don't walk to Egypt. They don't walk three times a year from Nazareth to Jerusalem either.

> Good Father [St. Joseph], I thank you for having watched over my Mother Mary while you were on earth.[2]
>
> — Servant of God Sr. Mary Martha Chambon

Young Husband of Mary

I don't agree with the traditional picture of St. Joseph as an old man, even though it may have been prompted by a desire to emphasize the perpetual virginity of Mary. I see him as a strong, young man, perhaps a few years older than Our Lady, but in the prime of his life and work.[1]

— St. Josemaría Escrivá

Have you ever read such a statement from a saint about the age of St. Joseph? Saint Josemaría has good reason for asserting that St. Joseph was a young man when he married Our Lady — and St. Josemaría is not the only one who thinks this way.

The Catholic Church has no formal, official teaching on the age of St. Joseph. You are free to believe that St. Joseph was an old man when he espoused Mary if you want to. You are also free to believe he was a young man. Personally, I find it very hard to believe that St. Joseph was an old man. The physical demands of his mission make the probability of him being an old man practically zero.

If you consider the titles that the Church gives St. Joseph in his Litany (Guardian of the Redeemer; Chaste Guardian of the Virgin; Guardian of Virgins; Model of Workmen; Terror of Demons; etc.), they lean in the direction that St. Joseph was young and strong. These titles are not descriptions of an elderly man. Is an old man capable of guarding virgins? Can an elderly man serve as a model of laborers? It takes strength to be a guardian; it takes health to be a worker. Can an old man do these things? As Mother Angelica said, "Old men don't walk to Egypt!" Neither do old men guard anything whose safekeeping requires mobility and strength. None of this implies any moral fault in elderly men, of course. The world is filled with countless holy old men who are virtuous, wise, and saintly. Yet old men are not known for their physical capacity to do the kinds of things that St. Joseph was required to do for the Holy Family.

Then why has the vast majority of art over the centuries depicted St. Joseph as an old man? The most articulate answer to this question is provided by Venerable Fulton J. Sheen. He writes:

> Was he [St. Joseph] old or young? Most of the statues and pictures we see of Joseph today represent him as an old man with a gray beard, one who took Mary and her vow under his protection with somewhat the same detachment as a doctor would pick up a baby girl in a nursery. We have, of course, no historical evidence

whatsoever concerning the age of Joseph. Some apocryphal accounts picture him as an old man; Fathers of the Church, after the fourth century, followed this legend rather rigidly …

But when one searches for the reasons why Christian art should have pictured Joseph as aged, we discover that it was in order better to safeguard the virginity of Mary. Somehow, the assumption had crept in that senility was a better protector of virginity than adolescence. Art thus unconsciously made Joseph a spouse chaste and pure by age rather than by virtue. But this is like assuming that the best way to show that a man would never steal is to picture him without hands …

But more than that, to make Joseph out as old portrays for us a man who had little vital energy left, rather than one who, having it, kept it in chains for God's sake and for his holy purposes. To make Joseph appear pure only because his flesh had aged is like glorifying a mountain stream that has dried. The Church will not ordain a man to his priesthood who has not his vital powers. She wants men who have something to tame, rather than those who are tame because they have no energy to be wild. It should be no different with God.

Furthermore, it is reasonable to believe that Our Lord would prefer, for a foster-father, someone who had made a sacrifice rather than someone who was forced to it. There is the added historical fact that the Jews frowned on a disproportionate marriage between what Shakespeare called "crabbed age and youth"; the Talmud admits a disproportionate marriage only for widows or widowers. Finally, it seems hardly possible that God would have attached a young mother, probably about sixteen or seventeen years of age, to an old man. If he did not disdain to give his mother to a young man, John, at the foot of the Cross, then why should he have given her an old man at the crib? A woman's love always determines the way a man loves: she is the silent educator of his virile powers.

Since Mary is what might be called a "virginizer" of young men as well as women, and the greatest inspiration of Christian purity, should she not logically have begun by inspiring and virginizing the first youth whom she had probably ever met — Joseph, the Just? It was not by diminishing his power to love but by elevating it that she would have her first conquest, and in her own spouse, the man who was a *man*, and not a mere senile watchman!

Joseph was probably a *young* man, strong, virile, athletic, handsome, chaste, and disciplined. Instead of being a man incapable of loving, he must have been on fire with love. Just as we would

give very little credit to the Blessed Mother if she had taken her
vow of virginity after having been an old maid for fifty years, so
neither could we give much credit to a Joseph who became her
spouse because he was advanced in years. Young girls in those
days, like Mary, took vows to love God uniquely, and so did
young men, of whom Joseph was one so preeminent as to be
called the "just." Instead, then, of being dried fruit to be served
on the table of the king, he was rather a blossom filled with
promise and power. He was not in the evening of life, but in its
morning, bubbling over with energy, strength, and controlled
passion. Mary and Joseph brought to their espousals not only
their vows of virginity but also two hearts with greater torrents
of love than had ever before coursed through human breasts ...

How much more beautiful Mary and Joseph become when we
see in their lives what might be called the first Divine Romance!
No human heart is moved by the love of the old for the young;
but who is not moved by the love of the young for the young?
In both Mary and Joseph, there were youth, beauty, and promise. God loves cascading cataracts and bellowing waterfalls, but
he loves them better, not when they overflow and drown his
flowers, but when they are harnessed and bridled to light a city
and to slake the thirst of a child. In Joseph and Mary, we do not
find one controlled waterfall and one dried-up lake but rather
two youths who, before they knew the beauty of the one and
the handsome strength of the other, willed to surrender these
things for Jesus. Leaning over the manger crib of the Infant
Jesus, then, are not age and youth but youth and youth, the
consecration of beauty in a maid and the surrender of strong
comeliness in a man.[2]

Wow! Fulton Sheen is brilliant! As far as I know, no other person
in the entire history of the Church has articulated a more convincing
argument for a young St. Joseph than Fulton Sheen. As he so clearly
states, theology and art only depicted St. Joseph as an old man in
order to protect the virginity of Mary.

Now, to be fair, the decision to depict St. Joseph as an old man,
whether in preaching, writing, or art, did work to safeguard Mary's
virginity and purity. As an extreme example of this, an ancient Coptic
text on the life of St. Joseph presents him as being 91 years of age
when he espoused Mary! However, all historians and theologians
acknowledge that the sources for presenting St. Joseph as an old man
come from apocryphal — that is, non-canonical — documents. Relying on apocryphal writings to offer an age for St. Joseph led to pre-
sentations of him as an old man, diminishing his virtue, importance,

and greatness in the minds of Christians. No wonder so few people have paid attention to St. Joseph over the centuries.

How drastic an effect did this approach to St. Joseph have? To this day, St. Joseph is rarely included in seminary classes on Christology, Mariology, soteriology, or ecclesiology. The man universally acclaimed as the most loving, just, chaste, prudent, courageous, obedient, and faithful man to ever live doesn't even get mentioned in classes on the theological or moral virtues. This needs to change! Thank God for the wisdom and insights of people such as St. Josemaría Escrivá, Mother Angelica, and Venerable Fulton Sheen. The Church needs to re-present to her children an image of St. Joseph that depicts him as strong, masculine, and young. The constant presentation of him as an old man has severely warped our understanding of the greatest saint (besides Mary) to walk this earth! It's time to reclaim St. Joseph!

Now, don't take this the wrong way. The Lord loves elderly men. God loves a man's years of hard work, service, selfless dedication, and sacrificial love. Calm, just, and peaceful societies rest on the foundations established by old men. Yet those men built the foundations and pillars of civilization when they were young, not when they were old. Likewise, the formative years of Jesus Christ were lovingly ruled by a strong young father named Joseph. It was this hardworking, caring, and virtuous father who laid the foundations for the human growth and development of Jesus Christ. While there is no doubt that an old man is just as capable of being holy as any young man, it takes a strong young father to teach a boy how to swing an axe, work with wood, carry lumber, walk great distances, and earn a living by the sweat of his brow.

> If earthly princes consider it a matter of so much importance to select carefully a tutor fit for their children, think you that the Eternal God would not, in his almighty power and wisdom, choose from out of his creation the most perfect man living [St. Joseph] to be the guardian of his divine and most glorious Son, the Prince of heaven and earth?[3]

> — St. Francis de Sales

Blessed William Joseph Chaminade echoes a similar idea, but looks at St. Joseph's manhood from the perspective of his marriage to Our Lady. He writes:

> If God had charged you with the honorable task of choosing from among the kings a husband for the Blessed Virgin, would

you not have given her the greatest mind in the world? And if he had ordered you to pick one of the saints, would you not have given her the greatest saint who ever trod the earth? Now, do you think that the Holy Spirit, who is the author of this divine marriage, is less concerned than you are to provide her with a husband suited to her merits?[4]

— Blessed William Joseph Chaminade

Makes a lot of sense, right? Sure it does. Saint Joseph was the loving husband of Mary, not a "retired" husband incapable of manual labor and long journeys on foot. Saint Joseph was known by everyone in Nazareth as the father of Jesus, not the grandfather of Jesus.

As the father of Jesus, St. Joseph was a zealous defender and strong protector of his beloved Son. Saint Joseph sacrificed everything — including the pleasures of conjugal love — to fulfill his mission as "Guardian of the Virgin" and "Guardian of the Redeemer." Incidentally, when popes and saints use the word "guardian" in reference to St. Joseph, they are using it in more than just a legal sense. They use it in the protective, fatherly, and manly sense. A guardian is someone who is strong, not only in mind and heart, but also physically. Saint John Henry Newman spoke of the guardianship of St. Joseph in the following way:

He [St. Joseph] was the Cherub, placed to guard the new terrestrial paradise from the intrusion of every foe.[5]

A man charged with guarding a territory from the intrusion of every foe needs to be a physically powerful man, not an elderly man requiring a cane. Like a powerful cherub, dedicated to the protection and service of the Queen of Angels, St. Joseph was given the task of guarding the temple of Mary's body, and in particular, her virginity. Mary's guardian had to be young and strong in order to successfully fulfill his mission. An elderly man would probably not have the strength to guard a young wife. Neither would an elderly man be likely to have the stamina needed to raise an infant son.

Saint Joseph's manhood was a protective shield, a protective cloak, for the Blessed Virgin. No man or beast could do any harm to the Virgin because St. Joseph stood attentive and ready to defend her, even to the point of death.

The cloud [that] in the Old Law overshadowed the tabernacle is a figure of St. Joseph's marriage with the Blessed Virgin. *The cloud covered the tabernacle of the covenant, and the glory of the*

Lord filled it (Ex. 40:32). Saint Joseph's marriage is a sacred veil which covers the mystery of the Incarnation. Everyone sees that Mary is a mother, but only Joseph knows that she is a virgin.[6]

— Blessed William Joseph Chaminade

As a young husband and father, St. Joseph modeled manhood for his Son, Jesus. Every boy should be able to look to his father to understand what it means to be a man. If St. Joseph had been an elderly man, would Jesus have observed in his father any physical strength or true love put into practice through heroic chastity, hard work, and bodily gestures of piety — kneeling, for example? If St. Joseph were two or three times the age of his wife, what would Jesus have observed in his father: afternoon naps and forgetfulness? Again, there's nothing wrong with old age. Growing old is part of human life. Saint Joseph himself aged as life went on, as happens to all men. But would God the Father entrust the upbringing and education of his Son — the Lion of Judah and King of Kings — to an elderly and fragile man? Probably not.

What the Church and the world can learn from a younger depiction of St. Joseph — especially in theology, preaching, literature, and art — is that young men can be chaste, heroic, and holy. Indeed, the Church has countless examples of young men who kept themselves chaste and pure for the sake of the Kingdom of Heaven. And St. Joseph was the greatest of them all. Saint Josemaría Escrivá tells us:

> You don't have to wait to be old or lifeless to practice the virtue of chastity. Purity comes from love; and the strength and gaiety of youth are no obstacle for noble love. Joseph had a young heart and a young body when he married Mary, when he learned of the mystery of her divine motherhood, when he lived in her company, respecting the integrity God wished to give the world as one more sign that he had come to share the life of his creatures. Anyone who cannot understand a love like that knows very little of true love and is a complete stranger to the Christian meaning of chastity.[7]

In my opinion, St. Joseph was a young husband, tender and loving toward his wife, but always chaste, modest, and pure. Mary loved her Joseph. His manly love for her was strong and always controlled by reason and faith. His virile powers, always held in restraint and service to God's will, made him the most virtuous husband and father ever to walk this earth. No woman ever had a greater man than St. Joseph.

God would not have given the most holy Virgin to Joseph as his wife unless he had been holy and righteous. What right-minded father would ever give his most beloved daughter in marriage to a man who was not moral and beyond reproach according to his rank and state in life?[8]

— St. Lawrence of Brindisi

So what are you to gain from this wonder of St. Joseph? Are you required to believe that St. Joseph was young? No, you are not. But do you understand, at least based on the physical demands his mission would have inevitably placed on him, why it makes more sense that St. Joseph was young rather than old when he married Our Lady? Regardless of which depiction of St. Joseph you prefer, know that St. Joseph is your loving, strong, and fearless spiritual father. Thank him for all that he did out of selfless love for Jesus and your spiritual mother, Mary. Thank him for all that he does for love of you.

I thank you, O holy patriarch Joseph, because we who are incapable of even knowing how to love Jesus and our Immaculate Mother, know and rejoice that you at least loved her as she deserved to be loved, the worthy and true Mother of Jesus.[9]

— Blessed Gabriele Allegra

The Consecrated Knight

Saint Joseph sweetly and continuously stimulates us to love, serve, and imitate the Queen of his heart, the Immaculate Mother of Jesus.[1]

— Blessed Gabriele Allegra

Saint Joseph is the most Marian of all saints. His love for Mary is greater than that of St. Bernard of Clairvaux, St. Louis de Montfort, St. Alphonsus Liguori, St. Maximilian Kolbe, and St. John Paul II combined. There has never been a greater Marian saint than St. Joseph, and there never will be.

Saint Joseph is the model for total consecration to Mary. Long before Calvary, when Jesus commanded all of his disciples to take Mary into their hearts and homes (see Jn 19:26-27), St. Joseph had already taken Mary into his heart and into his home. She is his heart; she is his home. Everything he did was done for Jesus and Mary. He lived and died for Jesus and Mary.

Like Joseph, do not be afraid to take Mary into your home.[2]

— Pope Benedict XVI

Saint Joseph is the first human person to have been totally consecrated to the Blessed Virgin Mary. If you were to ask Our Lady who is the one human person in all of Christianity who has loved her most, been the most devoted to her, and served her most faithfully, she would undoubtedly point to St. Joseph. He is the prototype, blueprint, and model for how to live a life of total consecration to Mary.

The various forms of Marian consecration promoted by saints down through the centuries — for example, those of St. Louis de Montfort, Blessed William Joseph Chaminade, St. Maximilian Kolbe, the Servant of God Joseph Kentenich, and others — all find their fulfillment and perfection in the person of St. Joseph.

Saint Louis de Montfort's program of Marian consecration teaches people to be slaves of Jesus and Mary; Blessed William Joseph Chaminade teaches people to act as the heel of Mary, crushing the head of Satan; the Servant of God Joseph Kentenich instructs people to become an "apparition" of Mary; and St. Maximilian Kolbe's method of Marian consecration instructs people to be the property of Mary. All of these forms are wonderful ways of describing the one fundamental dimension of all Marian consecration: *Be another Joseph for Mary.*

All the great Marian movements (the Militia Immaculatae, Schoenstatt, the Legion of Mary, the former Blue Army [now called the World Apostolate of Fatima], and so many others), have Marian chivalry at their core. To be chivalrous toward Mary is to be on the path of sainthood. A person who is chivalrous is noble, well-mannered, courageous in battle, and a refuge for the weak. Saint Joseph is the most chivalrous of all Christians, and he teaches us that everyone, including women and children, can be spiritual knights of the Queen of Heaven. He is, in fact, the first consecrated knight of the Holy Queen.

For centuries, Christians have referred to the Virgin Mary as "Our Lady." It's a term that acknowledges the great love, respect, honor, and reverence that is owed to Mary. It is a term that bespeaks chivalry. It should come as no surprise, then, that St. Joseph is the first man to speak of Mary as his lady. Mary is St. Joseph's woman. Before her feminine wonder and beauty, he bows in loving reverence. His mission is to have all hearts bow before her in love. For this reason, St. Joseph is the greatest knight of Our Lady.

During the Middle Ages, there were many stories and legends of knights traveling far and wide on heroic quests in search of the Holy Grail, the chalice that held the Blood of Jesus at the Last Supper. During the age of chivalry, no one but the priest drank the Blood of Jesus from the chalice at Mass. For this reason, as well as many others, the stories tell us that knights set out on quests in search of the lost Holy Grail, believing that if they drank from the chalice, they would be given eternal life. Their heroic quests were noble and well-intentioned, but unnecessary. All Catholics in a state of grace who receive the Body of Christ at Mass are assured everlasting life, even if they don't drink from the chalice; they must, however, remain in a state of grace, observe the 10 Commandments, and obey the teachings of the Church. The storied quests of the medieval knights were unnecessary for another reason as well. All they had to do in order to find the true chalice of our Lord's Precious Blood was to look to St. Joseph, the first and greatest knight of Our Lady! He knows where to find the living chalice containing the life-giving blood of Jesus Christ. The Holy Grail that St. Joseph possesses has not been lost. Saint Joseph stands ready to give this chalice to all his spiritual children.

What St. Joseph teaches his children is that the Virgin Mary is the Holy Grail! She is what every Christian knight seeks. Unlike the chalice used at the Last Supper, this vessel has not been lost. Mary, the Holy Grail, is easily found. Those who find her find Jesus because those who find her find Catholicism and its greatest treasure, Jesus in Holy Communion. Mary desires to lead all souls to Holy Mass where they can receive the Lamb of God and attain eternal life. All who imitate St. Joseph will discover Mary and the saving mystery of Holy Mass.

> Mary, my mother, Joseph, my father, give me your eyes to contemplate Jesus; give me your hearts and spirits to understand him, and to be impassioned for him.[3]
>
> — Venerable Francis Xavier Nguyễn Văn Thuận

From heaven, St. Joseph continues his quest to lead all souls to Jesus through Mary. From heaven, he looks for souls who are willing to be knights of the Holy Queen. He desires to raise up loving defenders and heroic champions of Jesus, Mary, and the Catholic faith. He wants men, women, children, priests, and nuns who will serve Mary and lead others to the Kingdom of Heaven. Valiant souls are needed today, Joseph-like souls, who zealously strive to lead others to the fountain of everlasting life.

To Jesus through Mary and St. Joseph!

He [St. Joseph] always favors with especial protection those souls who are enrolled beneath the standard of Mary![4]

— St. Mary Magdalen de Pazzi

When the Holy Virgin and St. Joseph intercede together it is very powerful![5]

— St. André Bessette

Grant that according to your example [St. Joseph] we may keep our eyes fixed on our mother Mary, your most sweet spouse.[6]

— Venerable Pope Pius XII

WONDER 4

VIRGINAL FATHER OF JESUS

Since there is nothing on record that he [St. Joseph] ever had any other spouse than the Virgin Mary, it is also certain that he remained a virgin all his life.

— St. Jerome

Feast of the Holy Spouses

No husband and wife ever loved one another so much as Joseph and Mary.[1]

— Venerable Fulton J. Sheen

Did you know there is a liturgical feast that celebrates the marriage of Mary and Joseph? It's called the "Feast of the Holy Spouses" (sometimes also referred to as the "Feast of the Espousals of Mary and Joseph").

The Feast of the Holy Spouses has a long history going all the way back to the 15th century. The day traditionally designated for the feast is January 23. In a few countries, the feast is celebrated on January 22 or November 26, but those dates tend to be exceptions. Nobody is exactly sure why January 23 was chosen as the day for the feast, but we are given a fascinating insight into the date in the mystical visions of Blessed Anne Catherine Emmerich (1774-1824).

In the accounts we have of her visions, Blessed Anne Catherine claims to have been transported to the marriage of Mary and Joseph and witnessed the ceremony. Blessed Anne Catherine offers details about the wedding and explicitly mentions the date of the marriage. She writes:

The espousals took place, I think, upon our 23rd of January. They were celebrated in Jerusalem, on Mount Zion, in a house used for such feasts.[2]

Another mystic, Venerable Mary of Ágreda (1602-1665), also claims to have had visions about the lives of Mary and Joseph. She wrote extensively about her mystical experiences and claims to also have been present at the wedding of Mary and St. Joseph. Her account of the wedding provides detailed descriptions of such things as the dress Our Lady wore, the stateliness and attractiveness of St. Joseph, and the joy experienced by everyone in attendance. Venerable Mary of Ágreda wrote the following about what she witnessed at the wedding of Mary and St. Joseph:

> By divine operation the two most holy and chaste spouses felt an incomparable joy and consolation [on their wedding day]. The heavenly princess, as one who is the Mistress of all virtues, lovingly corresponded to the desires of St. Joseph. The Most High also gave to St. Joseph new purity and complete command over his natural inclinations so that he might serve his spouse Mary.[3]

Why don't more people know about the liturgical feast of the Holy Spouses? Well, unfortunately, the feast is not on the universal liturgical calendar of the Church. The Feast of the Holy Spouses is only celebrated in a few shrines dedicated to St. Joseph (for example, the Oratory of St. Joseph in Montreal, Canada); a few dioceses where the local bishop has approved it; and in several religious communities dedicated to St. Joseph. One notable religious community that celebrates the Feast of the Holy Spouses is the Oblates of St. Joseph. Founded in Asti, Italy, by St. Joseph Marello in 1878, the Oblates of St. Joseph are a wonderful religious community of men serving the Church, and they celebrate the feast annually on January 23. Their founder, St. Joseph Marello, was a very holy bishop who had a tremendous love of and devotion to St. Joseph. He was canonized by St. John Paul II in 2001.

Interestingly, in 2002, St. John Paul II also offered the world the Luminous Mysteries of the rosary. The Luminous Mysteries were actually founded in 1957 by St. George Preca of Malta, but St. John Paul II offered them to the universal Church to help us call to mind important truths of Christianity that are under attack today. The Second Luminous Mystery is the Wedding Feast at Cana. In meditating on this mystery, we are reminded that marriage is between a man and a woman.

Since this perennial truth is so hotly contested today, the Church needs a universal liturgical feast that celebrates marriage. It would be truly wonderful if the Church placed the Feast of the Holy Spouses on the universal liturgical calendar. Such a feast would serve as a reminder to all men and women of the sanctity of Holy Matrimony. What a delight it would be to liturgically celebrate the holiest couple who ever lived! Let us pray that more places request permission to celebrate the Feast of the Holy Spouses, and that someday it may be placed on the universal liturgical calendar.

> Everything that refers to that marriage [of Mary and Joseph] happened by an intimate disposition of the Holy Spirit.[4]

> — St. Bonaventure

Virginal Father of Jesus

> It is perfectly in accordance with the faith and spirit of the Church, to honor as a virgin not only the Mother of God, but likewise Joseph.[1]

> — St. Peter Damian

The mother of Jesus is a virgin, a perpetual virgin. The perpetual virginity of Mary has been a very important teaching of Christianity from the beginning. How important? Well, in the fourth century, a bishop named Bonoso from Illyricum (that is, modern day areas of Albania, Montenegro, and Croatia) was rebuked by his brother bishops and stripped of his episcopacy for teaching that Mary and Joseph had more children after Jesus was born. The pope at the time, St. Pope Siricius, wrote a letter to the faithful bishops in Illyricum thanking them for disciplining the errant bishop. He wrote:

> We surely cannot deny that you were right in correcting the doctrine about children of Mary, and you are right in rejecting the idea that any other offspring should come from the same virginal womb from which Christ was born according to the flesh.[2]

The doctrine of Mary's perpetual virginity is such an important teaching of Christianity that St. Pope Martin I made it a dogma of the faith at the Lateran Council in 649.

With this in mind, did you know that there is a tradition in the Church that holds that St. Joseph was a perpetual virgin as well? It is a tradition that has been adhered to and promoted by saints, holy mystics, and popes for centuries. Before delving into this tradition, it is necessary to address common objections that are often raised against the virginity of Mary. In addressing these objections, a clearer picture of the virginity of St. Joseph will emerge.

First, some have stated that the passages in the New Testament that refer to the "brothers and sisters" of Jesus (see Mk 3:31; 6:3; Mt 13:55-56) are a clear indication that Mary did not remain a virgin. At first glance, these statements seem to contradict the perpetual virginity of Mary, as well as any possibility of St. Joseph being a virgin. However, the *Catechism of the Catholic Church* provides a concise answer to the question. It states:

> The Church has always understood these passages as not referring to other children of the Virgin Mary. In fact, James and Joseph, "brothers of Jesus," are the sons of another Mary, a disciple of Christ, whom St. Matthew significantly calls "the other Mary." They are close relations of Jesus, according to an Old Testament expression.[3]

The wisdom expressed in the *Catechism* is the fruit of centuries of study of the Scriptures. Learned biblical scholars familiar with Old Testament expressions have always held that when "brothers and sisters" is used in the New Testament to describe the relatives of Jesus, it is not referring to his biological brothers and sisters. Rather, the Old Testament expression "brothers and sisters" found its way into the New Testament as a way to describe the cousins of Jesus. Every biblical scholar knows that, in the ancient Greek versions of the Old and New Testaments, the word used for brothers and sisters is the same word used for cousins.

Saint Jerome, arguably the greatest biblical scholar in Church history, tackled this issue in the fourth century. He offers the following reflections:

> Certain people who follow the ravings of the apocrypha fancy that the brethren of the Lord are sons of Joseph from another wife, and invent a certain woman, Melcha or Escha. As it is contained in the book which we wrote against Helvidius, we understand as brethren of the Lord not the sons of Joseph but the cousins of the Savior, children of Mary [wife of Clopas, she who was] the Lord's maternal aunt, who is said to be the mother of James the Less and Joseph and Jude. They, as we read, were called brethren of the Lord in another passage of the gospel. Indeed, all scripture indicates that cousins are called brethren.[4]

Saint Jerome addresses several points in this statement. He notes that the "brothers and sisters" of Jesus were not Jesus' biological siblings, but his cousins, and also points out that the idea that St. Joseph had children from a previous marriage finds its origin in apocryphal (non-canonical and non-approved) documents.

Saint Bede the Venerable, one of the greatest historians of the eighth century, echoes the thought of St. Jerome:

> There were indeed heretics who thought Joseph, the husband of the ever Virgin Mary, had generated from another wife those whom Scripture calls the "brethren of the Lord." Others, with still more cunning, thought that he [St. Joseph] would have given birth to others from Mary herself after the birth of the Lord. But, my dearest brethren, without any fear on this question, we must know and confess that not only the Blessed Mother of God, but also the most holy witness and guardian of her chastity, remained free from absolutely all marital acts; in scriptural usage, the "brothers and sisters of the Lord" are called, not their children [of Mary and Joseph], but their relatives.[5]

Saint Jerome and St. Bede know what they are talking about. These great saints are not only defending a fundamental truth of Christianity — Mary's perpetual virginity — but are also affirming the tradition that St. Joseph remained a virgin his entire life.

Second, some have raised the objection that Mary could not have remained a virgin — and by association, neither could St. Joseph have remained a virgin — because several passages in the New Testament refer to Jesus as the "firstborn" of Mary (see Lk 2:7; Col 1:15). Once again, St. Jerome offers a biblical answer to the objection. He writes:

> Certain people have perversely conjectured that Mary [and Joseph] had other sons, for they assert that he alone who is to be called "firstborn" has brothers. However, it is customary in holy scripture to call "firstborn" not him whom brothers follow, but him who is first begotten.[6]

In other words, when Scripture refers to Jesus as the firstborn child of Mary, this is not meant to imply that there are second, third, or fourth-born children. Referring to Jesus as the firstborn Son of Mary is simply a biblical way of stating that Mary begat her first child. It doesn't mean that more children followed.

Third, some protest against the notion of Mary and St. Joseph having a virginal marriage because of the passage in the Gospel of Matthew that states that Joseph did not know his wife "until" Jesus was born. The passage reads:

> And Joseph rising up from sleep, did as the angel of the Lord had commanded him, and took unto him his wife. And he knew her not until she brought forth her firstborn son: and he called his name Jesus.
>
> — Mt 1:24-25

At first glance, the passage from Matthew does give the impression that Joseph engaged in marital relations with his wife after she gave birth to Jesus: "[H]e knew her not *until* she brought forth her firstborn son." However, as numerous Scripture scholars, saints, popes, and theologians have stated over the centuries, the use of the word "until" in Scripture does not necessarily mean that a subsequent action will occur in the future.

Saint Thomas Aquinas, the greatest theologian in the history of Christianity, tackled this specific issue in his *Summa Theologiae*. He wrote:

> "Until" does not necessarily have a determined temporal sense. When the psalmist says: "Our eyes are turned to the Lord until he have mercy on us" (Ps 122:2), this does not mean that, once we have obtained mercy from God, we shall take our eyes off him.[7]

There are several other passages in Scripture that attest that the use of the word "until" does not imply that an action will necessarily follow.

- 2 Sam 6:23: "And Michal the daughter of Saul had no child *until* the day of her death." (Does this mean that Michal had children after she died? Of course not!)
- 1 Tim 4:13: "*Until* I come, attend to the public reading of scripture, to preaching, and to teaching." (Does this mean Timothy should stop preaching on Jesus after Paul arrives? Of course not!)
- 1 Cor 15:25: "For he [Christ] must reign *until* he has put all his enemies under his feet." (Does this mean that Christ's reign will end? Of course not!)
- Mt 1:25: "And he [St. Joseph] knew her not *until* she brought forth her firstborn son." (Does this mean St. Joseph had relations with Mary after she gave birth to Jesus? No, it doesn't.)

The consistent teaching and tradition of the Church is that Mary and Joseph lived a virginal marriage. Their perpetually virginal marriage resulted in a perpetually virginal Son, Jesus Christ.

The teaching of the Church that Mary and St. Joseph lived a virginal marriage is the basis for the tradition that St. Joseph was a perpetual virgin. In fact, the tradition that holds that St. Joseph was a perpetual virgin also affirms that St. Joseph, in a similar fashion to Mary, had made a vow of virginity to God in his youth.

> Both Mary and Joseph had made a vow to remain virgins all the days of their lives; and God wished them to be united in the bonds of marriage, not because they repented of the vow already made, but to be confirmed in it and to encourage each other to continue in this holy relation.[8]
>
> — St. Francis de Sales

> Mary belonged to Joseph, and Joseph to Mary, so much so that their marriage was very real, since they gave themselves to each other. But how could they do this? Behold the triumph of purity. They reciprocally gave their virginity, and over this virginity they gave each other a mutual right. What right? To safeguard the other's virtue.[9]
>
> — St. Peter Julian Eymard

Mary and St. Joseph safeguarded each other's virtue for the sake of the mission of their virginal Son.

The idea that St. Joseph was a widower who brought children from his first marriage into his marriage with Mary has never been the official teaching of the Catholic Church. The Catholic Church has never advanced this idea because it is not in accord with the dominant tradition that St. Joseph was a perpetual virgin. It is very important to stress that the idea of St. Joseph as a man who had been previously married and fathered other children from a previous wife — as well as the claim that he was an old man when he espoused Mary — originates in apocryphal (non-approved) sources.

On occasion, apocryphal sources have been used by the Church to establish liturgical feasts — for example, the feast of Mary's parents, Sts. Joachim and Ann — but such instances are rare and only affirmed by the Church when they are in accord with tradition. It can't be denied that some Fathers of the Church — especially in the East — wrote favorably about St. Joseph having a previous marriage and children. However, this does not in any way mean that the Church embraced their ideas or promoted them as official teaching. On the contrary, the dominant tradition on this matter holds that St. Joseph was not a widower, but a virgin.

> The Church's constant tradition holds that St. Joseph lived a life of consecrated chastity. Some of the apocryphal gospels picture

him as an old man, even a widower. This is not the Church's teaching. We are rather to believe that he was a virgin, who entered into a virginal marriage with Mary.[10]

— Servant of God John A. Hardon

The tradition that St. Joseph was a perpetual virgin provides us with tremendous insights into St. Joseph's greatness and virtue — and it also affords us an insight into how old he probably was when he espoused Mary. A presentation of St. Joseph as a virgin presumes that he was young when he espoused Mary; young enough to make a sacrifice of his virile powers. A virginal St. Joseph conveys an image of a youthful man who had to exhibit heroic, supernatural virtue in order to remain a virgin — he espoused the most beautiful woman ever to live! An elderly man espousing a young virgin requires no sacrifice; the elderly man's virility and passion are waning. A strong, loving, youthful, and virginal man, on the other hand, would be required to make a tremendous sacrifice of his mind, body, senses, and heart in order to espouse a woman so pure and lovely.

Saints, mystics, Scripture scholars, and theologians are not the only ones to affirm the virginal fatherhood of St. Joseph. Several popes in the 20th century have done so as well.

On November 26, 1906, St. Pope Pius X approved a prayer invoking St. Joseph as the virgin father of Jesus. He even granted an indulgence to all who recite the prayer. It reads:

O Joseph, virgin father of Jesus, most pure spouse of the Virgin Mary, pray for us daily to the same Jesus, the Son of God that, armed with the weapons of his grace, we may fight as we ought during life, and be crowned by him at the moment of our death. Amen.[11]

On May 4, 1970, St. Pope Paul VI, speaking to a group in France, affirmed that Mary and St. Joseph lived a virginal marriage. He went so far as to offer an image of St. Joseph and Mary as the new parents of humanity, a type of new Adam and new Eve. He stated:

Whereas Adam and Eve were the source of evil which was unleashed on the world, Joseph and Mary are the summit from which holiness spreads over the earth. The Savior began the work of salvation by this virginal and holy union.[12]

Think about it: If the virgin Eve was entrusted by God to the care of a virginal husband (Adam), why would it be any different between

Mary and St. Joseph? Mary and St. Joseph are much greater than Adam and Eve. Unlike our first parents (Adam and Eve), the virginal union of our new parents (Mary and St. Joseph) did not result in the downfall of the human race but in mankind's elevation. The virginal, loving union of St. Joseph and Mary leads to our redemption. Their virginal union produced a virginal Son, Jesus Christ, the Savior of the world.

Catholic tradition has always taught that Mary's virginal love for God was so great that she consecrated her body to God at an early age through a vow of perpetual virginity. Mary entrusted her entire person to God and had absolute confidence in his plan for her life. She desired nothing in life other than God's will. Her confidence in God was so great that she trusted him to lead her into marriage with a man. She was certain that God would give her a man who would truly love both God and her, and so respect her vow; a man who would be completely dedicated to God's plan and protect her virginity. She never doubted God at all.

> The Virgin [Mary] has been wed to the virginal bridegroom [Joseph]. Yet she — who married Joseph out of obedience to her elders — has no fear for her virginity under Joseph's protection. Having placed her trust in God, she delegated to a man the safeguarding of the greatest treasure. She — who had dedicated the flower of virginity to God earlier in a solemn ceremony — had no doubt that she would have a virginal spouse.[13]
>
> — St. Stanislaus Papczyński

In St. Joseph, God prepared a spouse, a guardian, and a knight for Mary. According to God's design, it had to be this way. God did not come into the world in any other manner than through the marriage of a man and a woman, a virginal man and woman.

In St. Joseph, Mary experienced a perfect reflection and mirror of God's love for her. When Mary met St. Joseph, she knew that God had chosen him to be her loving (and beloved) husband. Trusting in God's plan, she fell in love with St. Joseph and gave him her Heart. Mary's body was reserved for God, but she had the freedom to give her Heart to St. Joseph, the only man worthy of her, the only man perfectly reflecting the pure love of God.

In the virtuous manhood of St. Joseph, Mary experienced purity, chastity, modesty, and sacrificial love. Mary's Heart and body were secure in the spousal love of St. Joseph. He is a mirror of the purity of God the Father. Like the Father eternally begets a Son without physical union with another person, St. Joseph fathers a Son without physical union with Mary. The virginal marriage of St. Joseph and Mary brings about spiritual motherhood, spiritual fatherhood, and virginal fecundity.

The greatest theological minds in all of Christianity have praised the virginal fatherhood of St. Joseph:

> A Son was born of the Virgin Mary to the piety and love of Joseph, and that son was the Son of God. Thus, should not the husband accept virginally what the wife brought forth virginally? For just as she was a virginal wife, so was he a virginal husband; just as she was a virginal mother, so was he a virginal father. Therefore, whoever says, "He should not have been called father because he did not generate the son" looks to concupiscence in the procreation of children, not to the inner sentiments of love. Let his greater purity confirm his fatherhood; let not holy Mary reprehend us, for she was unwilling to place her name before that of her husband but said, "Thy father and I have been seeking thee sorrowing." Therefore, let no perverse murmurers do what the virginal wife did not do. As he was a virginal husband, so he was a virginal father. Just as was the man, just so was the woman. The Holy Spirit, resting in the justice of both, gave a son to both.[14]
>
> — St. Augustine

> Joseph also was virginal through Mary in order that from a virginal marriage a virginal son might be born.[15]
>
> — St. Jerome

> I believe that this man, St. Joseph, was adorned with the most pure virginity, the most profound humility, the most ardent love and charity towards God.[16]
>
> — St. Bernardine of Siena

> In order to augment and support Mary's virginity the Eternal Father gave her a virginal companion, the great St. Joseph.[17]
>
> — St. Francis de Sales

> He [St. Joseph] was a virgin, and his virginity was the faithful mirror of the virginity of Mary.[18]
>
> — St. John Henry Newman

Saint Thomas Aquinas also believed that St. Joseph was a virgin. The Angelic Doctor offers an additional insight on the virginal fatherhood of St. Joseph, advancing the notion that it is only proper that Jesus entrusted his virgin mother to a virgin husband since the virgin mother was later entrusted to a virgin apostle (St. John the Apostle) at the foot of the Cross. Saint Thomas writes:

> We believe that just as the mother of Jesus was a virgin, so was Joseph, because he [God] placed the Virgin in the care of a virgin [St. John the Apostle], and just as he did this at the close [at the Cross], so did he do it at the beginning [at the marriage of Mary and Joseph].[19]

Saint Thomas Aquinas' reasoning makes sense. If you were God, wouldn't you entrust your mother to a virgin? Wouldn't you want your mother to be guarded and honored by a man absolutely pure, chaste, and a perfect reflection of God's love? Of course you would! Saint Albert the Great thought so, too. He wrote:

> As a virginal husband, he [St. Joseph] guarded his virginal wife.[20]

In the 17th century, the famed mystic Venerable Mary of Ágreda wrote *The Mystical City of God*. The book is a devotional masterpiece, portraying for us the life and wonders of the Virgin Mary. Venerable Mary of Ágreda reports that she was privy to conversations that took place between Mary and St. Joseph. In one such conversation, St. Joseph spoke to his beloved wife about the delight he took in her virginity, and revealed to her that he, too, had taken a vow of virginity in his youth. It reads:

> My Mistress, in making known to me thy chaste and welcome sentiments, thou hast penetrated and dilated my heart. I have not opened my thoughts to thee before knowing thy own. I also acknowledge myself under greater obligation to the Lord of creation than other men; for very early he has called me by his true enlightenment to love him with an upright heart; and I desire thee to know, Lady, that at the age of twelve years I also made a promise to serve the Most High in perpetual chastity. On this account I now gladly ratify this vow in order not to impede thy own; in the presence of his Majesty I promise to aid thee, as far as in me lies, in serving him and loving him according to thy full desires. I will be, with the divine grace, thy most faithful servant and companion, and I pray thee, accept my chaste love and hold me as thy brother, without ever entertaining any other kind of love, outside the one which thou owest to God and after God to me.[21]

Saint Joseph is the virginal spouse of Mary and the virginal father of Jesus. He is a perpetual virgin. Saint Joseph is your virginal father!

Santo Anello

Divine union between Our Lady and the glorious St. Joseph! By means of this union that good of eternal goods, Our Lord himself, belonged to St. Joseph as well as to Our Lady.[1]

— St. Francis de Sales

"Santo Anello?" Who is that?

Actually, Santo Anello is not a person. Santo Anello is a thing: the "holy ring" that St. Joseph gave Mary on their wedding day!

Yes, you read that right. The wedding ring that St. Joseph gave to Mary is still in existence today. It is reserved in a special gold and silver reliquary in the Cathedral of San Lorenzo in Perugia, Italy. Many people who go on pilgrimage to Assisi, Italy, are unaware that only a short distance away from Assisi (14 miles) is the holy ring.

The holy ring has been in Perugia since the 19th century. Prior to its term in Perugia, the ring was housed in various other locations throughout Italy. Until recently, the existence of the ring was not known to many people outside of Perugia. Even many saints did not know about the holy ring.

Thanks to the mystical visions of Blessed Anne Catherine Emmerich, people around the world now know about the Santo Anello and its exact location. Interestingly, Blessed Anne Catherine herself never saw the ring in person. She only saw the holy ring in her mystical visions, but never knew where the ring was located. Information about its precise location only came to light after her death.

Here's how.

It was reported that on July 29 and August 3, 1821, Blessed Anne Catherine received visions concerning the holy ring. Prior to the visions, she had had no idea that the ring St. Joseph had given Mary was still in existence. She said:

> [July 29, 1821] I saw the Blessed Virgin's wedding ring; it is neither of silver nor of gold, nor of any other metal; it is dark in color and iridescent; it is not a thin narrow ring, but rather thick and at least a finger broad. I saw it smooth and yet as if covered with little regular triangles in which were letters. On the inside

was a flat surface. The ring is engraved with something. I saw it kept behind many locks in a beautiful church. Devout people about to be married take their wedding rings to touch it.

[August 3, 1821] In the last few days I have seen much of the story of Mary's wedding ring, but as the result of disturbances and pain I can no longer give a connected account of it. Today I saw a festival in a church in Italy where the wedding ring is to be found. It seemed to me to be hung up in a kind of monstrance which stood above the tabernacle. There was a large altar there, magnificently decorated; one saw deep into it through much silverwork. I saw many rings being held against the monstrance. During the festival I saw Mary and Joseph appearing in their wedding garments on each side of the ring, as if Joseph were placing the ring on the Blessed Virgin's finger. At the same time, I saw the ring shining and as if in movement.[2]

According to the visions, Blessed Anne Catherine learned that the wedding ring was in a church in Italy, but she never knew what church or town in Italy, and she died without ever finding out. A few years after her death, people began searching for the locations of many of the things that Blessed Anne Catherine reportedly saw in her visions. Incredibly, the ring and its location were discovered! The ring was found in the Cathedral of San Lorenzo in Perugia, Italy. It was discovered to be housed in a beautiful reliquary resembling a monstrance, exactly as Blessed Anne Catherine had stated. The ring had been there for some time, but almost nobody outside of Italy knew about it. Her description of the ring was true as well. The ring appears iridescent and dark in color, a dark amber or yellow. On occasion, if there is a lot of sunlight in the Cathedral, the ring can appear to be milky white.

A fascinating aspect of Blessed Anne Catherine's reported visions are the dates that she saw the ring. Her visions of the ring occurred on July 29 and August 3. Unbeknownst to her, these dates coincide with the time of year when pilgrims visit the Cathedral in Perugia as they make their way to Assisi for the annual celebration of the Feast of the Holy Angels of the Portiuncula on August 2. The end of July and/or early August see large groups of people venerate the ring in a special way. Married couples, as well as those about to be married, are allowed to touch their wedding rings to the Santo Anello to receive a blessing on their marriage. Blessed Anne Catherine apparently witnessed this happening in her visions!

Today, pilgrims from around the world travel to Perugia to see the relic and venerate it. Blessed Pope Pius IX venerated the ring on May 10, 1857, when visiting Perugia; he also celebrated Mass at the Cathedral.

> O, what pure love the virgin spouses had for each other! More than Adam and Eve in the early days of their innocence, Joseph and Mary were the delight of the Lord, the ecstasy of angels in the humble home of Nazareth. Nazareth was similar to Eden in the first days of creation: everything was holy, everything was innocent, everything was beautiful![3]
>
> — Blessed Bartolo Longo

WONDER 5

JUST AND REVERENT MAN

Saint Joseph was "a just man," a tireless worker, the upright guardian of those entrusted to his care.

— St. John Paul II

Son of David

How great is the dignity of that son of David, Joseph, the husband of Mary![1]

— Blessed Gabriele Allegra

How great indeed is the dignity of St. Joseph! In the Litany of St. Joseph, he is given the title "Noble Offspring of David." In some translations, the title is rendered as "Renowned Offspring of David." Either way, the meaning is the same: Saint Joseph is a descendant of King David.

> He [St. Joseph] was the progeny of a patriarchal, regal, and princely stock according to the direct line. From this it is evident that the dignity of the patriarchs, kings, and princes terminated in Joseph.[2]
>
> — St. Bernardine of Siena

Saint Joseph has the blood of kings. What a noble father Jesus has in St. Joseph; what a noble father we have in St. Joseph. Our spiritual father is a descendant of royalty! Saint Joseph is the "Son of David."

The title "Son of David" is a Messianic title. Jesus is called the "Son of David" 17 times in the New Testament. Unlike Jesus, St. Joseph is not the Messiah, but he is the only other person in the New Testament referred to as the Son of David.

Saint Joseph is called the "Son of David" by the angel of God when he is instructed by the angel not to be afraid to take Mary into his home (see Mt 1:20). Why does the angel call St. Joseph the "Son of David," especially in light of the fact that it is a title associated with the Messiah? The reason the angel does it is because St. Joseph needs to be reminded of his royal ancestry at a very crucial moment in salvation history. Saint Joseph had recently discovered that his wife was pregnant and, in his humility, not fully understanding the origin of the child in her womb, he is about to take action by separating himself from her and the Child. The angel had to come to remind St. Joseph of who he was and let him know what role he had been given by God in the coming of the Messiah, lest he walk away from divine mysteries and the vocational call he had been created to fulfill. In other words, God planned for his Eternal Son to be known by those around him as the son of a man of the house of David. That man was St. Joseph.

> "Joseph, son of David, do not be afraid." Otherwise, while troubled in mind, you may fail to understand this mystery. "Joseph, son of David, do not be afraid." What you see in her is virtue, not sin. This is not a human fall, but a divine descent. Here is a reward, not guilt. This is an enlargement from heaven, not a detriment to the body. This is not the betrayal of a person, it is the secret of the Judge. Here is the victory of him who knows the case, not the penalty of torture. Here is not some man's stealthy deed, but the treasure of God. Here there is a cause not of death, but of life. Therefore, do not be afraid.[3]
>
> — St. Peter Chrysologus

Saint Peter Chrysologus' words are beautiful and thought-provoking. His reflection presumes that St. Joseph was suspicious of Mary's faithfulness, but as we will see in the section "Just and Reverent Man," many other saints provide a much more noble and virtuous explanation for Joseph's behavior. These saints hold that St. Joseph was in reverential awe at what was happening in Mary's womb, and he considered himself unworthy to be her husband and the putative father of the Child. He never suspected Mary of any wrongdoing whatsoever. On the contrary, St. Joseph knew he was in the presence of a great mystery. Humble and just, he planned to separate himself from Mary quietly in order not to get in the way of divine mysteries. Before he could take action, however, God sent his angel to remind Joseph of his royal lineage, a lineage needed for the Savior to be considered a descendant of David.

King David, St. Joseph's royal ancestor, had himself once taken a similar course of action. Considering himself unworthy to have the Ark of the Covenant in his city, King David sent the Ark away (see 2 Sam 6) for three months. To prevent something similar from happening in the marriage of Mary and St. Joseph, the angel reassured St. Joseph that God had chosen him to take the child and his mother into his home. Saint Joseph was not to send the ark away. Saint Joseph was not to do what King David had done. "Joseph, son of David, do not be afraid to take Mary your wife into your home" (Mt 1:20).

Just and Reverent Man

To be just is to be perfectly united to the Divine Will, and to be always conformed to it in all sorts of events, whether prosperous or adverse. That St. Joseph was this, no one can doubt.[1]

— St. Francis de Sales

To exercise the virtue of justice, as St. Francis de Sales rightly notes, a person needs to live in perfect accord with the Divine Will and, in the face of all sorts of events, whether advantageous or adverse, give God and others their due. The Church has always understood St. Joseph to be a just and holy man, loving God and neighbor as he ought, but it hasn't always understood the deeper theological significance of what those words actually mean, especially when applied to the actions of St. Joseph in the New Testament. It has taken the Church centuries to advance a theology of St. Joseph that shows his greatness and his holiness.

Today, the Church teaches that St. Joseph is the holiest human person after Mary and the "Most Just" of all the saints. He is our spiritual father, the Pillar of Families, the Glory of Domestic Life, the Patron of the Universal Church, and the Terror of Demons. For this reason, certain passages in the New Testament that present the actions of St. Joseph need to be reexamined in light of what is now unequivocally taught by the Church to be true about St. Joseph — namely, that St. Joseph, as he confronted all sorts of events, whether advantageous or adverse, always acted in accord with the Divine Will and gave God and others their due. He truly lived the love of God and neighbor that his Son would later teach.

What did he [St. Joseph] actually do? He loved. This is all he did, and it was sufficient for his glory. He loved God without limit and without lessening. This was his significance; this was his life here below. For this, he has been loved immeasurably.

Behold his glory for eternity! Go to him without hesitation. He is all-powerful in heaven. As for his goodness, you cannot doubt it when you think that he spent his life in the intimacy of the hearts of Jesus and Mary — the most loving and most kindly hearts there ever were.[2]

— Blessed Jean Joseph Lataste

One of the most important actions of St. Joseph in the New Testament is his response to discovering that his wife was pregnant. It is within the biblical recounting of this story that St. Joseph is called a just man.

Now the birth of Jesus Christ took place in this way. When his mother Mary had been betrothed to Joseph, before they came together she was found to be with child of the Holy Spirit; and her husband Joseph, being a just man and unwilling to put her to shame, resolved to send her away quietly. But as he considered this, behold, an angel of the Lord appeared to him in a dream, saying, "Joseph, son of David, do not fear to take Mary your wife, for that which is conceived in her is of the Holy Spirit; she will bear a son, and you shall call his name Jesus, for he will save his people from their sins." All this took place to fulfill what the Lord had spoken by the prophet: "Behold, a virgin shall conceive and bear a son, and his name shall be called Emmanuel" (which means, God with us). When Joseph woke from sleep, he did as the angel of the Lord commanded him; he took his wife.

— Mt 1:18-24

The translation provided is from the RSVCE (Revised Standard Version Catholic Edition). I offer the RSVCE translation because it does not state that St. Joseph desired to "divorce" his wife. Did you know that the Catholic Church has always allowed for multiple interpretations of Matthew 1:18-24? In particular, the Church allows for an interpretation that does not state that St. Joseph desired to divorce his wife. From the first centuries of Church history, there have been three theories posited about St. Joseph's plan of action when he discovered that his wife was pregnant. All three of the theories have been held by various saints and scholars, and all three theories originate in the early Church. The three theories are:

1) *The Suspicion Theory.* Saint Joseph suspects Mary of adultery, and as a result, he decides to obtain a divorce. According to Jewish law, if a just man wants to divorce his wife because she has been unfaithful, he is required to stone her. Saint

Joseph, being a just man, does not want to stone Mary, so he seeks to divorce her quietly. This theory was promoted in the apocryphal literature and held by several Fathers of the Church.

2) *The Stupefaction Theory.* Saint Joseph is perplexed and stupefied by Mary's pregnancy, but he does not doubt Mary's innocence. He is dumbfounded and doesn't know what to do. Confused, he decides to divorce Mary. Some Fathers of the Church adhere to this theory and greatly promote it. It becomes the most common theory and is known as "Joseph's Doubt."

3) *The Reverence Theory.* Saint Joseph discovers that Mary is pregnant, but he does not doubt her purity and innocence. Instead, he doubts his worthiness and ability to take care of Mary and the child. A just man, he knows that Mary belongs to God and he considers himself unworthy of living with Mary. He decides to separate himself from her quietly out of justice to God and reverence for Mary. He is willing to leave the picture so as not to reveal her mystery. Some Fathers of the Church, as well as many medieval saints, theologians, and mystics promote this theory.

Why does the Church allow for three theories on this important topic? Well, it all hinges on the translation of the Greek word *apoluo*. Biblical scholars all agree that the word *apoluo* is a very difficult word to translate. In Greek, *apoluo* can have multiple meanings, and the meaning chosen for a particular passage is usually determined by the context in which it appears. For example, according to the context, *apoluo* can mean "separate," "conceal," "hide," "distance oneself from," or "divorce." Interestingly, the majority of those who have translated the New Testament from Greek into other languages have chosen to translate *apoluo* as "divorce." However, now that the Church has a much greater understanding of the holiness of St. Joseph, especially as regards his privileges, virtues, and wonders, is this translation correct? In light of what we hold to be true of St. Joseph, can we really say that St. Joseph intended to divorce his beloved wife? The Church has come a long way in her understanding of St. Joseph, and in the opinion of many, the idea that he wanted to divorce Mary needs to be reexamined.

Now, to be fair, those throughout history who have translated *apoluo* as divorce did not do so out of bad intent or malice. Remember: Divorce is often a valid translation of the word according to the context of a particular passage. However, the only reason the word divorce was used in Matthew 1:14-28 is because the Church did not yet possess a developed theology of St. Joseph. Unfortunately, the effect of translating *apoluo* as divorce set in motion a centuries-long minimization of the importance of St. Joseph in the life of the Church. In fact, Matthew 1:18-24 is often described as "Joseph's Doubt" instead of the more noble description "St. Joseph's Annunciation." It's easy to understand, then, why St. Joseph hasn't been loved as much as he deserves, and has been so little honored, revered, and imitated throughout history.

"What's the big deal?" you ask. Well, there's a big difference between St. Joseph desiring to divorce his wife versus desiring to distance himself from her out of a sense of justice and reverence. The latter explanation of what he intended to do is what has caused many an erudite scholar to opt for a translation of *apoluo* that does not mean divorce. Today, in light of what the Church now clearly discerns to be true about St. Joseph, maintaining the position that St. Joseph desired to divorce his wife is very hard to reconcile with St. Joseph's virtues. After all, the idea that St. Joseph intended to divorce his wife places the very foundation of the new covenant of Jesus Christ on shaky ground! Divorcing Mary would have been an extremely unjust thing for St. Joseph to do. Mary was innocent and had done nothing wrong. How can the man the Church invokes as the "Pillar of Families" and the "Glory of Domestic Life" be the same man who desired to divorce the pure, innocent, immaculate Mother of God? It doesn't make sense.

Does this mean that for 2,000 years the Church was wrong about a very important aspect of Divine Revelation? No, it doesn't mean that at all. Remember, since the time that the New Testament was written, the Church has allowed for various translations of *apoluo* in the Gospel of Matthew. What it does mean, however, is that in light of the Church's development of a theology of St. Joseph, the Church needs to reexamine the issue and present a more theologically accurate interpretation of Matthew 1:18-24, an interpretation that has been there from the beginning.

What is it, then, that the Church now understands to be true about St. Joseph that is causing scholars and theologians to shy away from translating *apoluo* as divorce? Why are many scholars preferring to describe St. Joseph's intended plan of action as "distancing himself" from Mary? Well, the Church's recognition of the extraordinary obedience, justice, reverence, and humility of St. Joseph has provided the true context for how to correctly translate the word *apoluo* in Matthew's Gospel. In essence, understanding the extraordinary holiness of St. Joseph provides the correct interpretation of what St. Joseph intended to do. Saint Joseph's supernatural faith informed him that Mary had conceived by the Holy Spirit, and he was afraid of the mystery taking place inside her. He didn't want to divorce Mary. He believed he owed it to God, the originator of the mystery taking place inside her womb, to distance himself from her and the Child until a further revelation was given. The fact that the Church allows for this interpretation, and that many of the Fathers of the Church, medieval theologians, saints, and mystics have already interpreted the passage in this way, is what is causing many scholars to adhere to the Reverence Theory.

For example, Fr. René Laurentin, universally acclaimed as the greatest Mariologist of the 20th century, conducted thorough studies on Matthew 1:18-24 and concluded that it is theologically problematic to hold the position that St. Joseph desired to divorce his beloved wife. How could a truly just man have desired to divorce his innocent wife? Divorcing Mary would not have been a just act; it would have been an extremely unjust act! Father John McHugh, one of the most learned biblical scholars of the 20th century, reached the same conclusion, as has Fr. John Saward, a convert from Anglicanism and a scholar of the highest caliber.

Another such scholar is Fr. Ignace de la Potterie, SJ. Widely respected as a fine theologian and biblical scholar, Fr. de la Potterie conducted extensive studies on Matthew 1:18-24 and was so convinced of the truth of the Reverence Theory that he offered his own translation of the passage. His translation is an eyeopener! It elucidates St. Joseph's selfless and heroic exercise of the virtue of justice, as well as St. Joseph's profound reverential love for Mary and the Child in her womb. Father de la Potterie's translation reads:

> Concerning Jesus as Messiah, the origin took place in the following manner: His mother Mary was betrothed to Joseph; but before they had led a life in common she was found bearing (a child) in her womb, by the work of the Holy Spirit. But Joseph her spouse who was a just man, and who was unwilling to unveil

(her mystery), resolved to secretly separate himself from her. But as he had designed this plan, behold an angel of the Lord appeared to him in a dream and said to him: "Joseph, son of David, do not fear to take Mary your spouse into your home; for certainly that which has been begotten in her comes from the Holy Spirit, but she will bear a son (for you) and you will give him the name of Jesus. For it is he who will save his people from their sins." Now all this happened that what had been said by the Lord through the mouth of a prophet would be accomplished: "Behold: the virgin will bear in her womb and bring forth a son and they will give him the name of Emmanuel," which signifies in translation: "God-with-us." Now when Joseph was awakened from his sleep it happened as the angel of the Lord had prescribed and he took his spouse into his home.[3]

What a translation! It reads somewhat oddly in places because it is a very literal translation, but it is by far the best translation of the passage available. His translation recognizes the supernatural virtues of St. Joseph as the context demanding a more noble interpretation of the passage. Imagine if this translation had been placed in Bibles, preached in sermons, and included in liturgies over the centuries. Without a doubt, the faithful would have possessed a much more theologically accurate — and spiritually edifying — understanding of the blessed person of St. Joseph.

Again, those over the centuries who translated *apoluo* as divorce did not have bad intent. They simply lacked a true understanding of the supernatural greatness of St. Joseph because a theology of St. Joseph had not yet been developed. We can't change history, but now that the Church has begun to truly understand the greatness of St. Joseph, we can give direction for the future. Our understanding of St. Joseph's perfect, loving union with the will of God, as well as his justice and reverence, should exclude any interpretation that states that he desired to divorce his wife. Such an interpretation is theologically untenable because of what we now know to be true about St. Joseph.

Let's examine why this is the case.

The theological definition of the virtue of justice is that it disposes a person to always give God and others their due. In all sorts of events, whether advantageous or adverse, St. Joseph always did the will of God and perfectly exercised the virtue of justice. Thus, it is theologically impossible to hold that St. Joseph would have resolved to do something God hates.

For I hate divorce, says the Lord, the God of Israel, and the one who covers his garment with violence, says the Lord of hosts. You should be on your guard, then, for your life, and you must not break faith.

— Mal 2:16

(Now, for anyone reading this who has had a divorce, don't panic. God hates divorce, not you. It is true that the Catholic Church, following the teaching of Jesus Christ himself, says that divorce is impossible in the case of valid sacramental marriages [see Mk 10:2-12], and only tolerates civil divorce in extreme instances [see Mt 19:3-12; 1 Cor 7:10-16]. A Catholic annulment is not the same thing as a divorce. An annulment states that a true marriage never existed; a divorce, on the other hand, would dissolve a true marriage bond. The Church allows for the legal separation of validly married spouses [which is neither an annulment nor an attempt at divorce], as long as the separated spouses do not attempt to sever the marriage bond. To repeat: God doesn't hate you if you have had a civil divorce; he hates the divorce. It also needs to be noted that not everyone who desires or gets a civil divorce is committing a sin or a moral offense against God. The reason is because there can be unique circumstances in each particular case. Now, back to St. Joseph's marriage.)

Saint Joseph was undergoing a test. Saint Joseph's virtue and cooperation with grace needed to be put to the test because God intended to make St. Joseph a new Abraham, a spiritual father to a new covenant people. If St. Joseph passed the test by a loving willingness to sacrifice himself completely, God would bless him in a manner greater than he had blessed any other man who has ever lived.

Needless to say, St. Joseph passed the test! Many of the Fathers of the Church beautifully describe for us how St. Joseph passed the test through his supernatural justice and reverence.

Joseph was just, and the Virgin was immaculate: but when he wished to put her away, this happened from the fact that he recognized in her the power of a miracle and a vast mystery which he held himself unworthy to approach. Humbling himself therefore before so great and ineffable a phenomenon, he sought to retire, just as St. Peter humbled himself before the Lord and said, "Depart from me, O Lord, for I am a sinful man," and as the ruler confessed who sent word to the Lord, "I am not worthy that thou shouldst enter under my roof, for I have considered myself not even worthy to come to thee," or as St. Elizabeth said to the Most Blessed Virgin, "And how have I deserved that the mother of my Lord should come to me?" In like manner did the just man Joseph humble himself and fear to enter into a union with such exalted holiness.[4]

— Origen

Joseph discovered both Mary's pregnancy and its cause, namely, that it was of the Holy Spirit. Therefore, he feared to be called the husband of such a wife, and wished to put her away privately since he did not dare to reveal what had taken place in her. Yet because he was just, he desired a revelation of the mystery.[5]

— St. Basil the Great

But he thought especially of sending her away so as not to commit a sin in allowing himself to be called father of the Savior. He feared to live with her lest he dishonor the name of the virgin's son. That is why the angel said to him, "Do not fear to take Mary to your home."[6]

— St. Ephrem the Syrian

O inestimable tribute to Mary! Joseph believed in her chastity more than in her womb, in grace more than in nature! He plainly saw the conception, and he was incapable of suspecting fornication. He believed that it was more possible for a woman to conceive without a man than for Mary to be able to sin.[7]

— St. John Chrysostom

Saint Romanus the Melodist, a poet from the sixth century, wrote a beautiful poem that depicts St. Joseph's fear and reverence for Mary's mysterious pregnancy:

Then Joseph, who never knew the Virgin, stopped,
stunned by her glory,
and, gazing on the brilliance of her form, said:
"O shining one, I see that a flame and hot coals encircle you.
It frightens me, Mary. Protect me, do not consume me!
Your spotless womb has suddenly become a fiery furnace.
Let it not melt me, I beg you. Spare me.
Do you wish me, like Moses of old, to take off my shoes,
that I may draw nigh and listen to you, and taught by you say:
Hail, Bride unbridled!"[8]

Saint Joseph's love, faith, humility, justice, and reverence are so great that at no time did he suspect Mary of being unfaithful. Mary was pure and innocent, and he knew it. Nor did he consider it a possibility that another man had forced himself upon his wife. He was absolutely positive that Mary belonged to God, and God would take care of her. He trusted God and he trusted Mary. To divorce Mary would have been to abandon her and throw away his God-given marriage. For this reason, St. Joseph desired to distance himself from Mary, knowing that God, who had brought about the Child in her womb, would take care of her and the Child.

Saint Joseph loved Mary immensely, and it would have been torturous for him to contemplate distancing himself from her, but he loved God first. His immediate resolve was to give God what Joseph believed was God's due, that is, to distance himself from Mary since she belonged to God. Out of justice and reverence, he was willing to step out of the picture completely. These are the actions of St. Joseph that moved the heart of God, solidified St. Joseph's marriage, and made him our father in faith.

> Why did he [St. Joseph] wish to leave her [Mary]? Listen, now, no longer to my opinion, but to that of the Fathers [of the Church]. Joseph wanted to leave her for the same reason Peter begged the Lord to leave him, when he said, "Depart from me, Lord, for I am a sinful man," and for the same reason the Centurion kept him from his house, [saying,] "Lord, I am not worthy that you should come under my roof." Thus Joseph, considering himself unworthy and a sinner, said to himself that a man like him ought not to live under the same roof with a woman so great and exalted, whose wonderful and superior dignity filled him with awe. He saw with fear and trembling that she bore the surest signs of the divine presence, and, since he could not fathom the mystery, he wanted to depart from her. Peter was frightened by the greatness of the power; the Centurion feared the majesty of the presence. Joseph, too, as a human being, was afraid of the newness of the great miracle, the profundity of the mystery, and so he decided to leave her quietly. Are you surprised that Joseph judged himself unworthy of the pregnant Virgin's company? After all, have you not heard that St. Elizabeth, too, could not endure her presence without fear and awe? As she says, "Whence is this to me that the Mother of my Lord should come to me?" This then is why Joseph decided to leave her.[9]
>
> — St. Bernard of Clairvaux

According to [St.] Jerome and Origen, Joseph had no suspicion of adultery because he knew the modesty and chastity of Mary. Moreover, he had read in Scripture that the virgin would conceive and that "a shoot shall sprout from the stock of Jesse, and from his roots a bud shall blossom." He knew also that Mary was descended from the line of David. Thus it was easier for him to believe that Isaiah's prophecy had been accomplished in her than to think that she could have let herself descend into debauchery. This is why, considering himself unworthy to live with a person of such great sanctity, he wanted to send her away secretly — like when Peter says to Jesus, "Depart from me, Lord, for I am a sinful man!"[10]

— St. Thomas Aquinas

Joseph wanted to give the Virgin her liberty, not because he suspected her of adultery, but [because] out of respect for her sanctity he feared to live together with her.[11]

— St. Thomas Aquinas

In the mystical revelations of St. Bridget of Sweden, the Blessed Virgin herself spoke of the justice and reverence St. Joseph had exercised in response to discovering her pregnancy. Our Lady said the following to St. Bridget:

From the moment I [Mary] gave my consent to God's messenger, Joseph, seeing that, having conceived by the power of the Holy Spirit, I was pregnant and that I was growing, wondered greatly. Because he would not suspect evil but remembered the words of the prophet who foretold that the Son of God would be born of a virgin, he reputed himself unworthy to serve such a mother, until the angel in a dream commanded him not to fear but to minister to me with charity.[12]

Interestingly, what Mary told St. Bridget of Sweden is exactly what she would have told St. Matthew when he was writing his Gospel. Think about it: How else did St. Matthew find out about what is recounted in Matthew 1:18-24 if not from Mary? Saint Matthew did not know St. Joseph, and he was not present when everything happened. The source of the information had to be Mary, and Mary did not tell St. Matthew that her husband wanted to divorce her. She would have told him the exact same thing she told St. Bridget: namely, that St. Joseph did not suspect any wrongdoing and knew that Mary had conceived of the Holy Spirit. He was afraid of such holiness. Mary didn't tell St. Matthew that her husband wanted to divorce her. On the contrary, she told him that her husband considered himself unworthy of that great role and desired to distance himself from her out of justice and reverence.

Did St. Joseph fully understand what was going on in Mary's womb? No, he didn't. He would not have had all the information needed to give a theological discourse about how God was taking on human nature in Mary's womb, and he, a faithful, first century Jewish man, certainly would not have understood terms such as "hypostatic union" or "Incarnation" since those only emerged in the Church after centuries of thought, prayer, and discernment. However, he was convinced that what was happening in her was of God. He did not know how the Child came to be in her womb, but we are assured by saints and Fathers of the Church that he never doubted that Mary was pure or that God was at work in her. He did not doubt Mary; he doubted himself and his ability to be the husband of such a woman and the father of such a Child.

The greatness of St. Joseph is that he was willing to become a homeless wanderer out of love for God and Mary. He did not want to defame Mary by a divorce, even a quiet one. After Jesus Christ, St. Joseph is the humblest of all men, and he was willing to step out of the picture and disappear. If God wanted him to remain in the picture, it would take a divine revelation to make it known. With the exception of Jesus Christ, of course, there has never been a man so selfless and heroic in love, faith, justice, reverence, and humility as St. Joseph.

God, of course, already knew he had the right man in St. Joseph, but St. Joseph needed to hear it from heaven itself. And that's exactly what the angel did when he came to St. Joseph and spoke to him in his sleep. God let St. Joseph know that he needed to rely on St. Joseph's willingness to always do the will of God. Jesus himself would need to rely on the humility and sacrificial love of St. Joseph in order to accomplish his saving mission. There would come a time when St. Joseph would be removed from the picture so that Jesus could teach the world about his Heavenly Father, but that time was not yet. Yet St. Joseph had proven himself to be a man who was reliable and obedient in the face of all sorts of events, whether advantageous or adverse. God could trust him.

The Reverence Theory teaches us that, in the mind and heart of St. Joseph, God comes first. If giving to God what belongs to God required St. Joseph to sacrifice a future with Mary, then so be it. God comes first. Out of love for God, St. Joseph was willing to undergo a sacrifice greater than any Old Testament Patriarch or New Testament martyr could ever make. God wanted St. Joseph to be a new Abraham, a man willing to sacrifice everything for God's holy will. God rewarded St. Joseph's love, obedience, justice, reverence, and humility by confirming him as the Head of the Holy Family, the father of Jesus Christ, the Terror of Demons, and our spiritual father. Saint Joseph reaped an unparalleled type of spiritual fatherhood, and his children will be as numerous as the stars of the sky! God made him the spiritual father of a new creation. God made him the Increaser!

The saints, theologians, and mystics who have taught over the centuries that St. Joseph exhibited perfect love, justice, and reverential piety toward God and Mary give us a profound interpretation of Matthew 1:18-24 that is today being affirmed in what the Church teaches about St. Joseph. He is the greatest of all the saints, the "Pillar of Families" and the "Glory of Domestic Life." After Jesus Christ, St. Joseph is the "Most Just," loving, and reverent of all men!

> Through his complete self-sacrifice, Joseph expressed his generous love for the Mother of God, and gave her a husband's "gift of self." Even though he decided to draw back so as not to interfere in the plan of God which was coming to pass in Mary, Joseph obeyed the explicit command of the angel and took Mary into his home, while respecting the fact that she belonged exclusively to God.[13]
>
> — St. John Paul II

Saint Joseph, our spiritual father, is not a man of doubt who sought to divorce our spiritual mother. After his Son, St. Joseph is *the* model of supernatural love, faith, justice, reverence, and humility. He is a virtuous gentleman whose faith is constant and pure.

> As regards his [St. Joseph's] constancy, did he not display it wonderfully when, seeing Our Lady with child, and not knowing how that could be, his mind was tossed with distress, perplexity, and trouble? Yet, in spite of all, he never complained, he was never harsh or ungracious towards his holy spouse, but remained just as gentle and respectful in his demeanor as he had ever been.[14]
>
> — St. Francis de Sales

Saint Joseph's response to Mary's pregnancy is a model for us. Our spiritual father teaches us how to be just and reverent in the face of all sorts of events. He teaches us to give God his due even if it requires us to be willing to sacrifice everything we love. Our spiritual father teaches us that we should not act hastily or harshly when we encounter perplexing situations. We are to take everything to prayer, and wait on the Lord for guidance and light. If we are loving, faithful, reverent, and just, God will reveal everything to us and make us abundantly fruitful.

Who was holier than Joseph? Who was purer than the Most Holy Virgin? And yet he [St. Joseph] wanted to leave her secretly. But how prudently and righteously he wanted to do it! He did not want to separate from her openly, lest she be defamed, but clandestinely, that she may preserve her good name. You ought to learn from this holy and just man: although the deeds of others may seem evil to you and are said to be imperfect, you should judge them secretly, not openly, and judge in such a way that neither your conscience nor their good name be hurt. If you do so, you will not be lacking the light, so that you may judge rightly, as the righteous husband of the Most Holy Virgin did not lack light for comprehending the truth about how she had conceived.[15]

— St. Stanislaus Papczyński

Gifts of the Holy Spirit

There is a general rule concerning all special graces granted to any human being. Whenever the divine favor chooses someone to receive a special grace, or to accept a lofty vocation, God adorns the person chosen with all the gifts of the Spirit needed to fulfill the task at hand. This general rule is especially verified in the case of St. Joseph.[1]

— St. Bernardine of Siena

Saint Joseph had the loftiest of vocations, the greatest of missions. He was called to be the spouse of the Virgin Mary and the father of Jesus Christ. His mission required all seven gifts of the Holy Spirit (knowledge, understanding, counsel, fortitude, piety, fear of the Lord, and wisdom).

Consider that the Holy Spirit chose only Joseph to be the protector of the Blessed Virgin, to be her true husband and consequently, no created being can equal the glory of this great saint.[2]

— Blessed William Joseph Chaminade

Saint Joseph was not only chosen to be the protector of Mary, but also the protector of Jesus — and you! Jesus and Mary are in heaven, but you are not. This means that St. Joseph's mission is ongoing. From heaven, he watches over those entrusted to his loving care and asks the Holy Spirit to pour out gifts on his children.

You have a mission: to become holy, loving God truly and your neighbor mercifully. You need the seven gifts of the Holy Spirit in your life. They will help you resemble your spiritual father and reach heaven.

What specifically do the seven gifts of the Holy Spirit do for us though? Well, the Holy Spirit Fathers provide the answer for us. The Holy Spirit Fathers (also called Spiritans) are the religious community responsible for promulgating throughout the world a very powerful novena to the Holy Spirit that contains an excellent summary of what the gifts are and what they do for us. Reprinted with the permission of the Holy Spirit Fathers, listed below are the descriptions of the seven gifts of the Holy Spirit from the novena, as well as a beautiful prayer:

1. *The Gift of Knowledge* enables the soul to evaluate created things at their worth — in their relation to God. Knowledge unmasks the pretense of creatures, reveals their emptiness, and points out their only true purpose as instruments in the service of God. It shows us the loving care of God even in adversity, and directs us to glorify him in every circumstance of life. Guided by its light, we put first things first, and prize the friendship of God beyond all else.

2. *The Gift of Understanding* helps us to grasp the meaning of the truths of our holy religion. By faith we know them, but by understanding we learn to appreciate and relish them. It enables us to penetrate the inner meaning of revealed truths and, through them, to be quickened to newness of life. Our faith ceases to be sterile and inactive, but inspires a mode of life that bears eloquent testimony to the faith that is in us.

3. *The Gift of Counsel* endows the soul with supernatural prudence, enabling it to judge promptly and rightly what must be done, especially in difficult circumstances. Counsel applies the principles furnished by knowledge and understanding to the innumerable concrete cases that confront us in the course of our daily duty as parents, teachers, public servants, and Christian citizens. Counsel is supernatural common sense, a priceless treasure in the quest of salvation.

4. *The Gift of Fortitude* strengthens the soul against natural fear and supports us in the performance of duty. Fortitude imparts to the will an impulse and energy which move it to undertake without hesitancy the most arduous tasks, to face dangers, to trample underfoot human respect, and to endure without complaint the slow martyrdom of even lifelong tribulation.

Charity embraces all the other Virtues.

(5) *The Gift of Piety* begets in our hearts a filial affection for God as our most loving Father. It inspires us to love and respect for his sake persons and things consecrated to him, as well as those who are vested with his authority, his mother, St. Joseph, the saints, the Church and its visible head, our parents and superiors, our country and its rulers. He who is filled with the Gift of Piety finds the practice of his religion, not a burdensome duty, but a delightful service.

(6) *The Gift of Fear* fills us with a sovereign respect for God, and makes us dread nothing so much as to offend him by sin. It is a fear that arises, not from the thought of hell, but from sentiments of reverence and filial submission to our heavenly Father. It is the fear that is the beginning of wisdom, detaching us from worldly pleasures that could in any way separate us from God.

(7) *The Gift of Wisdom* embodies all the other gifts, as charity embraces all the other virtues. Wisdom is the most perfect of the gifts. Of wisdom it is written "all good things came to me with her, and innumerable riches through her hands." It is the Gift of Wisdom that strengthens our faith, fortifies hope, perfects charity, and promotes the practice of virtue in the highest degree. Wisdom enlightens the mind to discern and relish things divine, in the appreciation of which earthly joys lose their savor, while the Cross of Christ yields a divine sweetness.

Prayer for the Seven Gifts of the Holy Spirit

O Lord Jesus Christ, who, before ascending into heaven, did promise to send the Holy Spirit to finish your work in the souls of your apostles and disciples, deign to grant the same Holy Spirit to me that he may perfect in my soul, the work of your grace and your love. Grant me the Spirit of Wisdom that I may despise the perishable things of this world and aspire only after the things that are eternal; the Spirit of Understanding to enlighten my mind with the light of your divine truth; the Spirit of Counsel that I may ever choose the surest way of pleasing God and gaining heaven; the Spirit of Fortitude that I may bear my cross with you and that I may overcome with courage all the obstacles that oppose my salvation; the Spirit of Knowledge that I may know God and know myself and grow perfect in the science of the saints; the Spirit of Piety that I may find the service of God sweet and amiable; and the Spirit of Fear that I may be filled with a loving reverence towards God and may dread in any way to displease him. Mark me, dear Lord, with the sign of your true disciples and animate me in all things with your Spirit. Amen.

WONDER 6

SAVIOR OF THE SAVIOR

He [St. Joseph] guarded from death the Child threatened by a monarch's jealousy, and found for him a refuge.

— Pope Leo XIII

Seven Sorrows and Seven Joys

Because St. Joseph was associated with Mary in her glorious privileges, he also had to suffer like her and his heart too was pierced by seven swords.[1]

— St. Peter Julian Eymard

In the 16th century, a devotion to St. Joseph began in the Church called the Seven Sorrows of St. Joseph. No one seems to know the exact origins of the devotion, but it parallels a popular devotion to Our Lady called the Seven Sorrows of Mary.

As a devotion, the Seven Sorrows of St. Joseph consists of meditation on biblical passages from the life of St. Joseph that caused him sorrow. When meditating on the biblical passages, it is customary to pray an Our Father, a Hail Mary, and a Glory Be.

Saint Joseph was such a great lover of God, but was afflicted by much suffering which he endured with a wonderful fortitude.[2]

— St. Joseph Sebastian Pelczar

In the 18th century, Blessed Januarius Maria Sarnelli took the Seven Sorrows of St. Joseph devotion and added another dimension to it: the Seven Joys of St. Joseph. In his preaching, Blessed Januarius told the story of how two shipwrecked Franciscans had been lost at sea for several days, clinging to a plank so as not to drown. Suddenly, a man appeared to them and guided them safely to shore. When the Franciscans asked the man who he was, the man responded that he was St. Joseph. After revealing his identity, St. Joseph asked the Franciscans to honor his Seven Sorrows and Seven Joys on the Seven Sundays leading up to his feast on March 19. As a result of Blessed Januarius' preaching about the shipwrecked Franciscans, the Seven

Sorrows and Seven Joys of St. Joseph devotion became known as the Seven Sundays Devotion to St. Joseph and quickly spread throughout the entire Church.

> O most faithful saint who shared the mysteries of our redemption, glorious St. Joseph, the prophecy of Simeon regarding the sufferings of Jesus and Mary caused thee to shudder with mortal dread, but at the same time filled thee with a blessed joy for the salvation and glorious resurrection which, he foretold, would be attained by countless souls.[3]
>
> — Blessed Januarius Maria Sarnelli

The Seven Sorrows and Seven Joys of St. Joseph, the biblical references that go with them, and their order according to the Seven Sundays devotion are as follows:

1ST SUNDAY
1st Sorrow: *Saint Joseph Resolves to Leave Mary Quietly* (Mt 1:19)
1st Joy: *Saint Joseph's Annunciation* (Mt 1:20)

2ND SUNDAY
2nd Sorrow: *The Poverty of Jesus' Birth* (Lk 2:7)
2nd Joy: *The Birth of the Savior* (Lk 2:10-11)

3RD SUNDAY
3rd Sorrow: *The Circumcision* (Lk 2:21)
3rd Joy: *The Holy Name of Jesus* (Mt 1:25)

4TH SUNDAY
4th Sorrow: *The Prophecy of Simeon* (Lk 2:34)
4th Joy: *The Effects of the Redemption* (Lk 2:38)

5TH SUNDAY
5th Sorrow: *The Flight into Egypt* (Mt 2:14)
5th Joy: *The Overthrow of the Idols of Egypt* (Is 19:1)

6TH SUNDAY
6th Sorrow: *The Return from Egypt* (Mt 2:22)
6th Joy: *Life with Jesus and Mary at Nazareth* (Lk 2:39)

7TH SUNDAY
7th Sorrow: *The Loss of the Child Jesus* (Lk 2:45)
7th Joy: *The Finding of the Child Jesus* (Lk 2:46)

May he [St. Joseph] take charge of the affair of your salvation. Just as he led the Son of God in his travels, may he be your guide on the voyage of this life until you arrive at the haven of eternal happiness.[4]

— Blessed William Joseph Chaminade

Savior of the Savior

To give life to someone is the greatest of all gifts. To save a life is the next. Who gave life to Jesus? It was Mary. Who saved his life? It was Joseph. Ask St. Paul who persecuted him. Saint Peter who denied him. Ask all the saints who put him to death. But if we ask, "Who saved his life?" Be silent, patriarchs, be silent, prophets, be silent, apostles, confessors and martyrs. Let St. Joseph speak, for this honor is his alone; he alone is the savior of his Savior.[1]

— Blessed William Joseph Chaminade

"Savior of his Savior?" That sounds heretical, doesn't it? Don't worry: Blessed William Joseph Chaminade is not claiming that St. Joseph is God or greater than Jesus. Blessed William Joseph was a very holy priest and had a tremendous devotion to St. Joseph. He lived through the French Revolution and suffered many hardships during a very anti-Catholic era of France's history. Blessed Chaminade's love for Jesus, Mary, and St. Joseph gave him the strength to resist the evil intentions of the revolutionaries.

At the height of the French Revolution, Blessed Chaminade spread devotion to Mary and preached fervently about St. Joseph. He encouraged his religious confreres to act as the heel of Mary and crush the darkness of the revolution. He knew the power of St. Joseph as well, and encouraged everyone to seek refuge beneath the fatherly protection of St. Joseph.

Make him [St. Joseph] responsible for the protection of your person, he who saved the life of his Savior.[2]

— Blessed William Joseph Chaminade

To understand and justify Blessed Chaminade's description of St. Joseph as the "Savior of his Savior," we turn to the Gospel of Matthew.

When they had departed [from Bethlehem], behold, the angel of the Lord appeared to Joseph in a dream and said, "Rise, take the child and his mother, flee to Egypt, and stay there until I tell you. Herod is going to search for the child to destroy him." Joseph rose and took the child and his mother by night and departed for Egypt.

— Mt 2:13-14

Saint Joseph can be called the Savior of the Savior because he saved Jesus from the wicked intentions of Herod by taking Jesus to Egypt. Saint Joseph is the only saint who has the privilege of being called the Savior of the Savior — not even the Mother of God has such a title. God wanted St. Joseph to have the unique title all to himself. It is a title that shows the greatness of the fatherhood of St. Joseph. It teaches us his important paternal role in the plan of God.

To him [St. Joseph] was entrusted the Divine Child when Herod loosed his assassins against him.[3]

— Pope Pius XI

Blessed Chaminade is not the only one who called St. Joseph the Savior of the Savior. Saint Madeleine Sophie Barat made a similar statement. She wrote:

Jesus wished to become indebted to St. Joseph for the necessities of life, and of this holy patriarch alone it may be said that he saved the life of his Savior.[4]

Saint Alphonsus Liguori, a Doctor of the Church, went so far as to claim that because St. Joseph saved the Savior from Herod, Jesus will not refuse anything to those who go to St. Joseph for assistance. He writes:

The Apostle Paul writes, that in the next life Jesus Christ "will render to every man according to his works" (Rom 2:6). What great glory must we not suppose that he bestowed upon St. Joseph, who served and loved him so much while he lived on earth! At the last day our Savior will say to the elect, "I was hungry, and you gave me to eat. I was a stranger, and you took me in; naked, and you clothed me" (Mt 25:35). These, never-theless, have fed Jesus Christ, have lodged him or clothed him, only in the persons of the poor, but St. Joseph procured food, a dwelling, and clothes for Jesus Christ in his own person. More-over, our Lord has promised a reward to him who gives a cup of water to the poor in his name: "for whosoever shall give you to drink a cup of water in my name, he shall not lose his reward" (Mk 9:40). What, then, must be the reward of St. Joseph, who can say to Jesus Christ, "I not only provided thee with food, with a dwelling, and with clothes; but I saved thee from death, delivering thee from the hands of Herod." All this helps to increase our confidence in St. Joseph; it makes us reflect that, on account of so many merits, God will refuse no grace which St. Joseph asks of him for his devout clients.[5]

Wow! What confidence we should have in St. Joseph!

Ultimately, St. Joseph saved Jesus' life so that Jesus could save us. For his part, Jesus is extremely grateful to St. Joseph for all that he suffered to make the saving mission of our Lord possible: exile, poverty, hardship, fatigue, ridicule, and so many other hardships. Saint Joseph suffered so much for Jesus. Without the sufferings of St. Joseph, we would not have the Savior to set us free from sin and death. This is why Jesus grants every desire and wish of his beloved virginal father.

The sufferings of St. Joseph are rarely mentioned in homilies or writings on St. Joseph. Yet, if you think about it, being the father of the Savior could not have been easy. Saint Joseph's fatherly mission entailed tremendous suffering.

> How great a share had not the glorious St. Joseph in the chalice of Jesus' passion, by the services which he rendered to his sacred humanity![6]
>
> — St. Mary Magdalen de Pazzi

Saint Joseph's suffering began before our Lord was even born. When St. Joseph discovered that his beloved wife was pregnant, his heart, mind, and soul experienced excruciating sorrow. His sorrow did not come from suspecting Mary had been unfaithful; he never doubted Mary's love, fidelity, and holiness. Rather, his suffering came from knowing that he was not worthy to be the husband of so holy a woman; nor did he consider himself worthy to be the father of a heavenly Child. He realized that Mary belonged totally to God, and out of justice, he needed to give God his due by distancing himself from Mary. The thought of distancing himself from Mary caused more sorrow in his heart than any martyr could ever experience. Unlike the suffering of the martyrs who shed their blood for love of Christ, St. Joseph's suffering was interior, and of such intensity that it is more meritorious than the suffering of all Christian martyrs. Preparing to distance himself from Mary, the delight of his heart, caused him such deep sorrow that God had to send an angel to comfort and instruct him not to be afraid to take her into his home. Abraham was made the father of a multitude of nations because of his willingness to sacrifice his son; St. Joseph was made the father of the new covenant people because of his willingness to distance himself from his own beloved wife.

Saint Joseph's suffering continued for the remainder of his married life. When he traveled with his pregnant wife to Jerusalem for the census, he suffered greatly from not being able to provide a suitable place for his wife to give birth. What man wants his wife to give birth in a cold, dirty, and smelly animal stable? Yet a stable was all that St. Joseph could provide. Men, by nature, are providers. If a man is unable to provide as much or as well for the ones he loves as he wishes, he dies inside. Saint Joseph died daily.

Saint Joseph experienced sorrow when his Son was circumcised. When he and his wife saw the blood coming from their Son's body, they knew it was a foreshadowing of things to come. When and by what method, they did not know, but they were so attuned to divine mysteries and Old Testament prophecies that they knew there was more bloodshed to come. It would be confirmed when Jesus, Mary, and Joseph appeared before the priest at the Temple in Jerusalem for the ritual of the purification of a new mother. On what was supposed to be a joyful occasion, St. Joseph learned that his wife's Heart would be pierced and his Son was destined to be a sign of contradiction.

> The child's father and mother were amazed at what was said about him; and Simeon blessed them and said to Mary his mother, "Behold, this child is destined for the fall and rise of many in Israel, and to be a sign that will be contradicted, and you yourself a sword will pierce so that the thoughts of many hearts may be revealed."
>
> — Lk 2:33-35

Simeon's words were spoken to Mary, but St. Joseph heard them. When St. Joseph heard Simeon announce to Mary that Jesus would be a cause of division, and that Mary's Heart would be pierced by a sword, the prophetic words penetrated the loving heart of St. Joseph, causing him unspeakable sorrow. It was a sorrow that he would carry in his heart and soul for the rest of his life.

What man wants to hear that his wife and child are going to suffer ridicule and hatred? What husband would not experience tortures of the heart knowing that his wife is going to be pierced by a sword? Scripture tells us that Mary pondered the words of Simeon in her Heart (see Lk 2:19). Saint Joseph had to have pondered Simeon's words in his heart as well. No man could walk away undisturbed after hearing such shocking statements about his wife and son. The hearts of a husband and wife are one. What is of concern to one is of concern to the other. For decades, St. Joseph carried the sorrowful prophecy of Simeon in his heart. Because his love is great, St. Joseph's suffering was interior, intense, and long lasting.

> O most sensitive heart of St. Joseph, who, resembling the tender heart of Mary, felt the sorrows of the Most Holy Mother, tell me, what did you feel, hearing the terrible prophecy of Simeon? Yet with what generosity, with what silence and unalterable resignation did you accept from the hands of God even the sword of sorrow for our good! How can I show you my thanks? O my sweetest saint, I want to imitate your generosity, and to any painful news I will say with you: God's will be done.[7]
>
> — Blessed Bartolo Longo

Were it possible for St. Joseph to prevent his wife and Son from suffering, he would have done everything in his power to protect them. A good and loving husband is willing to stand in front of his wife and have the sword pierce his heart instead of hers. Yet, according to the plan of God, St. Joseph knew that he had to allow his wife's Heart and soul to be pierced. Such suffering was required so that a new humanity could be born. His immaculate bride had not suffered the pangs of birth at the manger in Bethlehem because she was free from all stain of original sin and exempt from all its penalties, but Simeon's prophecy had foretold that a day would come when St. Joseph's wife would endure a torturous type of birth-pang: spiritual birth-pangs. Saint Joseph's wife is the New Eve, and God was going to use her Heart as a spiritual womb. She would have to undergo spiritual birth pangs in order for humanity to be reborn in Christ. Simeon had prophesied it; St. Joseph knew it had to happen. His role was to prepare his wife and Son for the sacrifice.

No martyr's suffering has been greater than the suffering of St. Joseph. Simeon's prophecy had been addressed to Mary alone. Saint Joseph knew why, and the knowledge caused him even greater suffering. Saint Joseph understood that Simeon's prophecy meant that when the time came for Mary's Heart to be pierced, she would be without St. Joseph. The time, place, and manner of the piercing were unknown to St. Joseph, but he understood that he would not be there with Mary. In light of Simeon's prophecy, he must have spent his marriage lovingly consoling Mary and preparing her for the hours when she would suffer unparalleled sorrow and agony — her spiritual birth-pangs. Saint Joseph's sweet consolations helped prepare Mary for the sacrifice of Calvary. He could not prevent her maternal suffering, but he could prepare her for it. His years of love and devotion were a consolation to Mary's Immaculate Heart. Saint Joseph is the greatest consoler of the Heart of Mary.

> How beautiful and simple did you [St. Joseph] see this innocent dove [Mary]. And how greatly you suffered at the vision of her martyrdom without you, the solitude of the wife whom you loved so well. Oh what martyrdom wracked your soul at the fore-vision of the Passion and the seven swords which would pierce the Immaculate Heart of Mary. You dreamed of her alone, alone without Jesus — and this affliction embittered your happy life.[8]
>
> — Blessed Concepción Cabrera de Armida

The sword that was going to pierce Mary's Heart on Calvary needed to pierce the heart of St. Joseph as well, but in a different way. He would not be at Calvary, but the sword needed to pierce his paternal heart since it is fitting that the re-birth of mankind would involve both a mother and a father. Husbands do not experience labor pangs as a woman does, but every husband is called to journey with his wife throughout the pregnancy and prepare her for delivery. As a good husband, St. Joseph would see to it that his wife was well-prepared for her suffering. He spent decades preparing her for the painful delivery on Calvary.

At Calvary, Mary must have experienced great consolation and strength as she remembered all that her husband had done for her and their Son across the years. The consolation offered by John the Apostle, Mary Magdalene, and several others paled in comparison to the consolation offered to Mary by the man who was not even there. God spared St. Joseph the tortures of Calvary, but Mary brought him there in her Heart. Her Crucified Son, before whom she stood, was also Joseph's Son. Mary remembered her husband and stood strong in faith, hope, and love.

There were many memories of St. Joseph that would have flooded Mary's Heart at Calvary. They were all a source of consolation and strength for Mary. The memory of St. Joseph's own strength in suffering would have increased Mary's determination to witness and suffer with her Crucified Son. She would have remembered the slaughter of the innocents and how much that had wounded her husband's heart. Remember: When the angel came to St. Joseph and instructed him to take the Child and His mother to Egypt, St. Joseph was not told that children would be slaughtered and mothers would witness the death of their children. Mary would have remembered how bitterly St. Joseph had wept over the loss of so many precious children. It was a source of tremendous suffering to St. Joseph, but he remained firm in his resolution to do the will of God. At the foot of the Cross, Mary did likewise.

> Joseph and Mary had not yet crossed the mountains that sepa-
> rated them from the desert, when suddenly the painful moans,
> echoing through hills, reached their ears. These heartrending
> cries, which were the cries of the mothers of innocent saints
> slaughtered on the breasts and arms of their mothers, filled the
> hearts of Joseph and Mary with tremendous sadness.[9]

> — Blessed Bartolo Longo

At the foot of the Cross, Mary remembered how St. Joseph, as the head of the family, had taken her and Jesus to Egypt, and how strong St. Joseph had been in protecting and caring for their family. Walking to Egypt could not have been a safe or comfortable journey for the Holy Family. Egypt was a very dangerous place, notorious for bandits, thieves, and pagan practices. Saint Joseph's years of living there must have been very difficult. Saint Thomas Aquinas and St. Bonaventure believe that the Holy Family was in exile in Egypt for almost seven years. These years would have been filled with much suffering for St. Joseph. Mary remembered these years and how strong St. Joseph had been for love of God and their family.

At Calvary, Mary remembered all the sufferings St. Joseph had endured during their time in Egypt. According to the mystical revelations of Blessed Anne Catherine Emmerich, the hardships of the Holy Family in Egypt were especially felt by St. Joseph because he was the loving head of the family. The responsibility of taking care of the family was primarily St. Joseph's. Oftentimes unable to acquire sufficient work, food, clean water, or proper housing, the man of the house suffered greatly because he was unable to provide everything that was needed by his family.

In Egypt, St. Joseph was in a land which was not only foreign, but also hostile to Israelites. The Egyptians resented that the Israelites had escaped from their tyranny, and also that they had been the cause of many of their ancestors being drowned in the Red Sea.[10]

— St. Francis de Sales

In the accounts of the mystical visions of Blessed Anne Catherine Emmerich, we are told that in Egypt the Holy Family underwent the frightful experience of being surrounded by robbers with bad intentions. On Calvary, Mary remembered how strong her husband had been and how he was willing to die out of love for his family. In this memory, she would have found the strength to be a co-victim with Jesus.

Mary would have also recalled the memory of the time she and her husband had lost Jesus for three days. Losing a child is the worst nightmare a parent could ever face. For three days, the Hearts of Mary and Joseph were filled with anxiety and worry. Yet she remembered that, after three days of tremendous sorrow and suffering, she and her husband found Jesus in the Temple. Finding him, their hearts were filled with inexpressible joy. In some way, losing Jesus for those three days was a preparation for Calvary. Remembering this event, Mary once again would have found strength and consolation in her sweet St. Joseph.

At Calvary, the memory of all St. Joseph had done for his wife and Son must have been a consolation to Jesus, as well. Through the role model Joseph provided for him of long and faithful suffering, Jesus was better able to offer his own sacrifice on Calvary. Our Lord knew well that his father had saved him from Herod, carried tremendous burdens of love in his heart, consoled his mother, and helped Mary prepare for her suffering with Jesus. God did not require that St. Joseph be physically present at the sacrifice at Calvary, but Jesus knew that he would never have made it to Calvary without him. God made the sacrifice of Calvary dependent upon the fatherly sacrifices that St. Joseph had offered during the hidden years of the Holy Family. The fruit of St. Joseph's paternal love and suffering made him the spiritual father of the new covenant family. Similar to Mary, Jesus, too, would have had St. Joseph on his mind and in his Heart at Calvary.

The virginal Hearts of Jesus, Mary, and St. Joseph are one. As their Hearts are one, so is their mission. Jesus alone is the Savior of the world, but he wanted his mother and father to have a unique participation in the work of redemption. The union of the virginal and sorrowful Hearts of Jesus, Mary, and St. Joseph at Nazareth, Bethlehem, Egypt, and Calvary was the principal means that God chose to enable all of us to be born again. Jesus, Mary, and Joseph make it possible for us to be children of God.

What we learn from the sacrificial fatherhood of St. Joseph is that he is a man who takes care of those entrusted to him, no matter the cost. He offers consolation and strength to all his children. As your spiritual father, he wants to take care of you just as he took care of Mary and Jesus. He wants to console you and increase your capacity for self-sacrificing love.

God has given you a mission as a Christian. Your mission will require sacrifice, sorrow, and suffering. You will experience your own Calvary. With St. Joseph in your heart, you will find a father's consolation and the strength to endure all things for love.

Saint Joseph knows that as you seek to do God's will, Satan, a spiritual Herod, is going to unleash his assassins against you. You need St. Joseph to protect you. Your spiritual father will lovingly watch over you and never stop fighting for you. With his assistance, you can be victorious in suffering and overcome the enemy. Saint John Paul II emphasized this point in a homily he gave during a papal visit to the Shrine of St. Joseph in Kalisz, Poland. He said:

> The angel had warned him [St. Joseph] to flee with the child, because he was threatened by mortal danger. From the Gospel we learn about those who were threatening the child's life. In the first place Herod, but then also all his [Herod's] followers. Joseph of Nazareth, who saved Jesus from the cruelty of Herod, is shown to us in this moment as a great supporter of the cause of the defense of human life, from the first moment of conception to natural death. In this place, therefore, we wish to commend human life to Divine Providence and to St. Joseph, especially the life of children not yet born, in our homeland and throughout the world.[11]

You are going to suffer in life. Saint Joseph can't prevent all of your suffering, but he can prepare you for it and console you when you are in the midst of sorrow and pain. He offers a father's love and protection.

> Saint Joseph, with the love and generosity with which he guarded Jesus, so too will he guard your soul, and as he defended him

from Herod, so will he defend your soul from the fiercest Herod: the devil! All the care that the Patriarch St. Joseph has for Jesus, he has for you and will always help you with his patronage. He will free you from the persecution of the wicked and proud Herod, and will not allow your heart to be estranged from Jesus. *Ite ad Ioseph!* Go to Joseph with extreme confidence, because I do not remember having asked anything from St. Joseph, without having obtained it readily.[12]

— St. Pio of Pietrelcina

At the Shrine to St. Joseph in Kalisz, Poland, where St. John Paul II preached his inspiring homily on St. Joseph in 1997, in the crypt of the church, there is a museum dedicated to St. Joseph in thanksgiving for his role in saving the lives of many Catholic priests imprisoned in the Dachau concentration camp in World War II.

There were many priests (and bishops) in the Dachau concentration camp. According to official records, 2,579 Catholic priests were in Dachau. Of these, 1,034 of the priests died there. Saint Joseph helped them in their suffering and gave them the strength to offer their lives for love of Jesus. As for the other 1,545 priests who survived Dachau, all of them attribute their liberation from the camp on April 29, 1945, to the powerful intercession of St. Joseph.

Here's the story.

The first Catholic priests arrived in Dachau in 1939. In the following months and years, the numbers continued to grow because priests were transferred to Dachau from the Auschwitz and Sachsenhausen concentration camps. On December 8, 1940, the priests in Dachau made a communal act of consecration to St. Joseph, asking him to help them survive their ordeal and save them from death. They consecrated themselves to St. Joseph in particular because it was St. Joseph who had saved the Son of God from death when Herod wanted to kill him, and the priests knew that he had the power to save them from the Nazis as well.

The act of consecration to St. Joseph was frequently renewed. The imprisoned priests also renewed the consecration annually in a more solemn manner. Additionally, the priests prayed novenas to St. Joseph asking for help in their dire situation. When the camp was finally liberated in 1945, the remaining priests testified that it was St. Joseph who was responsible for their survival. In thanksgiving, many of the priests — especially the priests from Poland — organized a pilgrimage to the Shrine of St. Joseph in Kalisz, Poland, in 1948. The pilgrimage was such a memorable event that a second pilgrimage was organized in 1958, and subsequent pilgrimages followed. In 1995, the 37 remaining priests who had survived Dachau were present for the pilgrimage. Today, all the priests have died, yet their memory and tribute to St. Joseph lives on in the museum attached to the shrine.

Saint Joseph saved Jesus from Herod. Saint Joseph protected Mary from robbers. Saint Joseph consoled Jesus and Mary and prepared them for Calvary. Saint Joseph was in the Hearts of Jesus and Mary at Calvary. Saint Joseph consoled the many priests who suffered and died in Dachau. Saint Joseph helped many priests survive the camp. Saint Joseph, your spiritual father, wants to protect you, prepare you, console you, and help you make of your life a sacrifice for others.

> We all have in him [St. Joseph] a model and a protector.[13]
>
> — St. Peter Julian Eymard

> Let us say to the great Patriarch, "Here we are, we are all for you; may you be all for us. Show us the way, strengthen us in every step and lead us to where Divine Providence wants us to go.[14]
>
> — St. Joseph Marello

Saint Joseph's Workshop

Saint Joseph is the Glory of Domestic Life. He loved, educated, nourished, and protected his Son. He gave his entire life in loving service to Jesus and Mary.

On March 19, 1963 (the Solemnity of St. Joseph), St. Josemaría Escrivá gave a homily in honor of St. Joseph that has become very well-known. It is titled, "In Joseph's Workshop."

In the homily, St. Josemaría describes the wonderful relationship that St. Joseph and Jesus had as father and son. Below is a section of the homily.

> Joseph, caring for the child as he had been commanded, made Jesus a craftsman, transmitting his own professional skill to him. So the neighbors of Nazareth will call Jesus both *faber* and *fabri filius*: the craftsman and the son of the craftsman (see Mk 6:3; Mt 13:55). Jesus worked in Joseph's workshop and by Joseph's side. What must Joseph have been, how grace must have worked through him, that he should be able to fulfill this task of the human upbringing of the Son of God!

For Jesus must have resembled Joseph: in his way of working, in the features of his character, in his way of speaking. Jesus' realism, his eye for detail, the way he sat at table and broke bread, his preference for using everyday situations to give doctrine — all this reflects his childhood and the influence of Joseph.

It's not possible to ignore this sublime mystery: Jesus who is man, who speaks with the accent of a particular district of Israel, who resembles a carpenter called Joseph, is the Son of God. And who can teach God anything? But he is also truly man and lives a normal life: first, as a child, then as a boy helping in Joseph's workshop, finally as a grown man in the prime of life. "Jesus advanced in wisdom and age and grace before God and men" (Lk 2:52).

In human life, Joseph was Jesus' master in their daily contact, full of refined affection, glad to deny himself to take better care of Jesus. Isn't that reason enough for us to consider this just man, this holy patriarch, in whom the faith of the old covenant bears fruit, as a master of the interior life? Interior life is nothing but continual and direct conversation with Christ, so as to become one with him. And Joseph can tell us many things about Jesus. Therefore, never neglect devotion to him — *Ite ad Ioseph*: "Go to Joseph" — as Christian tradition puts it in the words of the Old Testament.

As master of the interior life, a worker deeply involved in his job, God's servant in continual contact with Jesus: that is Joseph. *Ite ad Ioseph*. With St. Joseph, the Christian learns what it means to belong to God and fully to assume one's place among men, sanctifying the world. Get to know Joseph and you will find Jesus. Talk to Joseph and you will find Mary, who always sheds peace about her in that attractive workshop in Nazareth.[1]

WONDER 7

ADORER OF CHRIST

What a sublime vision to have the Son of God ever before his [St. Joseph's] eyes! Ecstasy most rare! Rapture most marvelous!

— Blessed William Joseph Chaminade

Perpetual Adoration

Although he [St. Joseph] never adored our Lord under the Eucharistic species and never had the happiness of communicating [receiving Holy Communion], he did possess and adore Jesus in human form.[1]

— St. Peter Julian Eymard

If St. Joseph lived with Jesus for 30 years, his vocation was one of perpetual adoration. In many ways, the home of the Holy Family in Nazareth was the first Christian monastery.

Saint Peter Julian Eymard wrote an amazing book called *The Month of St. Joseph* that offers incredible insights on St. Joseph's life of prayer and adoration in Nazareth. It's a masterpiece.

Here's an excerpt from St. Peter Julian Eymard's book:

Saint Joseph was the first adorer, the first religious. Although he never adored our Lord under the Eucharistic species and never had the happiness of communicating [receiving Holy Communion], he did possess and adore Jesus in human form.

Saint Joseph knew our Lord more thoroughly than did all the saints together; he lived for him alone. In that lies his special glory, the keynote of his sanctity. In that, above all, he is our model, and in that too does his incomparable greatness consist.

When we see how close Joseph came to Jesus, how thoroughly he was transformed into him, we grasp his true greatness, his real sanctity. We find in him [St. Joseph], the perfect adorer, entirely consecrated to Jesus, working always near Jesus, giving Jesus his virtues, his time, his very life; it is thus that he is our model and our inspiration.

As foster-father of Jesus and husband of Mary, Joseph ranks among the elite of heaven. On earth he deserves the same recognition, for his mission, which will last as long as the Church itself, draws everyone within its scope. As adorers we have a right to a large share of his graces and protection, and careful study will show that all his special gifts aimed at making him a good adorer.

From his [Jesus'] entry into the world, even while still enclosed in Mary's womb as in a living ciborium, Jesus singled out Mary and Joseph to be his adorers. Joseph responded royally. He never ceased adoring Jesus in her womb. And after the child's birth at Bethlehem, Joseph and Mary adored him uninterruptedly as he lay before their eyes. They represented all mankind at the feet of Christ. Certainly Adam and Eve were well replaced!

At Nazareth Joseph's days were filled with work which [by] necessity took him away at times from his Infant God. During these hours Mary replaced him, but when evening brought him home again, he would pass the entire night in adoration, never tiring, only too happy for the chance to contemplate the hidden riches of Jesus' divinity. For he pierced the rough garments the child wore, until his faith touched the Sacred Heart. In profound adoration he united himself to the special grace of each one of the events in the life of Jesus. Have confidence, strong confidence in him [St. Joseph]. Take him as the patron and the model of your life of adoration.[2]

Saint Peter Julian Eymard is known as the "Apostle of the Eucharist." He was zealous in promoting Adoration of the Blessed Sacrament. Saint Peter Julian founded two religious communities to promote Adoration of the Blessed Sacrament: the Congregation of the Blessed Sacrament for men, and the Servants of the Blessed Sacrament for women.

> When we receive Holy Communion, let us consider that Jesus comes to us as a little baby, and then let us pray that St. Joseph helps us welcome him, as when he held him in his arms.[3]
>
> — St. Joseph Marello

Adorer of Christ

How many times did he [St. Joseph], like the lone sparrow, nestle on the roof of that holy temple of the divinity, contemplating this divine Child sleeping in his arms, and thinking of his eternal repose in the bosom of the heavenly Father?[1]

— Blessed William Joseph Chaminade

Wherever St. Joseph traveled with his wife and Son, his home became an Adoration chapel. Nazareth, Bethlehem, and Egypt are all places where St. Joseph contemplated the divine presence of Jesus Christ and welcomed others to do the same. In that sense, St. Joseph is the founder of Adoration chapels and, with his wife, is the first to conduct a procession with the Body and Blood of Christ.

Along with Jesus and Mary, St. Joseph gave the world the greatest Adoration chapel known to man, the Catholic Church. Thanks to Mary and St. Joseph, every Catholic church around the world has a tabernacle housing the Real Presence of Jesus Christ — Christ present in his Body, Blood, Soul, and Divinity.

> No one can describe the adoration of this [St. Joseph's] noble soul. He saw nothing, yet he believed; his faith had to pierce the virginal veil of Mary. So likewise with you! Under the veil of the Sacred Species your faith must see our Lord. Ask St. Joseph for his lively, constant faith.[2]
>
> — St. Peter Julian Eymard

In Nazareth, months before the angel revealed to St. Joseph that Mary was pregnant with a divine Child, St. Joseph was inches away from the tabernacled presence of God in Mary's womb. Saint Joseph's wife was a walking tabernacle. The Incarnate God was living and growing inside St. Joseph's wife's womb, and he didn't even know it. God was preparing him to be the loving father of the greatest treasure the world has ever known: the Incarnate Son of God.

As a newly married man, St. Joseph never wanted to be far away from his wife. Mary must have come to him and expressed a desire to visit her relative Elizabeth for three months, and this must have been quite a surprise to St. Joseph. When we read this episode in the New Testament, we tend to presume that Mary did not ask St. Joseph to accompany her to Elizabeth's. The sacred text, however, does not inform us of what exactly happened on this occasion, other than telling us that Mary went in haste to the hill country. We are not told if St. Joseph went or not.

Many saints and mystics — St. Bernard of Clairvaux, St. Bonaventure, St. Bernardine of Siena, St. Francis de Sales, Venerable Mary of Ágreda, Blessed Anne Catherine Emmerich, and others — believe that St. Joseph did accompany Mary to Elizabeth's. Why wouldn't he go with her? What kind of husband would he be if he let his young and beautiful wife make such a long journey unaccompanied by her husband? The New Testament does not explicitly tell us that St. Joseph went with Mary, but it also does not explicitly tell us that he didn't. From a marital perspective, how could he stand to be away from her for so long? It actually makes a lot of sense that St. Joseph would have accompanied Mary to Elizabeth's, and maybe even stayed there with her for the three months. It's a very long journey from Nazareth to the hill country where Elizabeth lived (nearly 100 miles). Horrible things could have happened to St. Joseph's beautiful bride on the journey. What newly married man would not be concerned about such a journey, especially one that involved walking and sleeping in dangerous places? No man in his right mind would stay behind.

In the mystical writings of Venerable Mary of Ágreda, Mary and St. Joseph engage in a delightful conversation about the Visitation:

> [Mary to St. Joseph:] "My lord and husband, it has pleased the Lord to enlighten me, informing me that my cousin Elizabeth, despite being infertile, is now expecting a long-desired child. Therefore I think it may be suitable that I go and visit her to be of assistance and spiritual comfort to her. If, my lord, this is in accordance with your will, I shall do so. Consider yourself what may be best and command me what I am to do."

> [St. Joseph to Mary:] "You well know, my lady and my wife, that your desires are mine and that I trust fully in your prudence, since your most honest will would incline to nothing that was not of the greatest satisfaction to the Most High. So I believe it to be with this journey. And so that it may not appear strange that you undertake it without the company of your husband, I shall follow you with joy to be of use to you on the way, until you have reached your destination."[3]

Even if St. Joseph did not remain with Mary at Elizabeth's for three months, it is very likely that he at least accompanied his wife to Elizabeth's to keep Mary safe from robbers and men with bad intentions. Upon arriving at Elizabeth's with Mary, he would have then returned to Nazareth alone. After three months, he would have made the return journey to Elizabeth's and safely escorted his wife back to their home in Nazareth. If these things did happen, St. Joseph unknowingly conducted the first procession with the Body and Blood of our Lord!

For the sake of meditation, let's say that St. Joseph at least accompanied Mary to Elizabeth's. What might he have experienced upon arriving at Elizabeth's? Well, he most likely would have heard Elizabeth's Spirit-filled greeting to Mary.

> Blessed are you among women, and blessed is the fruit of your womb! And who am I that the mother of my Lord should come to me? For behold, when the voice of your greeting came to my ears, the babe in my womb leaped for joy. Blessed is she who believed that what the Lord said to her would be fulfilled!
>
> — Lk 1:42-45

What would St. Joseph have thought of Elizabeth's greeting? Her words would have seemed strange to him. There is no way he would have understood their theological significance, because he had no idea that his wife was pregnant. Yet, as a man of deep prayer, he would have pondered her words and taken them to prayer. He didn't understand their significance at the time, but months later, when he noticed that Mary was pregnant, he would have recalled Elizabeth's words. Remembering that Elizabeth called Mary "mother of my Lord," St. Joseph's eyes would have been opened to the full reality of what was happening in the womb of his wife. As a devout Jew, St. Joseph was not ignorant of the Scripture that states that a virgin would bring forth the Messiah (see Is 7:14). Realizing this great wonder, he would have felt completely unworthy to be the husband and father of such a woman and Child.

The possibility that St. Joseph accompanied Mary and heard Elizabeth's Spirit-filled greeting helps us to understand why St. Joseph never doubted Mary or wanted to divorce her. As Elizabeth had been, he was overwhelmed with reverential awe at the revelation that his beloved wife was pregnant with a heavenly Child. A just and God-fearing man, St. Joseph did not consider himself worthy of living under the same roof as Mary and serving as the father of the Child in her womb. How could he possibly be worthy to be the husband of such a wife? How could he ever take such a mother and Child into his home and into his care? Nothing short of an angelic announcement would keep him from removing himself from the picture.

On the other hand, if St. Joseph did not accompany his wife to Elizabeth's house, imagine the loneliness he must have felt being without Mary for three months. A separation of such a duration would have been a torture to his heart. His heart must have longed to be reunited with his beloved. To hear her voice must have been on his mind day and night. How his heart must have beat wildly with joy at the return of his queen after three long months apart.

Whether he accompanied Mary to Elizabeth's or not, he most likely traveled with his wife and Son to see Elizabeth, Zechariah, and their son, John (the Baptist), on later "visitations." Such family visits are normal. Catholic intuition has always known this and depicted these visitations in art. Scenes of Mary, St. Joseph, the Child Jesus, and John the Baptist are prominent in Catholic art throughout the world. After all, Jesus and John were relatives. They would have played and prayed together during the many visits that took place over the years. Saint Joseph might not have been present to hear Elizabeth's greeting, or been present to witness the birth of John the Baptist, but St. Joseph would have seen and spoken with John the Baptist on the other family visits. Saint Joseph and St. John the Baptist had to have known each other.

If the first procession with Jesus was to Elizabeth's house, the second procession took place when St. Joseph journeyed with his pregnant wife to Bethlehem to be enrolled in the census. In this procession, St. Joseph established the world's first Adoration chapel: Bethlehem.

> Saint Joseph went in haste with Mary to Bethlehem which means "house of bread," so that the bread of eternal life might be born there.[4]
>
> — Venerable Joseph Mindszenty

How fitting it is that the first public exposition of the Living Bread from Heaven took place in Bethlehem. As Venerable Joseph Mindszenty notes, the word "Bethlehem" in Hebrew means "House of Bread." In Arabic, Bethlehem means "House of Meat" or "House of Flesh." Our Jesus, the true Bread come down from heaven, was born in poverty and placed in a manger for a reason. Our Lord is a humble king, and he wanted St. Joseph to place him in a poor manger because a manger is where animals feed. The word "manger" is related to the well-known Italian word *mangiare:* Eat!

> O most intimate familiarity to be always with God, to speak only to God, to work, to rest, to converse in the company and presence of God! How many times did the happy tutor of the Child Jesus, like a chaste bee, gather the nectar of pure devotion from this beautiful flower of Jesse? How many times did he [St. Joseph], like the dove, hide in the heart of this rock?[5]
>
> — Blessed William Joseph Chaminade

The first Adoration chapel was visited by local shepherds, followed closely by Wise Men who came from a distant land to pay homage to the newborn God-King lying in a feeding trough (manger). Saint Joseph would not only establish Adoration in the Holy Land though. Saint Joseph established the second Adoration chapel in pagan territory: Egypt.

Saint Joseph is bold!

When Jesus was born, Egypt was both pagan territory and the bread basket of the world. How fitting that God sent St. Joseph to Egypt! There, St. Joseph was responsible for raising the Living Host that would feed the world. The Joseph of the Old Testament had saved his people from starvation by dispensing grain out of Egypt. The new Joseph would offer the world the "grain" he lovingly helped grow in Egypt, the living Bread that gives eternal life!

After their time in Egypt, St. Joseph and Mary walked with Jesus to Nazareth. This long walk was, and remains, the grandest procession of the Body and Blood of Christ ever conducted. It was a procession that covered more than 120 miles!

Once in Nazareth, St. Joseph and his wife adored the divine presence of Jesus in their home for decades. In one sense, it was like a house of Perpetual Adoration and uninterrupted contemplation, even while they carried out all the daily tasks and chores of domestic life. The Adoration lasted for decades!

> If the two disciples going to Emmaus were inflamed with divine love by the few moments which they spent in company with our Savior, and by his words; so much so, that they said, "Was not our heart burning within us while he spoke to us on the way?" — what flames of holy love must we not suppose to have been enkindled in the heart of St. Joseph, who for thirty years conversed with Jesus Christ, and listened to his words of eternal life![6]
>
> — St. Alphonsus Liguori

Even if Jesus were outside the home, working, or on a journey, St. Joseph was still in the presence of God when he was near his wife.

Let me explain.

Have you heard of fetal microchimerism, sometimes also called fetomaternal microchimerism? It's a long, complicated term, I know, but it reveals something wonderful about the biological connection between a mother and a child. Fetal microchimerism is the scientific term that describes a process in which living cells of a child remain in the body of a mother after her pregnancy has ended. In the late 20th century, scientists discovered that when a woman becomes pregnant, and after she has given birth, there are cells from her baby that remain in the mother's body. Many of these cells remain in her body for the rest of her life! Scientists and researchers have also discovered that the cellular exchange occurs in the other direction as well; cells of the mother are exchanged with her children and remain in the bodies of her children for life. This is amazing!

Though St. Joseph knew nothing of fetal microchimerism, God continued to bless him with the presence of Jesus whenever he was in the presence of his wife. To be near Mary is to be near Jesus. Jesus lives in her! Mary has in her body some of her divine Son's living cells. Our Lord didn't need to be in the house for St. Joseph to remain in the presence of God. Wherever Mary was, Jesus was. Saint Joseph's wife is a living tabernacle, a walking monstrance, a veiled temple. No wonder demons do not dare come near Mary — she is never without the divine presence. God lives in her body!

> If the lily, by being exposed only for a few days to the light and heat of the sun, acquires its dazzling whiteness, who can conceive the extraordinary degree of purity to which St. Joseph was exalted, by being exposed as he was day and night for so many years to the rays of the Sun of Justice, and of the Mystical Moon who derives all her splendor from him [Jesus]?[7]
>
> — St. Francis de Sales

> I congratulate you, most holy Patriarch, for those delightful hours you spent joyfully contemplating Jesus and happily enjoying the beautiful interior and exterior beauty of Mary. Constantly you studied them, drawing sweetness, patience, and self-denial from their hearts.[8]
>
> — Blessed Concepción Cabrera de Armida

Priests, monks, and nuns are privileged to experience something of what it would have been like to be St. Joseph. Every monastery and/or convent has a tabernacle housing the divine presence; all tabernacles are basically a replica of Mary's bodily temple. It doesn't matter if the tabernacle is veiled or if the doors are closed: Jesus is still there. It was the same in the Holy House of Nazareth. God lived in Mary at all times, and St. Joseph was perpetually in the presence of Jesus.

The mark of the Christian is the willingness to look for the divine in the flesh of a babe in a crib, the continuing Christ under the appearance of bread on an altar.[9]

— Venerable Fulton J. Sheen

Mary, God's tabernacle, is replicated in every tabernacle in a Catholic church. What is often missing in front of these tabernacles, however, are souls who resemble St. Joseph — souls who adore Jesus present and hidden in the tabernacle. The Church needs more people like St. Joseph.

We must beg for good adorers; the Blessed Sacrament needs them to replace St. Joseph and to imitate his life of adoration.[10]

— St. Peter Julian Eymard

To be like St. Joseph, you, too, need to adore Christ. You can go to the nearest Catholic church where Jesus is present, Body, Blood, Soul, and Divinity, in the Blessed Sacrament. The Eucharist is Jesus Christ. The Blessed Sacrament is the source and summit of the Christian faith, and St. Joseph wants to lead you to a deeper relationship with Jesus in the Eucharist.

In 1997, St. John Paul II conducted a papal visit to the Shrine of St. Joseph in Kalisz, Poland, and informed those in attendance that, before each of his Masses, he prayed the following prayer to St. Joseph.

O happy man, St. Joseph, whose privilege it was not only to see and hear that God whom many a king has longed to see, yet saw not, longed to hear, yet heard not (cf. Mt 13:17), but also to carry him in your arms and kiss him, to clothe him and watch over him!

O God, who has conferred upon us a royal priesthood, we pray to you to give us grace to minister at your holy altars with hearts as clean and lives as blameless as that blessed Joseph who was found to hold in his arms and, with all reverence, carry your only-begotten Son, born of the Virgin Mary. Enable us this day to receive worthily the sacred Body and Blood of your Son, and equip us to win an everlasting reward in the world to come. Amen.[11]

Spend time in the presence of Jesus in the Blessed Sacrament. If there is Perpetual Adoration at a church in your area, sign up for a weekly holy hour. Adoration will change your life. If there isn't a church with Perpetual Adoration in your area, sometimes a parish will have Adoration for a few hours a day or on a particular day of the week. Go! If you are unable to find a church that offers exposition of the Blessed Sacrament at all, simply visit any Catholic church and pray before the tabernacle. Jesus is there night and day. He waits for you. Be another St. Joseph for Jesus and Mary!

> When you visit the Most Blessed Sacrament, approach Jesus with the love of the Blessed Virgin, St. Joseph, and St. John.[12]

— St. Joseph Sebastian Pelczar

> O Blessed Joseph, I adore with you the first words that came from the mouth of the Incarnate Word. I prostrate myself with you to kiss with reverence the first footprints left by his adorable feet. O infinite God, You became weak in order to give us strength; You desired to speak like other children in order to teach us the language of heaven! O Blessed Joseph, inspire me with your feelings for Jesus, and obtain for me the grace to love God like you. Amen.[13]

— Blessed Bartolo Longo

The Holy House of Loreto

> Has anyone ever visited Loreto who has not seen with his own eyes and heard with his own ears the mighty works of God, and felt them in his soul?[1]

— St. Peter Canisius

The holiest house in the world is in Italy.

You read that right. It used to be in the Holy Land, but it moved.

The family home of Jesus, Mary, and Joseph is located in the town of Loreto, Italy. How did it get there? Well, what you are about to read is the true story of how the home of the Holy Family in Nazareth was transported to Italy by angels. The story is so fascinating that you are probably going to want to go to Loreto after reading it.

According to historians, the home of the Holy Family remained in Nazareth for 13 centuries. Then, on May 10, 1291, it suddenly disappeared! All that remained of the house was the foundation. The sudden disappearance of the house was noticed by everyone in Nazareth, leaving the entire community completely baffled. For a person or group of persons to remove it so quickly without anyone noticing was impossible.

According to tradition, the Holy House was tr&
Nazareth by angels. In the reports of her mystical exp&
Anne Catherine Emmerich spoke about the angelic t&
the house. She states:

> I have often in vision witnessed the transporting of the Holy
> House to Loreto. For a long time, I could not believe it, and
> yet I continued to see it. I saw the Holy House borne over the
> sea by seven angels. It had no foundation, but there was under
> it a shining surface of light. On either side was something like
> a handle. Three angels carried it on one side and three on the
> other; the seventh hovered in front of it, a long train of light
> after him.[2]

Fascinating stuff! What Blessed Anne Catherine did not observe
in her visions, however, is that the angels first took the Holy House
from Nazareth to the town of Trsat, an area in modern day Croatia.
At the time, Croatia was known as Illyria or Dalmatia. Why did the
angels take it there? What was the point in moving it at all?

The Holy House was moved in 1291. The reason for its transportation by angels out of Nazareth became clear three years later. In
1294, the entire town of Nazareth was sacked by invading Muslims.
If the Holy House had remained in Nazareth, the Muslims would
have completely destroyed it. God anticipated the act of sacrilege and
sent his holy angels to relocate the house to another location.

Throughout the centuries, God has used people such as St.
Helena to remove relics (holy objects associated with Jesus, Mary,
and the saints) from the Holy Land and relocate them to safer places.
Saint John Henry Newman once visited the Holy House and offered
a very insightful statement about its relocation. He wrote:

> He who floated the Ark [of Noah] on the surges of a world-wide
> sea and enclosed in it all living things, who has hidden the ter-
> restrial paradise, who said that faith might move mountains, who
> sustained thousands for forty years in a sterile wilderness, who
> transported Elias and keeps him hidden till the end, could do
> this wonder also. And in matter of fact we see all other records of
> our Lord and his saints gathered up in the heart of Christendom
> from the ends of the earth as paganism encroached on it (that
> is, his relics). Saint Augustine leaves Hippo, the prophet Samuel
> and St. Stephen leave Jerusalem, the crib in which our Lord lay
> leaves Bethlehem with St. Jerome, the Cross is dug up, St. Atha-
> nasius goes to Venice. In short, I feel no difficulty in believing it.[3]

But why did it go to Croatia first, though? Why didn't the angels take it directly to Italy? No one really knows the answer. Perhaps God wanted to bless the land of Croatia with the presence of the Holy House before taking it to its final location. Jesus once healed a deaf man in stages and not immediately. The angels' moving of the Holy House to several locations before finally placing it in Loreto has the effect of supplying a multitude of witnesses to the miraculous disappearance and reappearance of the house. In other words, God allowing the house to be moved several times before having it placed in Loreto shows that it wasn't being moved by man, but by God's holy angels.

Let's take a closer look at all the miraculous transportations associated with the Holy House.

On May 10, 1291, the day the Holy House disappeared from Nazareth, people in the village of Trsat, Croatia, witnessed the sudden appearance of a new house in the village. Not one person in the village knew how it got there. Interestingly, the villagers observed that the four walls of the house were resting on the dirt. The house had no foundation.

After being in Croatia for three years, the house miraculously disappeared again on December 10, 1294. No one in the village saw the house leave. The only thing that was left at the spot where the house once stood was the outline of the house in the dirt. To this day, a monument marks the exact spot in Trsat, Croatia, where the Holy House was located for three years.

Where did the house go after Croatia? It was taken by angels across the Adriatic Sea to the town of Piceno, Italy. Incredibly, the same thing happened in the town of Piceno: Nobody witnessed the house arrive, and nobody knew where it had come from. The house remained in this location for eight months. It was only in Piceno for eight months because robbers began to steal from the pilgrims (many from Croatia) who were coming to the Holy House. In August 1295, the house disappeared again. It reappeared on a hill not far from the town of Piceno. However, the hill where the house was placed was owned by two brothers, and they began to fight over ownership of the house. Unable to resolve their dispute, the brothers started to exploit the pilgrims for financial gain. The Holy House only remained on their property for several months before it miraculously disappeared again!

Near the end of December 1295, the Holy House was taken by angels a stone's throw away from the previous location, far enough not to be on the property of the two brothers. This location is known as Loreto, the town where the house is located today. (The miracle of the Holy House being transported by angels four times is the reason the Catholic Church has declared Our Lady of Loreto the patron of aviation.)

How do we know all this is true? Well, in 1296, one year after the Holy House arrived in Loreto, the Catholic Church appointed 16 envoys to investigate everything. The envoys visited Loreto, Croatia, and Nazareth, and conducted extensive studies in order to verify the events. The envoys went to Loreto first.

At the site in Loreto, they took precise measurements of the house, noting every detail. The envoys then traveled to Trsat, Croatia, to the place where the house had rested, and took measurements of the marks left in the dirt by the house. Next, they traveled to Nazareth to compare the measurements from Loreto and Trsat to the original foundation. Incredibly, at all three locations (Loreto, Croatia, and Nazareth), the measurements were exactly the same! There were no discrepancies whatsoever. Everything matched perfectly.

Centuries later, scientists conducted a chemical analysis of the stones of the walls of the Holy House in Loreto. Chemical studies on the wood used for the ceiling of the Holy House were done as well. Guess what they discovered? The walls of the Holy House are made from stones unique to the area of Nazareth, and the wood in the ceiling of the house comes from the exact area of Nazareth! Even the mortar used for the house was determined to be made of material originating in the Holy Land.

As a result of the studies, a larger church began to be built around the house to accommodate the many pilgrims arriving in Loreto. Further attesting to the truthfulness of these miraculous events, pilgrims continued to travel to Loreto from Trsat, Croatia, every year, asking heaven to bring the Holy House back to Croatia.

After the arrival of the Holy House in Loreto, Italy, in 1295, nearly 50 popes have affirmed its miraculous transportation by angels, sometimes referring to the transportation as the "translation" of the Holy House. In the 15th century, two popes were miraculously cured at the Holy House. In the 16th century, a fortified basilica was completed around the Holy House to protect it from Muslim attacks. Later, to fortify the structure even more, the Holy House was encased in Carrara marble.

Nearly all of the popes after Pius II [one of the popes from the 13th century who was miraculously healed] have spoken of its miraculous translation.[4]

— St. Alphonsus Liguori

Why have God and the Church taken such measures to preserve this house? Because it is the site of the Incarnation! Tradition holds that Mary was born and raised in the Holy House, and that it was in that house that the Archangel Gabriel appeared to the Virgin, and the Word became flesh. It is a house of supernatural wonders!

She [Mary] is said to have been born in the city of Nazareth itself, and, indeed, in the same chamber in which, overshadowed by the Holy Spirit, she afterwards conceived at the Angel's salutation.[5]

— St. Jerome

It is in reality the House of Nazareth that is venerated at Loreto, that House dear to God by so many claims, built originally in Galilee, separated from its foundations, and carried by Divine power across the seas into Dalmatia first, and thence into Italy — the blessed House where the most Holy Virgin, predestined from all eternity and perfectly exempt from original sin, was conceived, was born, was brought up; where heaven's messenger saluted her as full of grace; where she became the mother of the only son of God.[6]

— Blessed Pope Pius IX

The Holy House is also where the Holy Family lived in Nazareth. The house is often called the "Holy House of Mary," but it also deserves to be called the "Holy House of Joseph." When and how St. Joseph came into possession of the house is not certain, but it most likely occurred as a result of his marriage to Mary. In fact, recent excavations near the Basilica of the Annunciation offer clues as to how Mary's childhood home became the home of the Holy Family.

When pilgrims travel to the Holy Land, they usually journey to Nazareth to see the Basilica of the Annunciation (where the Holy House used to be and where the foundation of the chamber of the Incarnation remains). What many pilgrims are completely unaware of is that very close to the Basilica is the workshop of St. Joseph.

Tradition holds that when Joseph and Mary were engaged, but before they lived together, Joseph lived and worked in his own house nearby. Once Mary and Joseph began to live together, they chose to live in Mary's childhood home, and Joseph used the other house as his workshop. This helps us to understand why St. Joseph was not present when the angel came to Mary at the Annunciation; he was not living with her at the time.

The Holy House is a unique relic that hundreds, if not thousands, of saints have visited. Prior to its being transported to Loreto, St. Francis of Assisi and St. Helena visited the house in Nazareth. Since its mystical transportation to Loreto, countless saints have made a pilgrimage to Loreto to see it, including:

- St. Ignatius of Loyola
- St. Francis Xavier (He made a pilgrimage to Loreto before setting off on his missionary journey to India.)
- St. Francis Borgia
- St. Charles Borromeo
- St. Peter Canisius (He defended the truth of the Holy House against the Protestants who called it a legend.)
- St. Aloysius Gonzaga
- St. James of La Marca
- St. Stanislaus Kostka
- St. Francis de Sales
- St. Louis Guanella
- St. Lawrence of Brindisi
- St. Benedict Joseph Labre (He is called the "Saint of Loreto" because he visited the Holy House so frequently.)
- St. Francis Caracciolo
- Blessed Anthony Grassi (He grew up near the Holy House. On one occasion, while kneeling in prayer at the house, he was struck by lightning. The lightning strike miraculously cured his life-long acute pain from indigestion. As a result of the healing, he vowed to visit the Holy House once a year on pilgrimage.)
- St. Alphonsus Liguori (He once stated that he "left his heart" in Loreto.)
- St. Maximilian Kolbe
- St. Josemaría Escrivá (He visited the Holy House seven times and consecrated Opus Dei to Mary in Loreto.)
- St. Pope John XXIII
- St. John Paul II

Saint Thérèse of Lisieux visited the Holy House in 1887 as she made her way to Rome with her father. She wrote about her visit in her autobiography:

I was indeed happy when on the way to Loreto. Our Lady had chosen an ideal spot in which to place her Holy House. Everything is poor, simple, and primitive; the women still wear the graceful dress of the country and have not, as in the large towns, adopted the modern Paris fashions. I found Loreto enchanting. What shall I say of the Holy House? I was overwhelmed with emotion when I realized that I was under the roof that had sheltered the Holy Family. I gazed on the same walls Our Lord had looked on. I trod the ground once moistened with the sweat of St. Joseph' toil, and saw the little chamber of the Annunciation. I even put my rosary into the little porringer used by the Divine Child. How sweet these memories![7]

The Holy House is a powerful relic. Jesus, Mary, and Joseph lived, slept, ate, and prayed there. It's so powerful that the devil wants nothing to do with it. Blessed Baptist Spagnoli of Mantua (1447-1516), head of the Carmelite Order from 1513-1516, and a priest very devoted to the Holy House, offered the following eyewitness account of an exorcism performed on a woman in the Holy House of Loreto on July 16, 1489:

I will not pass over a thing which I saw with my own eyes and heard with my own ears. It happened that a French lady of some means and of gentle birth named Antonia, who had long been possessed by evil spirits, was brought into the holy place by her husband that she might be delivered. Whilst a priest named Stephen, an exemplary man, was reading over her the usual exorcisms, one of the demons who boasted that he had been the instigator of the massacre of all the Innocents, being asked to his confusion whether this had been the Immaculate Virgin's chamber, replied that it had been so indeed, but that he owned [confessed] it against his will, compelled by Mary to confess the truth. He moreover pointed to the places in the Holy House where Gabriel, and where Mary, had each of them been.[8]

The Holy House even has its own liturgical feast day. On April 12, 1916, Pope Benedict XV issued a decree establishing December 10 as the annual liturgical Feast of the Translation of the Holy House. To this day, the Feast of the Translation of the Holy House is celebrated with great festivity every December 10 in Loreto.

In that most blessed House took place the beginnings of man's salvation by the great and admirable mystery of God made man. Amid the poverty of this retired dwelling there lived those models of domestic life and harmony.[9]

— Pope Leo XIII

Is it not by an unparalleled miracle that this Holy House was brought over land and sea from Galilee into Italy? By a supreme act of benevolence on the part of the God of all mercy, it has been placed in our pontifical domain, where for so many centuries it has become the object of the veneration of all the nations of the world and is resplendent with incessant miracles.[10]

— Blessed Pope Pius IX

The Holy House of Loreto is the dwelling in which the divine Word assumed human flesh, and which was translated by the ministry of angels. Its authenticity is proved by ancient monuments and unbroken tradition as by the testimony of Sovereign Pontiffs, the common consent of the faithful, and the continual miracles which are there worked even to the present day.[11]

— Pope Benedict XIV

WONDER 8

SILENT WITNESS

He [St. Joseph] is truly the saint who carried out his duty in
silence but with angelic fervor.

— Blessed Gabriele Allegra

A Miraculous Staircase in New Mexico

He [St. Joseph] took his [Jesus'] little hands and raising them to
heaven he said: "Stars of heaven, behold the hands which created
you; O Sun, behold the arm that drew you out of nothingness."[1]

— Blessed William Joseph Chaminade

Saint Joseph is the Guardian of Virgins. As a good father, he looks
after their needs. An example of his fatherly protection is evidenced
in what he did for a group of religious sisters in New Mexico in 1878.

In 1873, the Sisters of Loretto operated a girl's academy in
Santa Fe, New Mexico. The academy was very successful, so the
sisters wanted to build a new chapel. They hired a well-known archi-
tect to complete the task. The building project took five years to
complete. However, once the chapel was finished, the sisters realized
that the chapel lacked a way to get to the upper choir loft without
the use of a very long ladder; the choir loft was 20 feet above the
main floor. Climbing such a ladder was very difficult for the sisters,
who wore a floor-length religious habit. They also realized that there
was no room left in the main chapel area for a staircase to be built
because of the many pews, and the sisters could not rehire the man
who had built the chapel because he died shortly after the chapel was
completed. What were they to do?

Well, the sisters prayed to St. Joseph for help. They began a
novena to St. Joseph asking him to send a carpenter to help them.
Remarkably, on the final day of the novena, a mysterious man arrived
at the convent and stated that he was interested in building a staircase
to the choir loft for the sisters. The gentleman had only one request:
He wanted to work alone and behind closed doors. The sisters readily
accepted his offer and hired him.

It took the man three months to build the staircase. Once the project was completed, the man could not be found. He simply vanished from the town. No one saw him leave, and no one knew who he was. The sisters looked for him everywhere but could not find him. They even ran an ad in the local newspaper to try and locate him. It didn't work.

Unsuccessful, the sisters went to the lumberyard to inquire who had obtained the lumber for the staircase, as well as to pay for the lumber. When questioned, not one person at the lumberyard knew what they were talking about. The sisters were informed that the lumberyard had never sold any wood to a man building a staircase for a chapel.

Perplexed, the sisters remembered how odd it was that the man had only had a T-square, a saw, a hammer, and a few other basic tools. Come to think of it, none of the sisters ever did see how the lumber arrived at the chapel either. Intrigued, the sisters and others from the town inspected the staircase and realized that the mysterious man had constructed something quite unique. It was a spiral staircase that didn't interfere with the pews on the main floor in any way. It had 30 steps, no center support or load-bearing column, and appeared to be floating in air. It also contained no nails! It was found to be held together by square wooden pegs. The staircase is an architectural wonder. It's a carpenter's masterpiece!

So where did the wood come from? Well, in 1996, a study was done by Forrest N. Easley, a forester and wood technologist for the United States Forest Service and the United States Naval Research Laboratory. His extensive study found that the wood of the staircase is spruce, but unlike any other spruce in the world. Additional studies were undertaken, and it was determined that the spruce that most resembles the kind found in the spiral staircase is only found in Israel.

Who was the mysterious man who built the staircase? The Sisters of Loretto believe that it was St. Joseph. After praying and asking their spiritual father to send someone to construct a staircase for them, St. Joseph came himself and built it for the consecrated virgins. The staircase remains intact to this day.

Silent Witness

The Gospel does not record a single word from him [St. Joseph];
his language is silence.[1]

— St. Pope Paul VI

We honor St. Joseph as the man who taught Jesus how to speak.
Jesus must have spoken in a style similar to his earthly father,
using the same colloquialisms and having the same accent as St.
Joseph. Yet we do not have a single one of St. Joseph word's recorded
in the New Testament. Actions speak louder than words.

Saint Joseph's silence and humility are the foundation of his
greatness. Of all the men God could have chosen to be the earthly
father of Jesus Christ, God selected St. Joseph, the most silent of
all men.

Saint Joseph, although the greatest of saints, is the humblest and
most hidden of all.[2]

— St. Peter Julian Eymard

You would think that to protect this precious treasure [Jesus],
the omnipotent God would equip him [St. Joseph] with thun-
derbolts. Wrong. Joseph sees in his arms a fugitive God and he
follows him. He finds consolation only in his submission and in
his confidence.[3]

— Blessed William Joseph Chaminade

Saint Joseph never wanted to be in the forefront of the drama
of salvation. He preferred to remain hidden. His desire is for all the
attention to be given to Jesus and Mary. The silence and humility
of St. Joseph are one-of-a-kind, revealing his power, greatness, and
influence with God.

In the 17th century, Bishop Jacques-Bénigne Bossuet of France
extolled the wonders of the silence and humility of St. Joseph. He
wrote:

Jesus was revealed to the apostles that they might announce him
throughout the world; He was revealed to St. Joseph who was
to remain silent and keep him hidden. The apostles are lights
to make the world see Jesus. Joseph is a veil to cover him; and
under that mysterious veil are hidden from us the virginity of
Mary and the greatness of the Savior of souls. He who makes the
apostles glorious with the glory of preaching, glorifies Joseph by
the humility of silence.[4]

Bishop Bossuet thought so highly of St. Joseph that he considered him to be the greatest human being in Christianity after Jesus and Mary. Although St. Joseph's holiness is hidden and unknown to many, Bishop Bossuet reminds us that the holiest object of Christianity is that which is hidden and veiled. He states:

> The most illustrious thing the Church has is that which she hides most.[5]

Bishop Bossuet is referring to the hidden Most Blessed Sacrament, reserved in every tabernacle around the world. It is interesting, however, that as exposition of the Blessed Sacrament has increased, so too has St. Joseph been brought to the forefront of the Church's attention and devotion. The unveiling of St. Joseph reveals one of the greatest treasures of Christianity. Previous generations would have been delighted with the development of the Church's understanding of Joseph's role and devotion to Joseph in modern times because, even though their understanding and devotion to Joseph was in a rudimentary stage, they still loved him and would have welcomed more light had it been available to them at the time.

There have been "unveilings" of the greatness of St. Joseph in the past. In the 14th century, many saints and scholars brought to the Church's life and theology a greater awareness of the wonders of St. Joseph through their own devotion and personal testimony. In the 17th century, St. Joseph himself made an appearance in Europe that would become world famous and bring about an even greater appreciation of the importance of St. Joseph.

On June 7, 1660, in Cotignac, France, St. Joseph appeared to a shepherd, spoke to him, and worked miracles and wonders of healing. As the story goes, in the middle of a scorching hot day, a shepherd named Gaspard Ricard sought refuge in the shade under the trees on Mount Bessillon near the southeastern French town of Cotignac. Extremely thirsty, Gaspard did not know what to do to quench his thirst. Suddenly, a man of dignified appearance appeared to him, pointed to a rock, and said to him: "I am Joseph. Lift this rock and you shall drink." The rock was extremely large, and Gaspard told the man that he would not be able to lift it by himself. Undeterred, the man repeated his order for Gaspard to move the rock. Gaspard reluctantly approached the rock and, to his astonishment, was able to move it. Immediately, clear water began to gush out from the spot where the rock had been. Gaspard consumed the water with great enthusiasm and rose to thank the man, but the man had vanished.

Not knowing where the man had gone, Gaspard ran to the village to tell the people what had taken place, fully expecting to be ridiculed and mocked. His story was so intriguing that many people from the village followed him and saw the spring flowing with clear water. They also took note that the large rock had been moved; they could even see where the rock had once been located. For better access to the water, men from the village tried to move the rock a little further. It took eight grown men to move it! It was then that it dawned upon Gaspard that he had been visited by the great St. Joseph!

As word got out about what had taken place, people began to come to the spring from all over France, and many miracles occurred because of the faith of the people. They prayed to God for healing, and God worked wonders through St. Joseph and the miraculous spring. The king of France, King Louis XIV, heard about what was happening in the village and was deeply impressed. He was so moved that he consecrated all of France to St. Joseph on March 19, 1661. He also declared the Feast of St. Joseph a national holiday throughout all of France. The site quickly became so popular that the local people built a shrine to St. Joseph around the miraculous spring. For over a hundred years, it was a place of great pilgrimage, but at the time of the French Revolution, the shrine was abandoned and fell into ruins. It was restored in 1978 and is now operated by Benedictine nuns.

On occasion, God has also taught the Church about the greatness of St. Joseph through the writings of saints and mystics, such as St. Bridget of Sweden, Venerable Mary of Ágreda, and Blessed Anne Catherine Emmerich. On one occasion, the Virgin Mary instructed St. Bridget about the greatness of St. Joseph, especially emphasizing the wonder of his silence. Our Lady said to St. Bridget:

> Saint Joseph was so reserved and careful in his speech that not one word ever issued from his mouth that was not good and holy, nor did he ever indulge in unnecessary or less than charitable conversation. He was most patient and diligent in bearing fatigue; he practiced extreme poverty; he was most meek in bearing injuries; he was strong and constant against enemies; he was the faithful witness of the wonders of heaven.[6]

In modern times, God has continued to unveil the greatness of St. Joseph through the writings of two of the most well-known and beloved saints of the Church: St. Thérèse of Lisieux and St. Faustina Kowalska. Their respective autobiographies are among the most popular writings of modern saints.

Saint Thérèse describes her love for St. Joseph in *The Story of a Soul*. She tells her readers that she had a tremendous devotion to St. Joseph from her childhood. She recounts the story of how, when she was a little girl, she was miraculously healed through the intercession of St. Joseph. Later, as a Carmelite nun, St. Thérèse wrote about how she prayed to St. Joseph every day, crediting him with granting her countless favors.

In the Divine Mercy apparitions given to St. Faustina Kowalska, St. Joseph frequently appeared to St. Faustina and reassured her of his protection over her important mission of making God's mercy known and trusted. Similar to St. Thérèse, Faustina, too, prayed to St. Joseph every day and wrote about her experiences in her *Diary*. Without a doubt, the saints and mystics of the Church have done much to reveal the greatness of St. Joseph. However, above them all, it is the Virgin Mary herself who seems to be doing the most to make her husband known and loved.

Think about it: Centuries ago, Mary was the first person to "unveil" the greatness of St. Joseph by telling St. Matthew and St. Luke about aspects of the life of St. Joseph of which they otherwise would have had no knowledge. Saint Matthew and St. Luke never knew St. Joseph personally; they never met him or talked to him. The most likely explanation for how St. Joseph ended up in the New Testament at all is that Mary told St. Matthew and St. Luke about St. Joseph. The wife of St. Joseph is *the* source of information about St. Joseph in the New Testament. Mary wanted her husband to be included in the New Testament. Saint Joseph didn't speak much, but his wife spoke for him.

Today, Mary is at it again. Through her various apparitions, Mary is making her husband known by bringing him with her and teaching the Church about his importance. The Holy Trinity is the one behind it, of course, but there can be no doubt that Mary greatly delights in it and wants it as well. It seems Mary is once again asking Jesus to provide more wine for the wedding!

> In our time, Our Lady has helped us comprehend and love her dear and chaste husband, St. Joseph. She has told us of the mystery surrounding him and of his greatness. She has let us know something of her love for St. Joseph, that most lovable saint who for years held the Word made flesh in his arms.[7]
>
> — Blessed Gabriele Allegra

Let's take a look at several of the apparitions referred to by Blessed Gabriele Allegra, as well as a few that have taken place since his death.

On August 21, 1879, the Virgin Mary appeared to 15 people in Knock, Ireland. The apparition is popularly known as the apparition of Our Lady of Knock, but St. Joseph and St. John the Apostle were also present. No words or messages were given by Our Lady or the other heavenly visitors. The apparition occurred in the pouring rain and lasted for many hours. According to the sworn testimony of those who witnessed the apparition, St. Joseph wore white, was barefoot, and had his hands folded in prayer with his head slightly bent toward Mary as if honoring her great dignity as the Mother of God. It's a mysterious and intriguing apparition, but one that is fully approved by the Church.

In 1917, the Virgin Mary appeared in Fatima, Portugal. On October 13, 1917, during the last of the six Marian apparitions given to the three young visionaries, St. Joseph made an appearance as well. Similar to Knock, the skies were pouring rain on October 13 when St. Joseph made his appearance. It was also on that day that the famed Miracle of the Sun took place. More than 70,000 people witnessed the sun gyrate and spin as though it were going to crash into the earth. It was shortly before the Miracle of the Sun took place that St. Joseph appeared, holding the Christ Child, and together they blessed the world. All three visionaries of Fatima testified that St. Joseph and the Christ Child simultaneously blessed the world.

The significance of Jesus appearing as a child and blessing the world with St. Joseph cannot be underestimated. The message of Fatima has great significance for our times. Sister Lucia, the longest-lived visionary of the Fatima apparitions, stated that the final battle between good and evil would be over marriage and the family. Heaven taught us on October 13, 1917, that Jesus works miracles, gives peace, and blesses the world through St. Joseph. What St. Joseph's presence at Fatima also signifies is that a crucial component of the Triumph of the Immaculate Heart of Mary — a promise Our Lady made during the July 13 apparition to the three visionary children — is for the world to receive the simultaneous blessing of St. Joseph. When the Church recognizes the blessing of St. Joseph's fatherhood, Jesus will reign in hearts, and Mary's Immaculate Heart will triumph.

In 1968, there were a series of apparitions of Jesus, Mary, and St. Joseph in Zeitoun, a suburb of Cairo, Egypt. The town of Zeitoun is believed to have been one of the places the Holy Family visited during their sojourn in Egypt centuries earlier. Incredibly, thousands of Zeitoun's inhabitants — including Christians, Muslims, Jews, and government officials — witnessed the apparitions of the Holy Family. As at Knock, there were no words spoken and no messages given. The apparitions took place above and around a Coptic church, and were approved by the local Coptic ecclesial authorities.

Perhaps the most significant of all St. Joseph's appearances in modern times were the alleged apparitions given to Sr. Mildred Mary Neuzil (also known as Sr. Mary Ephrem) in the United States in the 1950s. These apparitions are known as the apparitions of "Our Lady of America."

The alleged apparitions given to Sr. Mary Ephrem occurred in Ohio and took place over many years; Sr. Mary Ephrem died in 2000. At the heart of the messages is a call to prayer, conversion, purity, consecration to Our Lady as the Immaculate Conception, and devotion to St. Joseph. In 1956 and 1958, St. Joseph himself spoke to Sr. Mary Ephrem.

The messages of St. Joseph to Sr. Mary Ephrem are extremely important for our times. Saint Joseph spoke to her of his virginity, purity, obedience, and love for his spouse. He also informed Sr. Mary Ephrem that God desires that the world have a greater appreciation for the sufferings the heart of St. Joseph underwent in union with the Hearts of Jesus and Mary. Saint Joseph spoke of the importance of devotion to his heart and spiritual fatherhood, as well as how God desires to bless all fatherhood through St. Joseph. The recognition of the wonders of St. Joseph is of such great importance that St. Joseph instructed Sr. Mary Ephrem that God wants St. Joseph to be honored on the First Wednesday of every month, especially by the recitation of the Joyful Mysteries of the rosary and the reception of Holy Communion.

The messages given by St. Joseph to Sr. Mary Ephrem on March 18 and March 19, 1958, are of such spiritual importance and magnitude that they need to be presented here in their entirety. Sister Mary Ephrem wrote:

> On March 11, 1958, Our Lady said to me: "St. Joseph will come on the eve of his feast. Prepare yourself well. There will be a special message. My holy spouse has an important part to play in bringing peace to the world."

[March 18, 1958]

St. Joseph came as was promised, and these are the words he spoke at this time: "Kneel down, my daughter, for what you will hear and what you will write will bring countless souls to a new way of life. Through you, small one, the Trinity desires to make known to souls its desire to be adored, honored, and loved within the kingdom, the interior kingdom of their hearts. I bring to souls the purity of my life and the obedience that crowned it. All fatherhood is blessed in me whom the Eternal Father chose as his representative on earth, the Virgin-Father of his own Divine Son. Through me the Heavenly Father has blessed all fatherhood, and through me he continues and will continue to do so till the end of time. My spiritual fatherhood extends to all God's children, and together with my Virgin Spouse I watch over them with great love and solicitude. Fathers must come to me, small one, to learn obedience to authority: to the Church always, as the mouthpiece of God, to the laws of the country in which they live, insofar as these do not go against God and their neighbor. Mine was perfect obedience to the Divine Will, as it was shown and made known to me by the Jewish law and religion. To be careless in this is most displeasing to God and will be severely punished in the next world. Let fathers also imitate my great purity of life and the deep respect I held for my Immaculate Spouse. Let them be an example to their children and fellow men, never willfully doing anything that would cause scandal among God's people. Fatherhood is from God, and it must take once again its rightful place among men."

As St. Joseph ceased speaking I saw his most pure heart. It seemed to be lying on a cross which was of brown color. It appeared to me that at the top of the heart, in the midst of the flames pouring out, was a pure white lily. Then I heard these words: "Behold this pure heart so pleasing to him who made it." St. Joseph then continued: "The cross, my little one, upon which my heart rests is the cross of the Passion, which was ever present before me, causing me intense suffering. I desire souls to come to my heart that they may learn true union with the Divine Will. It is enough, my child; I will come again tomorrow. Then I will make known to you how God wishes me to be honored in union with Jesus and Mary to obtain peace among men and nations. Good night, my little one."

On the evening of the next day, March 19, 1958, St. Joseph again appeared to me as he had promised and addressed me in these words: "My child, I desire a day to be set aside to honor my fatherhood. The privilege of being chosen by God to be the Virgin-Father of his Son was mine alone, and no honor, excluding that bestowed upon my Holy Spouse, was ever, or will ever, be as sublime or as high as this. The Holy Trinity desires thus to honor me that in my unique fatherhood all fatherhood might be blessed. Dear child, I was king in the little home of Nazareth, for I sheltered within it the Prince of Peace and the Queen of Heaven. To me they looked for protection and sustenance, and I did not fail them. I received from them the deepest love and reverence, for in me they saw him whose place I took over them. So the head of the family must be loved, obeyed, and respected, and in return be a true father and protector to those under his care. In honoring in a special way my fatherhood, you also honor Jesus and Mary. The Divine Trinity has placed into our keeping the peace of the world. The imitation of the Holy Family, my child, of the virtues we practiced in our little home at Nazareth is the way for all souls to that peace which comes from God alone and which none other can give."

Then suddenly, as he ceased speaking, I was favored with a unique and marvelous vision of the glorious St. Joseph. He seemed suspended, as it were, a short distance above what had the appearance of a large globe with clouds moving about it. His head was slightly raised, the eyes gazing upward as if in ecstasy. The hands were in a position similar to that of the priest during the celebration of Holy Mass, only they extended upward somewhat more. The color of his hair as also of his rather small and slightly forked beard seemed a very dark brown. His eyes resembled in color the hair and beard. He was clothed in a white robe that reached to his ankles. Over this he wore a sort of cloak which did not come together at the throat, but covering the shoulders and draped gracefully over each arm, reached to the hem of the robe. The cloak at times had, or seemed to have, the appearance of a brown, sometimes a purple, hue, or perhaps a slight blending of the two. The belt about his waist was of a gold color, as were his sandals. His appearance, though quite youthful, gave at the same time the impression of rare maturity combined with great strength. He seemed a bit taller than medium height. The lines of his face appeared strong and purposeful, softened somewhat by a gentle serenity. I also saw his most pure heart at this time. Moreover, I saw the Holy Spirit in the form of a dove hovering above his head. Standing sideways, facing each other, were two angels, one on the right, the other on the left. Each carried what appeared to be a small pillow in a satin covering, the pillow on the right bearing a gold crown, the one on the left, a gold scepter. The angels were all white, even their faces and hair. It was a beautiful whiteness that reminded me of the stainlessness of heaven. Then I heard these words: "Thus should he be honored whom the King desires to honor."[8]

Whoa! If you didn't get that, read it again. Everything that modern man needs to know about the greatness of St. Joseph is contained in the messages given to Sr. Mary Ephrem: Saint Joseph's spiritual fatherhood, virginal fatherhood, youthful appearance, kingship, crown, heart, and cloak. Saint Joseph speaks of his protection of the family, the importance of fatherhood, and heaven's desire that a special feast day in honor of St. Joseph's fatherhood be established. God wants St. Joseph to be known and loved!

My friends, do you realize what this means? The fatherhood of St. Joseph is a game-changer! The significance of a feast day in honor of St. Joseph's fatherhood would do so much spiritual good for the Church, families, and the world. Saint Joseph is worthy to be crowned by his beloved children!

The apparition to Sr. Mary Ephrem also teaches us that St. Joseph has an essential role in bringing peace to the world. Saint Joseph is evidently an integral part of the Triumph of the Immaculate Heart of Mary (hence, his appearance at Fatima on Oct. 13). Our Lady's Heart will triumph when the restoration of the family, and God's rightful place in it, takes place. None of this will happen until St. Joseph's fatherhood is fully recognized by the Church. Now is the time of St. Joseph!

> He that is the lesser among you, he is the greater.
>
> — Lk 9:48

> Let us allow ourselves to be filled with St Joseph's silence! In a world that is often too noisy, that encourages neither recollection nor listening to God's voice, we are in such deep need of it.[9]
>
> — Pope Benedict XVI

Sleeping St. Joseph

In vain is your earlier rising, your going later to rest, you who toil for the bread you eat: when he pours gifts on his beloved while they slumber.

— Psalm 127:2

G od loves sleep. He made it.

Your Heavenly Father has designed you so that approximately one-third of your life should be spent asleep. He himself rested after creating the heavens and the earth (see Gen 2:2-3).

God is a father. He delights in his children when they sleep. God communicates with his children when they sleep. It's a biblical fact. In the life and mission of St. Joseph, God chose to speak to him as he slept. On four occasions, God communicated through an angel to St. Joseph very important messages in his dreams (see Mt 1:20; 2:13, 19, 22).

Saint Joseph's sleep is so important and powerful that Satan fears it. Christianity has always held that Satan, a rebellious creature, chose not to serve God, arrogantly declaring, "*Non serviam*" ("I will not serve"; Jer 2:20). In contrast, the Virgin Mary utters her humble "*Fiat mihi secundum verbum tuum*" ("Be it done to me according to your word" [Lk 1:38]). The great St. Joseph responds more with obedient action than with words: "*Fecit sicut præcepit ei angelus Domini*" ("He did as the angel of the Lord commanded" [Mt 1:24]). Saint Joseph's sleep is a game-changer!

According to the New Testament, St. Joseph's sleep is prayer. In heaven, St. Joseph no longer sleeps, of course, but in eternity he does "rest in the Lord." Is not the afterlife called "eternal rest"?

In recent times, a popular devotion to St. Joseph under the title "Sleeping St. Joseph" has developed in the Church. It involves obtaining a statue depicting St. Joseph asleep, asking St. Joseph's intercession for a particular intention, writing the intention on a piece of paper, and placing the piece of paper underneath the statue of Sleeping St. Joseph. In doing this, a person is asking St. Joseph to bring his or her intention to God. The Sleeping St. Joseph devotion is a wonderful way to stay connected to your spiritual father and ask him to pray (sleep) on your intentions.

The French poet Charles Péguy wrote about the importance of sleep in an incredible poem, titled *The Portal of the Mystery of Hope.*

The poem is written from God's perspective and is meant to remind modern man that God delights in his children when they sleep. Here's an excerpt:

> Just sleep. Why don't people make use of it?
> I've given this secret to everyone, says God. I haven't sold it.
> He who sleeps well, lives well. He who sleeps, prays.
> He who works, prays too. But there's time for everything. Both for
>   sleep and for work.
> Work and sleep are like two brothers. And they get on very well
>   together.
> And sleep leads to work just like work leads to sleep.
> He who works well sleeps well, he who sleeps well works well.
>
> ∞∞∞∞
>
> And yet they tell me that there are men who don't sleep.
> I don't like the man who doesn't sleep, says God.
> Sleep is the friend of man.
> Sleep is the friend of God.
> Sleep may be my most beautiful creation.
> And I too rested on the seventh day.
> He whose heart is pure, sleeps. And he who sleeps has a pure heart.
> This is the great secret to being as indefatigable as a child.
>
> ∞∞∞∞
>
> Yes, they tell me that there are men who work well and who sleep poorly.
> Who don't sleep. What a lack of confidence in me.
>
> ∞∞∞∞
>
> I'm talking about those who work and who don't sleep.
> I pity them. I'm talking about those who work, and who thus
> in doing this are following my commandment, poor children.
> And who, on the other hand, don't have the courage, don't have the
>   confidence to sleep.
> I pity them. I hold it against them. A bit. They don't trust me.
> As a child lays innocently in his mother's arms, thus do they not lay
>   innocently in the arms of my Providence.
> They have the courage to work. They don't have the courage to do
>   nothing.
> They possess the virtue of work. They don't possess the virtue of doing
>   nothing.
> Of relaxing. Of resting. Of sleeping.
> Unhappy people, they don't know what's good.[1]
>
> — Charles Péguy

The sleep of St. Joseph can teach modern man important lessons about life. One of the most important lessons it teaches us is that it is okay to rest. Being a workaholic is never a good thing. Saint Joseph was not a workaholic. He liked to sleep. Sleep refreshed his soul. God communicated with St. Joseph when he slept, and he was a holier husband and father because of it.

You are not wasting time when you rest. Sleep is pleasing to God. God will speak to you and refresh your soul when you sleep.

If you are able, obtain a statue of "Sleeping St. Joseph" (see page 324 to order one from the Marian Fathers). Write down your intentions and place them in the care of St. Joseph. Let him communicate with God about you.

> O Saint Joseph, you are a man greatly favored by the Most High. The angel of the Lord appeared to you in dreams, while you slept, to warn you and guide you as you cared for the Holy Family. You were both silent and strong, a loyal and courageous protector. Dear Saint Joseph, as you rest in the Lord, confident of his absolute power and goodness, look upon me. Please take my need into your heart, dream of it, and present it to your Son. Help me then, good Saint Joseph, to hear the voice of God, to arise, and act with love. I praise and thank God with joy. Saint Joseph, I love you. Amen.

WONDER 9

PATRON OF A HAPPY DEATH

Saint Joseph is the patron and protector of a happy death. Those who pray to him are certain to die in good dispositions. He is the model of those who wish to die in the Lord.

— St. Peter Julian Eymard

Votive Masses

This glorious saint [Joseph] has great influence in heaven with him who raised him there in body and in soul.[1]

— St. Francis de Sales

The Holy Sacrifice of the Mass is the most powerful of all prayers. It is the prayer of Jesus offering his Body, Blood, Soul, and Divinity to the Heavenly Father for sinful mankind.

A long-standing tradition in the Church has designated each day of the week with a particular theme to be recognized at the Holy Sacrifice of the Mass.

SUNDAY — Resurrection of Jesus
MONDAY — Souls in Purgatory
TUESDAY — Holy Angels
WEDNESDAY — St. Joseph
THURSDAY — Eucharist
FRIDAY — Passion of Jesus
SATURDAY — Our Lady

Why is Wednesday set aside for St. Joseph? Well, Wednesday is the halfway point between Sunday (the day of the Lord) and Saturday (the day set aside to honor Mary). Blessed Anna Maria Taigi was so devoted to St. Joseph that she attended Mass every Wednesday in his honor and fasted on bread and water the entire day.

Have you ever attended Mass on a Wednesday in honor of St. Joseph? It's a great way to give special honor to St. Joseph at the midpoint of the week. In days of old, all priests celebrated a votive Mass in honor of St. Joseph on Wednesdays (so long as they were not impeded by an obligatory feast, of course). Today, many priests no longer continue this tradition, not out of ill-will, but because they are not aware such a tradition ever existed. It would be wonderful to see more priests return to this practice.

Regardless of whether your pastor celebrates a votive Mass in honor of St. Joseph on a Wednesday or not, your intention can still be to honor St. Joseph at a Wednesday Mass. By going to a Mass on Wednesday in St. Joseph's honor, you can draw close to your spiritual father and ask him for particular needs and intentions. Saint Joseph is so neglected in the spiritual life that he longs to assist those who pour out their hearts to him.

Saint Joseph also has his own month dedicated to him: March. The Virgin Mary is honored in a special way during the month of May because she is our spiritual mother, and May is the month of flowers. Saint Joseph is honored in a special way during the month of March because he is our spiritual father, and the greatest feast day of St. Joseph is celebrated on March 19: the Solemnity of St. Joseph.

Do you honor St. Joseph in a particular way during the month of March? You should. It doesn't have to be anything extravagant or costly. Simply placing flowers near a statue of St. Joseph in your home or at your parish will suffice. Renewing your consecration to St. Joseph, praying the Joyful Mysteries of the rosary more frequently, or making a pilgrimage to a local shrine dedicated to St. Joseph are all ways that you can remember St. Joseph during his month in a special way. Sicilians have a wonderful tradition called "St. Joseph's Altar." Centuries ago, a severe drought occurred in Sicily, and the inhabitants prayed to St. Joseph for help. To everyone's surprise, it rained, and crops began to grow again. In commemoration of the event, Sicilians annually decorate altars dedicated to St. Joseph with flowers, candles, food, and bread as a way of remembering how St. Joseph helped them. Often, the food that is collected for St. Joseph's Altar is given to the poor. The Sicilian tradition has found its way into cultures around the world, and is always celebrated on March 19.

Another aspect of devotion to St. Joseph of which many people seem to be unaware is that St. Joseph is not only the Patron of the Dying; he is also a tremendous intercessor for those who have died and are in purgatory. This aspect of St. Joseph's powerful intercession is an untapped treasure in the Church's devotional life.

A very holy 19th-century woman named Blessed Mary of Providence offers a powerful witness to how St. Joseph aids the Holy Souls in purgatory. Blessed Mary was given a special charism to help the Holy Souls, and combined her zeal for helping the souls in purgatory with her devotion to St. Joseph. She founded a religious community dedicated to this purpose, the Helpers of the Souls in Purgatory, and placed it under the patronage of St. Joseph.

The monks of St. Joseph Abbey in France recount the story of how St. Joseph helped Blessed Mary found her religious community. They write:

> On November 2, 1853, a plan was laid to establish a religious congregation, whose chief aim would be to come to the aid of the poor souls [in purgatory] by work, prayer, and suffering. The saintly Curé of Ars [St. John Vianney], delighted with the idea, gave it his entire support, often sending counsel and advice to the holy foundress who would become Blessed Mary of Providence.
>
> A promise was made to St. Joseph that, if the work took shape, the first statue to be placed in the mother-house of those conse-crating themselves entirely to the relief of the souls in purgatory, would be his. Saint Joseph took good care not to forget this promise. Providence brought about the acquisition of a residence in Paris, and the Sisters took the name of Helpers of the Souls in Purgatory (*Auxilatrices des Ames du Purgatoire*). As early as the following day, a postman arrived and delivered a statue of the saint, sent by a person who knew nothing of either the pious intention or even the acquisition. Thus St. Joseph was pleased to declare himself the protector of this heroic work, pursuing a hidden ministry in the heart of the great city of Paris.[2]

Just like Blessed Mary of Providence, we need to invoke the holy intercession of St. Joseph for the souls in purgatory. He is an extremely powerful intercessor, one whose aid we, too, will need after we die. Saint Joseph once spoke to the Servant of God Sr. Mary Martha Chambon about this and assured her that all who were devoted to him in life would continue to receive his intercession after death. Saint Joseph told her the following:

> If the soul who prayed to me still has debts to pay to the Sover-eign Judge, I shall ask for grace on its behalf.[3]

God listens to St. Joseph's requests. Nothing is refused to St. Joseph.

Remember to specially honor and invoke St. Joseph on Wednes days, in the month of March, and when you pray for the souls in purgatory.

He was chosen by the eternal Father as the trustworthy guardian and protector of his greatest treasure, namely, his divine Son and Mary, Joseph's wife. What then is Joseph's position in the whole Church of Christ? Is he not a man chosen and set apart? Through him and, yes, under him, Christ was fittingly and honorably introduced into the world. Holy Church in its entirety is indebted to the Virgin Mother because through her it was judged worthy to receive Christ. But after her we undoubtedly owe special gratitude and reverence to St. Joseph.[4]

— St. Bernardine of Siena

Patron of a Happy Death

Since we all must die, we should cherish a special devotion to St. Joseph that he may obtain for us a happy death.[1]

— St. Alphonsus Liguori

Nobody knows when they are going to die. We don't even know when St. Joseph died. Tradition holds that he died sometime before Jesus initiated his public ministry, but we don't know the exact timeframe. Saint Bernardine of Siena offers a few insightful thoughts on St. Joseph's death. He writes:

Though we do not read in Scripture when St. Joseph died, yet it may be believed that he probably died before our Lord's Passion. For he would not have been absent from the Savior's Cross had he been alive; nor would it have been becoming for Christ, from his cross, to have placed Mary in another's care.[2]

Saint Bernardine's thoughts make a lot of sense. Were St. Joseph alive when his Son was crucified, he most certainly would have been at Calvary to comfort his wife and be a source of consolation to Jesus. As St. Bernardine points out, if St. Joseph was present at Calvary, the entrustment of Mary to St. John would have been very confusing for the early Church. God taking St. Joseph out of the picture before the public ministry and Passion of Jesus was clearly part of the divine plan.

"Why did God take St. Joseph before the Passion of Jesus?" you might wonder. Well, according to God's plan, it was fitting that St. Joseph already be deceased so that Jesus could entrust his mother to St. John — and also entrust St. John (symbolizing all souls) to his mother. Were St. Joseph present at the Cross, the entrustment of souls to Mary as our spiritual mother would not have been as clear or understandable to the followers of Jesus. The filial relationship that each soul is called to have with Mary might have been obscured had St. Joseph been present. In addition, had St. Joseph been present at the Cross, Jesus would have also said to John the Apostle, "Behold, your father." This entrustment would have caused tremendous confusion for the followers of Jesus regarding the difference between the Heavenly Father and St. Joseph. Jesus wants his disciples to have a filial relationship with St. Joseph as well as Mary, but the recognition of St. Joseph's spiritual fatherhood would have needed to wait until the Church was mature enough to begin to understand it.

As it is fitting that St. Joseph died before the Passion of Jesus, so it is also fitting that his death should have taken place before Jesus' public ministry. If St. Joseph were alive during the public ministry of Jesus, it would have been confusing for people to hear Jesus speak about his desire to take them to his Father. In order to avoid obscuring the primacy of the Heavenly Father, Joseph had to die before the public ministry of Jesus began.

Though we do not know exactly when St. Joseph died, saints and holy mystics do provide insights into the manner of his death.

> It may be piously believed that at the moment of his [St. Joseph's] death, Jesus and the most Blessed Virgin, his spouse, were present. What exhortations! What consoling words! What promises! What luminous and enflamed words! In this moment of his passage toward eternity, what revelations on eternal goods must he have received from his most holy spouse and from Jesus, the most loving Son of God! I leave the contemplation and consideration of all this to your own devotion.[3]
>
> — St. Bernardine of Siena

> He [St. Joseph] never preached, but he gave his entire life to the service of Jesus and died in his arms. If Jesus cried over Lazarus, must he not have cried over [the death of] St. Joseph?[4]
>
> — St. Peter Julian Eymard

> When Joseph was dying, Mary sat at the head of his bed, holding him in her arms. Jesus stood just below her near Joseph's breast. The whole room was brilliant with light and full of angels. After his death, his hands were crossed on his breast, he was wrapped from head to foot in a white winding sheet, laid in a narrow casket, and placed in a very beautiful tomb, the gift of a good man.[5]
>
> — Blessed Anne Catherine Emmerich

Blessed Anne Catherine Emmerich's reported mystical insights about St. Joseph's death have intrigued many people. Her idea that St. Joseph's body was placed in a tomb has led many people to wonder if the tomb still exists. While it's certainly probable that St. Joseph's body was placed in a tomb, to date, we have no idea where the tomb of St. Joseph is located. Not one person in all of Christianity has ever claimed to know where the body of St. Joseph was placed after death. Isn't that fascinating? We know where the tombs of the ancient patriarchs Abraham, Isaac, and Jacob are located because they are described in detail in the Old Testament, but as for St. Joseph's tomb, we have no idea where it is.

If St. Joseph's body is in a tomb, it would certainly be incorruptible, right? Blessed Anne Catherine Emmerich thought so, and offered an interesting thought about it. She states:

> Only a few men followed the coffin [of St. Joseph] with Jesus and Mary; but I saw it accompanied by angels and environed with light. Joseph's remains were afterward removed by the Christians to Bethlehem, and interred. I think I can still see him lying there incorrupt.[6]

Hmmm ... interesting. Blessed Anne Catherine's notion that St. Joseph's body might be incorrupt and lying somewhere in a tomb on earth has led some people to speculate that the incorrupt body of St. Joseph will be discovered one day and, when discovered, bring great rejoicing to the Church. Can you imagine? What a phenomenal day of rejoicing that would be! Yet, as wonderful as such an event would be, there's a very good reason why we don't know where the tomb of St. Joseph is located. It's more probable that Joseph's body is not lying incorrupt in a tomb on earth somewhere. Rather, it is more probable that his body is in heaven with Jesus and Mary.

Many saints believe that St. Joseph was assumed into heaven in a manner similar to the Assumption of the Blessed Virgin Mary. It makes a lot of sense if you think about it. There are no relics of Mary's body on earth — we have only pieces of her veil, sash, or other fragments of her garments — because she was assumed into heaven, body and soul. Likewise, there are no bodily relics of St. Joseph on earth — we have only pieces of his garments or other items associated with him; for example, his staff — because he, too, was most likely assumed into heaven, body and soul. If Jesus assumed his mother's body into heaven, why would he not do the same for his beloved father? What son, if he had divine power, would take his mother's body to heaven and leave his father's body in a tomb?

Saint Bernardine of Siena supported belief in the assumption of St. Joseph into heaven. He was quick to point out that such a belief can't be held as doctrine (at least not in St. Bernardine's time), but he did acknowledge that it was okay for the faithful of his era to piously believe it. He wrote:

> We may piously believe, but not assert, that the Most Holy Son of God crowned his foster-father with the same privilege which he gave his mother; that as he assumed her into heaven bodily and glorious in soul, so also on the day when he [Jesus] arose he took Joseph up with him in the glory of the Resurrection.[7]

A few centuries after St. Bernardine lived, St. Francis de Sales took the pious belief in the bodily assumption of St. Joseph to the next level. Saint Francis de Sales' statement on the topic is probably the boldest claim ever made by a saint regarding St. Joseph being assumed into heaven. He stated:

> We can never for a moment doubt that this glorious saint has great influence in heaven with him who raised him there in body and in soul — a fact which is the more probable because we have no relic of that body left to us here below! Indeed, it seems to me that no one can doubt this as a truth, for how could he who had been so obedient to St. Joseph, all through his life, refuse him this grace?[8]

Saint Francis de Sales expanded on his thought and asserted the following:

> If it is true, as we are bound to believe, that in virtue of the Blessed Sacrament which we receive, our bodies will come to life again on the day of judgment (Jn 6:55), how could we doubt that Our Lord raised up to heaven, in body and soul, the glorious St. Joseph? For he had the honor and the grace of carrying him so often in his blessed arms, those arms in which Our Lord took so much pleasure.[9]

In modern times, a saintly pope, John XXIII, has asserted that St. Joseph was assumed bodily into heaven. In a homily given on May 26, 1960, the Solemnity of the Ascension, he stated:

> It [the Ascension of Jesus] corresponds, also, to those deceased from the Old Testament who were closest to Jesus. We name

two who were the most intimate in his life; John the Baptist, the Forerunner; and Joseph of Nazareth, his putative father and custodian. It [the Ascension] corresponds to them, as well, and can be piously believed. It is an honor and a privilege for them to experience this admirable path to heaven.[10]

Why would saints and popes believe that St. Joseph was assumed into heaven in body and soul? Well, there are several reasons. One is found in the New Testament itself. In the Gospel of Matthew, we are told about an incredible event that happened to many people after the Resurrection of Jesus. It reads:

> And behold, the veil in the sanctuary was torn in two from top to bottom. The earth quaked, rocks were split, tombs were opened, and the bodies of many saints who had fallen asleep were raised. And coming forth from their tombs after his resurrection, they entered the holy city and appeared to many.
>
> — Mt 27:51-53

It's an intriguing passage, to say the least. Who are the saints that came forth from their tombs at the death of Jesus? Well, we don't know exactly who they were because no names are given, but the Church has often thought that they are the prophets of the Old Testament, as well as St. John the Baptist and St. Joseph. It certainly makes sense that St. Joseph would be among their number.

If people rose from the dead at the death of Jesus — a fact that is clearly stated in the passage from Matthew's Gospel — would not St. Joseph have been one of them? Why would our Lord raise others from the dead and leave his own beloved father in a tomb? Saint Joseph is greater than all the Old Testament prophets, including St. John the Baptist. Saint Joseph is even greater than the grandparents of Jesus, Sts. Joachim and Anne. It should come as no surprise, then, that St. Bernardine of Siena, St. Francis de Sales, St. Pope John XXIII, and St. George Preca believed that St. Joseph rose from the dead at the death of Christ and, after appearing to many in Jerusalem, was assumed into heaven, body and soul, after the Resurrection of Christ.

> If the Resurrection of Christ, as we read in the Gospel of Matthew, caused the bodies of certain saints to rise and appear to many, isn't it likely that St. Joseph shared in this privilege since he died before Christ?[11]
>
> — St. George Preca

Taking it one step further, if St. Joseph is one of the saints mentioned in the Gospel of Matthew who rose from the dead at the Resurrection of Jesus, entering the holy city of Jerusalem and appearing to many, who would St. Joseph most likely have gone to see? Why, his wife, of course! All this is speculation, but it does make for delightful meditation. Imagine the sweet reunion, the chaste, tear-filled embrace!

There is yet another reason to believe that St. Joseph was assumed into heaven. It comes from the idea that St. Joseph was sanctified in the womb of his mother, as St. John the Baptist was sanctified in the womb of his mother. This idea has been affirmed by many saints as well.

> If God, as I firmly believe, so sanctified all the patriarchs because the Messiah was to be born from them, and sanctified all the prophets to foretell mysteries concerning the Messiah, and sanctified Jeremiah in the womb, and filled John the Baptist with the Holy Spirit to be the herald of the Messiah, and above all sanctified the Blessed Virgin to be the mother of Christ, why would he not also sanctify Joseph, the father of Christ?[12]

> — St. Lawrence of Brindisi

> If Jeremiah had the privilege of being sanctified before birth, if St. John the Baptist received the same grace in preparation for his service as precursor of the Messiah, are we not to believe that the one who served as the father of the Savior, and husband of the Queen of virgins, was treated with equal love and mercy?[13]

> — Blessed Bartolo Longo

Now, to be clear, neither St. Joseph nor any other saint experienced an immaculate conception anything like Our Lady's. After the fall of man, the Virgin Mary was the first to be free of all stain of sin from the first moment of her existence. She and her Son alone have had that unique privilege. Yet St. Lawrence of Brindisi, Blessed Bartolo Longo, and many others affirm that God did give extraordinary gifts of holiness to certain saints immediately after they were conceived because of the mission that God had entrusted to them. Since this is the case, not only would St. Joseph have been on the list of saints who were sanctified in the womb, but he would have been the "most sanctified" of them all. His mission of love was far greater than those of any of the Old Testament prophets, and even greater than the mission of St. John the Baptist.

The belief that St. Joseph was sanctified in the womb has led many people to ponder the cause of St. Joseph's death. In other words, what did he die from, old age or other causes? According to many saints, there's a lot more to St. Joseph's death than we think. They claim that his death was both natural and supernatural. He died from a natural cause (illness or advanced age), but also from a supernatural cause (love).

Love was the real cause of the death of St. Joseph.[14]

— Venerable Mary of Ágreda

What does that mean? How can a person die from love? Actually, this kind of death should come as no surprise. Poets and musicians have written and sung about dying of love from time immemorial. For St. Joseph, it was more than poetic; it was real.

Let's explore this a bit more.

Saint Joseph's main purpose in life was to get his wife (the New Eve) and his divine Son (the New Adam) to Calvary. There, they could offer their sacrifice and redeem the world. Saint Joseph's physical presence, however, was not necessary at Calvary. God required St. Joseph to make his sacrifice beforehand. Sure, God could have kept St. Joseph alive to suffer with Jesus and Mary at Calvary, but God exercised great mercy toward St. Joseph in sparing him from being a witness to the Crucifixion of his Son and the piercing of his wife's Heart. Saint Joseph had already done his suffering.

Adhering to God's plan, St. Joseph had already offered his loving sacrifice before Jesus and Mary offered their sacrifice on Calvary. His mission required that he die to self every day in order to get Jesus and Mary to Calvary so that they could make their sacrifice. Saint Joseph had done all he could do, and though his body was surely giving out due to the limits of human nature, his death was more about love than anything else. His mind, heart, soul, and body could endure no more suffering. He was exhausted from love. For decades, he had poured out all his heart for Jesus and Mary. Love had consumed him. Love "killed" him.

No one has suffered more for Jesus and Mary than St. Joseph. You might ask, "How is this possible? He was not a martyr. Nor was he pierced by a lance, whipped, burned, or drawn and quartered as other martyrs have been throughout history." Yes, it is true that he wasn't a martyr by blood. However, St. Joseph's suffering for Jesus and Mary lasted for decades and was of such interior intensity that no martyr's blood can ever compare to the sacrificial love that the father of Jesus offered for so many years. He lived with the never-ending knowledge that his wife's Heart would be pierced and his Son mocked, ridiculed, and hated. He was not ignorant of the prophecy of Simeon. He knew it well. He carried it in his heart for decades. The purer your heart, the purer your sacrifice. The greater your soul, the greater your suffering.

Saint Joseph is the greatest saint after Mary because he suffered more than any other saint for Jesus. Before St. John the Baptist offered his head to the axe and the early Christians surrendered their bodies to the lions, St. Joseph had already given his heart and soul as a sacrifice for Jesus. The Desert Fathers observed rigorous methods of penance and years of asceticism, but the glorious St. Joseph had already lived extreme poverty, exile, and hardship for love of Christ. Saint Francis Xavier sailed across the high seas to evangelize foreign lands, suffering for the Gospel in a distant country, but St. Joseph had already been the first and greatest missionary. Saint Thérèse of Lisieux taught the world the "little way" of holiness and childlike simplicity, but St. Joseph long before her had already perfected the spirituality of childlike confidence in God. Saint Joseph gave everything for Jesus and Mary. He poured himself out. When completely exhausted from love, he died from having loved so much.

> We may well call St. Joseph the martyr of the hidden life, for no one ever suffered as he did. But why so much sorrow in his life? Simply because the holier a person is, the more he must suffer for the love and glory of God. Suffering is the flowering of God's grace in a soul and the triumph of the soul's love for God. Therefore, St. Joseph, the greatest of saints after Mary, suffered more than all the martyrs. The source of his suffering lay in his deep, tender, and enlightened love for Jesus and in his veneration for the Virgin Mary. All the elect must climb the hill of Calvary, and it is only through the wounds in His hands and feet that they reach the heart of Jesus. It is not so much a question of penitence as of love; penitence only pays a debt, but love goes further and crucifies itself with Jesus and for Jesus. It is a truth then that the more a soul loves, the more it suffers. That is why St. Joseph's Calvary lasted thirty years with no respite whatever. When he was honored with the dignity of foster-father of Christ, the Cross was set up in his heart and he labored in its shadow for the rest of his life.[15]

> — St. Peter Julian Eymard

Were it the will of God, St. Joseph would have eagerly desired to stay on earth and suffer even more with Jesus and Mary at Calvary. However, it was not God's will.

> Saint Joseph foresaw Mary's tears and misery. He would have desired to stay by her side, and he must have begged Jesus to be allowed to remain on earth that he might climb Calvary and sustain Mary.[16]
>
> — St. Peter Julian Eymard

God accepted St. Joseph's years of sacrificial love and filled his heart with such extraordinary graces that he died of love and was spared the tortures of Calvary. As a good son (indeed, as *the* good Son!), Jesus showed great mercy to his earthly father. Jesus, the Son of Joseph, did not desire for his earthly father to witness Calvary.

> God was pleased to take to himself St. Joseph before our Savior's Passion, to spare him the overwhelming grief it would have caused him.[17]
>
> — St. Bernardine of Siena

> Joseph had of necessity to die before the Lord, for he could not have endured his crucifixion; he was too gentle, too loving.[18]
>
> — Blessed Anne Catherine Emmerich

Mary, as the New Eve and Mother of All the Living, had to be at Calvary; St. Joseph, a New Adam, had already given himself and offered his loving sacrifice. Unlike St. Joseph, Mary's presence at the Cross was absolutely necessary. She had to be there in order to give birth to the Church. As (according to a venerable tradition) God had kept St. Joseph's eyes from seeing the birth of Christ at Bethlehem, so (according to Scripture) he also hid from St. Joseph's eyes the Crucifixion of his beloved Son on Calvary. Calvary would have been a double-torture to St. Joseph's heart.

> Poor St. Joseph! He had to submit to death and leave behind him Jesus and Mary: Jesus to be crucified and abandoned by his people; Mary, to suffer alone, unassisted. How his love for them was crucified![19]
>
> — St. Peter Julian Eymard

Venerable Mary of Ágreda had a vision of being transported to the bedside of St. Joseph so as to witness his last breath and final words to his loving wife. In a statement that is sure to move your heart and touch your soul, Venerable Mary of Ágreda related that St. Joseph said the following goodbye to Mary before he died.

> Blessed art thou among all women. Let angels and men praise thee; let all the generations know, praise, and exalt thy dignity; and may the Most High be eternally praised for having created thee so pleasing in his eyes and in the sight of all the blessed spirits. I hope to enjoy thy sight in the heavenly fatherland.[20]

Pious Union of St. Joseph

Will he, the great saint whom Jesus and Mary obeyed, who provided Jesus and Mary with their daily bread, be invoked in vain? No![1]

— St. Luigi Guanella

Saint Joseph is never invoked in vain. Jesus had total confidence in the comforting love of his virginal father. Jesus wants us to experience the wonders of living in union with St. Joseph as well.

> Which one of you would hand his son a stone when he asks for a loaf of bread, or a snake when he asks for a fish? If you then, who are wicked, know how to give good gifts to your children, how much more will your heavenly Father give good things to those who ask him.

— Mt 7:9-11

In the Scripture passage above, Jesus is teaching us about the love of his Heavenly Father. Yet this teaching of Jesus also applies to our spiritual father, St. Joseph. He is an icon of the Heavenly Father. In St. Joseph's steadfast love, we can have total confidence.

The life and work of St. Luigi Guanella offer us an example of having total confidence in St. Joseph. Born and raised in Italy, St. Luigi spent his entire priesthood doing corporal and spiritual works of mercy for others. He looked after orphans, cared for those with mental and physical disabilities, helped abandoned elderly people, clothed the homeless, and fed the poor. Zealous to help everyone in need, he founded two religious congregations to continue performing the works of mercy, the Servants of Charity and the Daughters of Mary.

Devotion to St. Joseph was at the heart of St. Luigi's life and mission. He made certain that both of the religious communities he founded strove to be in constant union with St. Joseph, seeing in him a model and a patron for all their charitable works. In the many homes St. Luigi established to meet the needs of others, he emphasized that devotion to St. Joseph needed to flourish, especially devotion to St. Joseph as the Patron of the Dying, because he believed that the works of mercy were fruitless if they did not help people acquire a relationship with the Lord and experience a holy and happy death like that of St. Joseph.

Saint Luigi's devotion to St. Joseph was so well known that St. Pope Pius X invited him to build a church near the Vatican in honor of St. Joseph. Saint Luigi was delighted by the invitation of the pope and began construction immediately. Not surprisingly, St. Luigi dedicated the new church to honoring St. Joseph's holy and happy death. The church took four years to complete and was consecrated on March 19, 1912.

The church St. Luigi built in honor of St. Joseph is located in the Trionfale region of Rome. It is known as San Giuseppe al Trionfale. Saint Pope Pius X had also encouraged St. Luigi to initiate an apostolate that would offer daily prayers for the suffering and the dying. In 1913, St. Luigi launched an international association of intercessors for the suffering and the dying. He named the association the Pious Union of St. Joseph, and St. Pope Pius X became the first official member. The headquarters of the Pious Union of St. Joseph is located right next to the church of San Giuseppe al Trionfale. International branches of the Pious Union of St. Joseph are located throughout the world. In the United States, the Pious Union of St. Joseph is headquartered in Grass Lake, Michigan (see page 287).

> My dear St. Joseph, be with me living, be with me dying, and obtain for me a favorable judgment from Jesus, my merciful Savior.[2]
>
> — Pope Leo XIII

> Saint Joseph, my dear father, gaze upon me from heaven. Detach me from the things of earth, obtain for me purity of heart, love of God, and final perseverance.[3]
>
> — Blessed Bartolo Longo

WONDER 10
TERROR OF DEMONS

Saint Joseph is most powerful against the demons which fight against us.

— St. Alphonsus Liguori

Saint Joseph the Worker

Like all Christians at that time, I too was happy and grateful at the Church's decision to declare a liturgical feast in honor of St. Joseph the Worker. This feast, which ratifies the divine value of work, shows how the Church publicly echoes central truths of the Gospel which God wishes men to meditate on, especially in our own time.[1]

— St. Josemaría Escrivá

The "time" St. Josemaría Escrivá mentions was the year 1955. It was the year the Church called upon her great protector to overcome a great evil: communism.

In the first half of the 20th century, communism had gained support from many leaders around the world, and entire nations had succumbed to its ideas. In 1937, Pope Pius XI realized the serious threat that communism posed to the common good and called upon St. Joseph to protect the Church from the many errors of communism. He wrote:

We place the vast campaign of the Church against world communism under the standard of St. Joseph, her mighty protector.[2]

As a result of Pope Pius XI's words, Catholics fervently began to pray to St. Joseph, specifically under the title "Terror of Demons," to combat the atheistic ideas of communism. They also invoked the help of St. Joseph in the cause of workers' rights. Both of these issues were major topics of concern in the mid-20th century.

On a related note, did you know that in the mid-19th century, May 1 was celebrated by many countries around the world as a secular holiday? It was called "May Day" and was neither a religious nor a political holiday. Sadly, in the mid-20th century, communists wanted to take over the secular holiday and re-designate it as "Communist Worker's Day." Renaming the holiday and emphasizing the ideas of communism were viewed as a way of influencing the masses. This development greatly concerned the Church because a celebration honoring the communist idea of work would have long-lasting effects on workers and negatively impact society and the family. At the time, the threat of worldwide communism was felt by everyone, including the pope.

The Vicar of Christ, Venerable Pope Pius XII, turned to St. Joseph, as his predecessor had done, and denounced the falsehoods of communism by elevating the dignity of workers in a very specific way.

On May 1, 1955, Pope Pius XII declared May 1 to be the liturgical feast of St. Joseph the Worker. He wrote:

> We are happy to announce to you our determination to institute — as in fact we do institute — the liturgical feast of St. Joseph the Worker, assigning it as the first day of May. Are you pleased with this our gift, beloved workers? We are certain that you are, because the humble workman of Nazareth not only personifies before God and the Church the dignity of the man who works with his hands, but is always the provident guardian of you and your families.[3]

Saint Joseph is, indeed, a light in the darkness and the Model of Workmen. He brings to light the malice of the enemies of the family. He brings light into the darkness of erroneous movements that seek to strip people of their human dignity and eliminate God from the minds and hearts of families and nations. Whether he is confronting communism, fascism, or any other kind of political ideology, St. Joseph is the protector of human dignity. He is the Terror of Demons!

> God our Father, creator and ruler of the universe, in every age you call man to develop and use his gifts for the good of others. With St. Joseph as our example and guide, help us to do the work you have asked and come to the rewards you have promised.
>
> — Opening Prayer for the Memorial of St. Joseph the Worker

Terror of Demons

O glorious St. Joseph, pray for me, assist me, and defend me from Satan.[1]

— St. Anthony Mary Claret

A fter the Virgin Mary, demons fear St. Joseph more than any other saint. The devil fears St. Joseph more than he fears the pope. How is this possible? Isn't the pope the Vicar of Christ? Yes, but the pope is only the Vicar of Christ; he is not the father of Christ. The Vicar of Christ has authority over the Mystical Body of Christ (the Church), but St. Joseph has the extraordinary gift and power of paternal intercession in heaven.

> The power of St. Joseph is greater than that of the ancient Joseph, of Moses, of Joshua, and of St. Peter.[2]

— Blessed William Joseph Chaminade

The power of St. Joseph is truly extraordinary. He alone bears the title "Terror of Demons." What makes this unique title of St. Joseph so extraordinary is that St. Joseph was not a pope, a priest, a monk, or a martyr. Saint Joseph is a layman. Like most laymen, he is a father and a husband. It is his loving fatherhood, in particular, that gives St. Joseph extraordinary intercessory power.

Have you heard of Blessed Bartolo Longo, who lived during the late 19th and early 20th century? He was born in Latiano, Italy, to a devout Catholic family. As a young man, he studied law at the University of Naples. After being swept away by various political ideologies, he became anti-Catholic, radically opposed to what he believed were the "old wives' tales" of Catholicism. Within a short period of time, he went from adhering to nationalistic ideologies to becoming involved in spiritualism. This led him to attend séances and become an ordained priest of Satan.

Bartolo's involvement with the occult and spiritualism left him empty and unhappy. He suffered from hallucinations, torturous nightmares, frazzled nerves, bodily ailments, and severe depression. Seeking guidance, he turned to a friend and a Dominican priest, and began to experience a radical conversion. Fearing for his soul, he renounced spiritualism and its practices, and turned back to the Catholicism of his youth. In gratitude for having been delivered from the occult, he became a Third Order Dominican and dedicated his life to the spread of the rosary, especially by renewing the Catholic faith in the ancient city of Pompeii and building there the Basilica of Our Lady of the Rosary. He was very devoted to St. Joseph, prayed to him every day, and was particularly fond of his title "Terror of Demons." Bartolo had such a great love for St. Joseph that he wrote a lengthy book of meditations and prayers to St. Joseph to be used for the month of March. Bartolo Longo, the former satanic priest, was beatified by St. John Paul II in 1980.

> It is a great blessing for souls to be under the protection of the saint whose name makes demons tremble and flee.[3]
>
> — Blessed Bartolo Longo

> Pronounce often and with great confidence the names of Jesus, Mary, and Joseph. Their names bring peace, love, health, blessings, majesty, glory, admiration, joy, happiness, and veneration. Their holy names are a blessing to angels and men, and a terror to demons. Christians should always have the names of Jesus, Mary, and Joseph in their hearts and on their lips.[4]
>
> — Blessed Bartolo Longo

The life of Blessed Bartolo Longo gives us more proof that the wonders of St. Joseph are without number and the devil is terrorized by all of them.

> The fatherhood of St. Joseph terrorizes the devil.
> The humility of St. Joseph terrorizes the devil.
> The charity of St. Joseph terrorizes the devil.
> The poverty of St. Joseph terrorizes the devil.
> The purity of St. Joseph terrorizes the devil.
> The obedience of St. Joseph terrorizes the devil.
> The silence of St. Joseph terrorizes the devil.
> The suffering of St. Joseph terrorizes the devil.
> The prayer of St. Joseph terrorizes the devil.
> The name of St. Joseph terrorizes the devil.
> The sleep of St. Joseph terrorizes the devil.

Of the wonders, two in particular need to be emphasized in our day: the fatherhood of St. Joseph and the purity of St. Joseph. These wonders of St. Joseph need to be highlighted because all men (laymen and clergy) need to realize the power that fatherhood and purity have over the forces of darkness.

All fatherhood is a threat to Satan. For centuries, the devil "delighted" in the reality that so few Christians prayed to St. Joseph and called upon his paternal intercession. Today, God wants to make St. Joseph's fatherhood known and replicated in the world. This terrifies Satan. The devil knows what the intercession of St. Joseph is capable of doing. If men resemble St. Joseph, the kingdom of Satan will be destroyed.

Satan hates motherhood, too, of course, especially disdaining and fearing the Virgin Mary. Women are the bearers of life, and the devil hates life. Satan hates fatherhood because of the inherent power in all fatherhood. All fatherhood has its origin in God and finds its earthly model in St. Joseph. All fatherhood has the power to combat evil. Lucifer fears the fatherhood of St. Joseph more than any other creaturely fatherhood because the devil knows that there is no created person who has a greater participation in the fatherhood of God than St. Joseph.

The devil is infuriated by the fact that God humbled himself to become a man and submitted himself to the fourth Commandment.

> Honor your father and your mother.
>
> — Ex 20:12

In taking on human nature, the Second Person of the Blessed Trinity chose a life of submitting to, obeying, and honoring mortals. The fact that the King of Kings and Lord of Lords obeyed the fourth commandment and submitted himself to the authority of St. Joseph on earth is incomprehensible to Satan. God lowered himself to obey and serve creatures made from dust. The filial obedience of Jesus to St. Joseph was met with the disdain of the devil.

Saint Joseph's fatherhood has power. The devil hates that Jesus and Mary obeyed the loving directives of St. Joseph. Now, in heaven, the intercessory power of St. Joseph poses a serious threat to the wiles of the devil and the devil knows it.

> The Eternal Father shares with St. Joseph the authority which he has over the Incarnate Word, just as God shared with Adam his authority over creatures.[5]
>
> — Blessed William Joseph Chaminade

> In the Holy Family he [St. Joseph] represented the heavenly Father.[6]
>
> — Blessed James Alberione

The two greatest personages who ever lived on this earth subjected themselves to him [St. Joseph].[7]

— St. Madeleine Sophie Barat

Saint Joseph was called by God to serve the person and mission
of Jesus directly through the exercise of his fatherhood.[8]

— St. John Paul II

In the home of Nazareth, St. Joseph's directives were akin to
paternal commands. In heaven, Jesus continues to listen to his virginal
father because St. Joseph's desires are always in accord with God's
most holy will. Satan is terrified that St. Joseph continues to exercise
paternal influence in heaven through his extraordinary intercession
with the Son of God.

The devil hates God the Father and every reflection of his fatherhood. This hatred incites the devil to destroy fatherhood in all men,
laymen as well as priests. Undoubtedly, the devil has a tremendous
fear of zealous popes, holy priests, and the blood of the martyrs, but
he also greatly fears laymen who pattern their fatherhood off of St.
Joseph. The last thing the devil wants is for men to be apparitions
of St. Joseph, increasing the presence of St. Joseph in the world.
If a man allows himself to be an apparition of St. Joseph, imitating
the virtues of St. Joseph, Satan becomes powerless in his attacks
against the family (the domestic church) and the Mystical Body of
Christ (the Church). When laymen, priests, and bishops pattern their
paternal authority after that of St. Joseph, the Church will experience
tremendous victories over evil.

The loving and merciful fatherhood of St. Joseph serves as the
model for all men, teaching them the proper use of paternal authority
and cooperation with Jesus and Mary in the salvation of the world.

> Saint Joseph was not only destined as a relief to the Mother of
> God, who had so many tribulations on earth; not only was he the
> supporter of Jesus Christ, but he was also destined to cooperate,
> in a way, in the redemption of the world.[9]
>
> — St. Alphonsus Liguori

The purity of St. Joseph also terrorizes Satan.

It is a tragedy that the majority of art depicting St. Joseph has
presented him as an elderly man. Sadly, sometimes he is even presented as soft and effeminate. This is far from the truth of who St.
Joseph is as a man. Saint Joseph is a dragon-slayer! His lily is not the

cane of an old man; it is the lance of a knight! Rare is the artist who has depicted the lily of St. Joseph as a sharp weapon piercing the serpent dragon. What the Church needs today are images that depict St. Joseph as a dragon-slayer. He worked with manly tools, chopped wood, and swung a sharp axe! Such images are needed in homes and churches today to convey the real manhood of St. Joseph. (See the commissioned artwork on pages 311 to 320.)

The purity of St. Joseph is a weapon against the filth and perversions of the devil. Satan is a filthy, perverse, and pornographic creature. Purity repulses him. It pierces him.

The number one sin among men today is impurity. It is a spiritual plague destroying the minds and hearts of men on a global scale. The spiritual plague of impurity involves pornography, immoral actions with oneself, homosexual acts and lifestyles, pedophilia, cohabitation, contraception, and abortion. These sins leave men powerless and spiritually impotent.

Men who are impure have no power. Impure men pose no threat to the devil because they are spiritually impotent. This explains why so many men today have no strength to fight evil. The devil doesn't fear many men today. Satan has nothing to fear from a man who has freely chosen to let demons into his life through lust, pornography, immoral desires, and every other form of perversion. A filthy heart blinds a person to the countenance of God. If men want to see God and have power over darkness, they must strive to have a chaste and loving heart like St. Joseph.

Blessed are the pure of heart, for they shall see God.

— Mt 5:8

Saint Joseph sees the face of God and has power over evil because he is pure. On earth, he gazed upon the face of Jesus for decades. In heaven, he gazes upon the divine countenance forever. The radiance of St. Joseph's face blinds the demons of hell.

The Church and the world need men who are terrors of demons! It will only happen when men imitate the purity of St. Joseph. If men do this, the world will be renewed. If priests and bishops do this, the Church will be renewed. When priests and bishops have pure hearts that reflect the knight-like spirit and the warrior-like purity of St. Joseph, parishes will once again be filled with throngs of people zealous for the things of God. When bishops imitate the purity, zeal, and fatherhood of St. Joseph, mankind will once again look to the

Church as the moral compass of the world. All men can become terrors of demons if they imitate St. Joseph.

> Valiant and strong is the man who, like St. Joseph, perseveres in humility; he will be conqueror at once of the devil and of the world, which is full of ambition, vanity, and pride.[10]

> — St. Francis de Sales

Men who want to be pure, pray. Without prayer, no one (male or female) can be pure. Pope Leo XIII understood this very well. At the end of the 19th century, Satan unleased a spiritual deluge of filth, immodesty, and impurity on the world. Pope Leo XIII desired to fight it and forged together two of the greatest spiritual weapons the Church has in her arsenal: the rosary and St. Joseph. This prophetic pope requested that the following prayer to St. Joseph be prayed at the end of the rosary in the month of October:

> To you, O Blessed Joseph, we have recourse in our affliction, and having implored the help of your most holy spouse, we now, with hearts filled with confidence, earnestly beg you to take us under your protection. Through that sacred bond of charity which united you to the Immaculate Virgin Mother of God, and by that fatherly love with which you embraced the Child Jesus, we humbly beg you to look graciously upon the beloved inheritance which Jesus Christ purchased by his blood, and to aid us in our necessities with your power and strength.

> Defend, O most watchful guardian of the Holy Family, the chosen children of Jesus Christ. Keep from us, O most loving father, all blight of error and corruption. Aid us from on high, most valiant defender, in this conflict with the powers of darkness. And just as you once saved the Child Jesus from mortal danger, so now defend God's Holy Church from the snares of the enemy and from all adversity. Shield us by your constant protection, so that, supported by your example and strengthened by your help, we may be able to live a virtuous life, die a happy death, and obtain everlasting bliss in heaven. Amen.[11]

The Church needs to constantly invoke the aid of St. Joseph to overcome the devil. Saint Joseph is more powerful in heaven than he was on earth!

> It is true that the other saints enjoy great power in heaven, but they ask as servants, and do not command as masters. Saint

Joseph, to whose authority Jesus was subject on earth, obtains what he desires from his kingly foster Son in heaven.[12]

— St. Thomas Aquinas

What could Jesus Christ refuse St. Joseph who never refused him anything during his mortal life on earth?[13]

— St. Augustine

The Lord wants us to understand that just as he was subject to St. Joseph on earth — for since bearing the title of father, being the Lord's tutor, Joseph could give the child commands — so in heaven God does whatever he commands.[14]

— St. Teresa of Avila

Since it is written that God "will do the will of them that fear him," how can he refuse to do the will of St. Joseph who nourished him for so long with the sweat of his brow?[15]

— St. Ambrose

We must be convinced that, in consideration of his great merits, God will not refuse St. Joseph any grace he asks for those who honor him.[16]

— St. Alphonsus Liguori

Whenever the divine favor chooses someone for a special grace or an exalted position, it endows the person thus chosen with all the gifts necessary for him and for his task. This was pre-eminently verified in St. Joseph, the foster father of Jesus Christ and true spouse of the Queen of Heaven and Mistress of Angels. He was chosen by the Father as the faithful foster father and guardian of his principal treasures, that is, his son and his spouse. If you compare him to the whole Church of Christ, is he not that chosen and unique man through whom and under whom Christ was brought into the world with due order and honor? If then, the entire holy Church is in debt to the Virgin Mother, because, through her, she was made worthy to receive Christ, after Mary, she owes him gratitude and singular veneration. For he is the key of the Old Testament, in whom the dignity of the patriarchs and the prophets attain its promised fruit. There can be no doubt that in heaven Christ did not deny Joseph that familiarity, reverence, and exalted dignity which he tendered him as a son to his father while he lived among men. He rather increased and perfected it.[17]

— St. Bernardine of Siena

Saint Joseph, with the love and generosity with which he guarded Jesus, so too will he guard your soul, and as he defended him from Herod, so will he defend your soul from the fiercest Herod: the devil! All the care that the Patriarch St. Joseph has for Jesus, he has for you and will always help you with his patronage. He will free you from the persecution of the wicked and proud Herod, and will not allow your heart to be estranged from Jesus. *Ite ad Ioseph!* Go to Joseph with extreme confidence, because I do not remember having asked anything from St. Joseph, without having obtained it readily.[18]

— St. Pio of Pietrelcina

Your name, Joseph, is the joy of heaven, the honor of earth, and the comfort of mortals. Your name invigorates the weak, comforts the afflicted, heals the sick, softens hardened hearts, helps us in temptation, frees us from the snares of the devil, obtains every gift, and shares in the power of the holy names of Jesus and Mary.[19]

— Blessed Bartolo Longo

Saint Joseph, Terror of Demons, pray for us!

Privileges of Devotion to St. Joseph

Love St. Joseph a lot. Love him with all your soul, because he, together with Jesus, is the person who has most loved our Blessed Lady and been closest to God. He is the person who has most loved God, after our Mother. He deserves your affection, and it will do you good to get to know him, because he is the Master of the interior life, and has great power before the Lord and before the Mother of God.[1]

— St. Josemaría Escrivá

Jesus wants you to love St. Joseph. Our Lady wants you to love St. Joseph. They both want this so that your virtue and holiness may increase. No matter what your vocation or state in life may be, you will be blessed if you maintain a fervent devotion to St. Joseph. The privileges of devotion to St. Joseph are tremendous, and they are yours for the taking!

Devotion to St. Joseph is powerful because he gives his protection, his example, and his blessing.[2]

— St. George Preca

Blessed Maria Teresa of St. Joseph loved St. Joseph and received extraordinary graces from heaven because of her reliance on his intercession. Anna Maria Tauscher van den Bosch (her name before she entered religious life) was born in Germany in 1855. She was raised in a staunchly Protestant family, and her father was a Lutheran minister. Over time, Anna Maria fell in love with the teachings of Catholicism and made it known to her father that she wanted to become a Catholic. Her father was not happy with her decision at all, telling her that he was ashamed of her for abandoning her Protestant upbringing. He didn't even want her living in his house anymore.

On one occasion, when she was living on her own but before she was yet a Catholic, her father visited her in an attempt to dissuade her from joining the Catholic Church. On that visit, he discovered a book on St. Joseph in her room. After a quick look at the book, he put it down, and later that night at dinner, he ridiculed and mocked St. Joseph in front of his daughter. In her autobiography, Anna Maria recounts the event. She writes:

> During the dinner my father said: "How can anyone pray to such an outlandish man?" This expression, "outlandish" or "foreign" made a deep impression on me. I thought more and more of St. Joseph, and I conceived such a great, tender devotion to dear Father St. Joseph, as I called him, that I thought I ought to make reparation for the coldness of all unbelievers toward him.[3]

After converting to Catholicism, Anna Maria's supervisor at work, a Lutheran, fired her because she had become a Catholic. He was so mean that after he had fired her, he continued to speak ill of her to others so that she was unable to find work anywhere. As a result, Anna Maria had no money and no place to live. Her great love for St. Joseph was not diminished, though. She daily sought comfort in the love of her Father St. Joseph. Eventually, she was given permission to move into an Augustinian convent and do menial tasks as a way of paying for her room and meals. She wrote:

> The recollection of my father asking how anyone could pray to such an "outlandish" person sank deep into my heart, and out of it came a great love for him [St. Joseph] and also a great trust in him. I entrusted myself more and more to his paternal care, and many times did St. Joseph prove his solicitude for me.[4]

Anna Maria eventually became a nun, taking the name Sr. Maria Teresa of St. Joseph. In time, she would found a new religious community, the Carmelite Sisters of the Divine Heart of Jesus. She would also establish charitable institutes around the world. For the remainder of her life, she always referred to St. Joseph as "Father St. Joseph." She attributed everything she was able to accomplish to the intercession of St. Joseph, her spiritual father. Pope Benedict XVI beatified her in 2006.

In the 17th century, Venerable Mary of Ágreda wrote about the extraordinary graces God gives to those who are devoted to St. Joseph. Venerable Mary of Ágreda was a mystic and the acclaimed author of a work detailing the life of the Virgin Mary, titled *The Mystical City of God*. Her work is truly a devotional masterpiece. In the book, she wrote extensively about St. Joseph and was given many insights into the blessings that await those who are devoted to St. Joseph. She wrote:

> I have been informed concerning certain privileges conferred upon St. Joseph by the Most High on account of his great holiness, which are especially important to those who ask his intercession in a proper manner. In virtue of these special privileges the intercession of St. Joseph is most powerful:
>
> 1. First, for attaining the virtue of purity and overcoming the sensual inclinations of the flesh;
> 2. Second, for procuring powerful help to escape sin and return to the friendship of God;
> 3. Third, for increasing the love and devotion to most holy Mary;
> 4. Fourth, for securing the grace of a happy death and protection against the demons in that hour;
> 5. Fifth, for filling the demons with terror at the mere mention of his name by his clients;
> 6. Sixth, for gaining health of body and assistance in all kinds of difficulties;
> 7. Seventh, for securing issue of children in families.
>
> These and many other favors God confers upon those who properly and with good disposition seek the intercession of the spouse of our Queen, St. Joseph. I beseech all the faithful children of the Church to be very devoted to him and they will experience these favors in reality, if they dispose themselves as they should in order to receive and merit them.[5]

The seven privileges of devotion to St. Joseph are stupendous! Venerable Mary of Ágreda heard Our Lady herself speak about them, saying:

> My daughter, although thou hast described my spouse, St. Joseph, as the most noble among the princes and saints of the heavenly Jerusalem; yet neither canst thou properly manifest his eminent sanctity, nor can any of the mortals know it fully before they arrive at the vision of the Divinity. Then all of them will be filled with wonder and praise as the Lord will make them capable of understanding. On the last day, when all men shall be judged, the damned will bitterly bewail their sins, which prevented them from appreciating this powerful means of their salvation, and availing themselves, as they easily could have, of this intercessor to gain the friendship of the just Judge. The whole human race has much undervalued the privileges and prerogatives conceded to my blessed spouse and they know not what his intercession with God is able to do.
>
> That which my spouse asks of the Lord in heaven is granted upon the earth and on his intercession depend many and extraordinary favors for men, if they do not make themselves unworthy of receiving them. All these privileges were to be a reward for the amiable perfection of this wonderful saint and for his great virtues, for divine clemency is favorably drawn forth by them and looks upon St. Joseph with generous liberality, ready to shower down its marvelous mercies upon all those who avail themselves of his intercession.[6]

In the 20th century, Blessed Concepción Cabrera de Armida, a famed mystic from Mexico, wrote meditations for the purpose of instructing and inspiring the faithful. In one meditation, Blessed Concepción offered a perspective on the importance of devotion to St. Joseph, placing the following words on the lips of Our Lady:

> Love him [St. Joseph], my child, and make him much loved. If you seek to please me, you cannot do anything that makes me happier than to have a filial devotion to him, to give him honor in your home, and to imitate his virtues. Take him as the patron of your interior and spiritual life, and you will advance greatly towards perfection.[7]

PART III
Prayers to St. Joseph

LITANY OF ST. JOSEPH

Lord, have mercy.   *Lord, have mercy.*
Christ, have mercy.   *Christ, have mercy.*
Lord, have mercy.   *Lord, have mercy.*
Christ, hear us.   *Christ, graciously hear us.*

God, the Father of Heaven,   *have mercy on us.*
God the Son, Redeemer of the world,   *have mercy on us.*
God the Holy Spirit,   *have mercy on us.*
Holy Trinity, One God,   *have mercy on us.*

Holy Mary,   *pray for us.*
Saint Joseph,   *pray for us.*
Noble Offspring of David,   *pray for us.*
Light of Patriarchs,   *pray for us.*
Spouse of the Mother of God,   *pray for us.*
Chaste Guardian of the Virgin,   *pray for us.*
Foster-Father of the Son of God,   *pray for us.*
Zealous Defender of Christ,   *pray for us.*
Head of the Holy Family,   *pray for us.*

Joseph Most Just,   *pray for us.*
Joseph Most Chaste,   *pray for us.*
Joseph Most Prudent,   *pray for us.*
Joseph Most Courageous,   *pray for us.*
Joseph Most Obedient,   *pray for us.*
Joseph Most Faithful,   *pray for us.*

Mirror of Patience,   *pray for us.*
Lover of Poverty,   *pray for us.*
Model of Workmen,   *pray for us.*
Glory of Domestic Life,   *pray for us.*
Guardian of Virgins,   *pray for us.*
Pillar of Families,   *pray for us.*
Comfort of the Afflicted,   *pray for us.*
Hope of the Sick,   *pray for us.*
Patron of the Dying,   *pray for us.*
Terror of Demons,   *pray for us.*
Protector of the Holy Church,   *pray for us.*

Lamb of God, who takes away the sins of the world,

Spare us, O Lord.

Lamb of God, who takes away the sins of the world,

Graciously hear us, O Lord.

Lamb of God, who takes away the sins of the world,

Have mercy on us.

V. He has made him lord of his household,

R. And prince over all his possessions.

Let us pray. *O God, who, in your loving providence, chose Blessed Joseph to be the spouse of your most Holy Mother, grant us the favor of having him for our intercessor in heaven whom on earth we venerate as our protector. You, who live and reign forever and ever. Amen.*

Litany of St. Joseph (Latin)

Kýrie, eléison.	*Kýrie, eléison.*
Christe, eléison.	*Christe, eléison.*
Kýrie, eléison.	*Kýrie, eléison.*
Christe, audi nos.	*Christe, exaudi nos.*
Pater de caelis, Deus.	*Miserére nobis.*
Fili, Redémptor mundi, Deus.	*Miserére nobis.*
Spiritus Sancte, Deus.	*Miserére nobis.*
Sancta Trínitas, unus Deus.	*Miserére nobis.*
Sancta María.	*Ora pro nobis.*
Sancte Ioseph.	*Ora pro nobis.*
Proles David ínclyta.	*Ora pro nobis.*
Lumen Patriarchárum.	*Ora pro nobis.*
Dei Genetrícis Sponse.	*Ora pro nobis.*
Custos pudíce Vírginis.	*Ora pro nobis.*
Filii Dei nutrície.	*Ora pro nobis.*
Christi defénsor sédule.	*Ora pro nobis.*
Almae Famíliae praeses.	*Ora pro nobis.*
Ioseph iustíssime.	*Ora pro nobis.*
Ioseph castíssime.	*Ora pro nobis.*

Ioseph prudentíssime.	*Ora pro nobis.*
Ioseph fortissíme.	*Ora pro nobis.*
Ioseph oboedientíssime.	*Ora pro nobis.*
Ioseph fidelíssime.	*Ora pro nobis.*
Spéculum patiéntiae.	*Ora pro nobis.*
Amátor paupertátis.	*Ora pro nobis.*
Exémplar opíficum.	*Ora pro nobis.*
Doménsticae vitae decus.	*Ora pro nobis.*
Custos vírginum.	*Ora pro nobis.*
Familiárum cólumen.	*Ora pro nobis.*
Solátium miserórum.	*Ora pro nobis.*
Spes aegrotántium.	*Ora pro nobis.*
Patrónc moriéntium.	*Ora pro nobis.*
Terror daémonum.	*Ora pro nobis.*
Protéctor sanctae Ecclésiae.	*Ora pro nobis.*

Agnus Dei, qui tollis peccáta mundi. *Parce nobis, Dómine.*

Agnus Dei, qui tollis peccáta mundi. *Exáudi nobis, Dómine.*

Agnus Dei, qui tollis peccáta mundi. *Miserére nobis.*

Constítuit eum dóminum domus suae. *Et príncipem omnis possessiónis suae.*

Orémus: *Deus, qui in ineffábili providéntia beátum Ioseph sanctíssimae Genetrícis tuae Sponsum elígere dignátus es, praesta, quaésumus, ut quem protectórem venerámur in terris, intercessórem habére mereámur in caelis: Qui vivis et regnas in saécula saeculórum. Amen.*

Acts of Consecration to St. Joseph

Act of Consecration to St. Joseph

O Glorious Patriarch and Patron of the Church! O Virgin Spouse of the Virgin Mother of God! O Guardian and Virginal Father of the Word Incarnate! In the presence of Jesus and Mary, I choose you this day to be my father, my guardian, and my protector.

O great St. Joseph, whom God has made the Head of the Holy Family, accept me, I beseech you, though utterly unworthy, to be a member of your "Holy House." Present me to your Immaculate Spouse; ask her also to adopt me as her child. With her, pray that I may constantly think of Jesus, and serve him faithfully to the end of my life. O Terror of Demons, increase in me virtue, protect me from the evil one, and help me not to offend God in any way.

O my Spiritual Father, I hereby consecrate myself to you. In faithful imitation of Jesus and Mary, I place myself and all my concerns under your care and protection. To you, after Jesus and Mary, I consecrate my body and soul, with all their faculties, my spiritual growth, my home, and all my affairs and undertakings. Forsake me not, but adopt me as a servant and child of the Holy Family. Watch over me at all times, but especially at the hour of my death. Console and strengthen me with the presence of Jesus and Mary so that, with you, I may praise and adore the Holy Trinity for all eternity. Amen.

Act of Consecration to St. Joseph
by Fr. Donald Calloway, MIC

On this day, before the great multitude of heavenly witnesses, I, _____, a repentant sinner, consecrate myself, body and soul, to you, St. Joseph.

I turn to you as my spiritual father and place my life and my salvation into your hands. Confident in your goodness, I place myself under your paternal cloak and ask you to protect me from the world, the flesh, and the devil.

Saint Joseph, you are the virginal husband of the Mother of God! Help me to love her with tender affection and filial devotion. Mary is my spiritual mother and the surest, fastest, and easiest way to Jesus. Keep me close to her and, together with her, bring me closer to Jesus.

Never depart from me, St. Joseph. Nourish me with the Bread of Life, instruct me in the wisdom of the saints, help me carry my cross, and keep me always in the Catholic Church. When I die, take me to the Kingdom of Heaven to see Jesus and Mary.

From this day onward, I will never forget you. I will speak of you often, spend time with you in prayer and, with your help, earnestly strive to sin no more. Should I fall, help me to repent and go to Confession. Should I go astray, guide me back to the truth.

Before heaven and earth, my soul cries out: Praise to the Holy Trinity who has made you prince over all their possessions! Praise to the Virgin Mary who loves you and longs to see you loved! Praise to you, my spiritual father, the great St. Joseph!

I give everything to you, St. Joseph. Take me as your own. I am yours. Amen!

Act of Consecration to St. Joseph
by Fr. Donald Calloway, MIC

I, _____, a child of God, take you, St. Joseph, to be my spiritual father. I am confident that Jesus and Mary have led me to you; to know you, to love you, and to be totally consecrated to you.

Therefore, having come to know and love you, I consecrate myself entirely to you, St. Joseph. I want you in my life; I need you in my life. Take me as your spiritual child, O great St. Joseph! I desire to hold nothing back from your protective fatherhood.

As the husband of Mary, you provided for my spiritual mother. Thank you for always being faithful to her. Thank you for loving her and giving your entire life for her service.

As the virginal father of Jesus, you cared for my Lord and protected him from evil men. Thank you for guarding the life of my Savior. Thanks to you, Jesus was able to shed his blood for me on the Cross. Thanks to you, St. Joseph, I have hope of everlasting life in heaven.

As my spiritual father, I know that you will guide and protect me, too. Please instruct me in the ways of prayer, virtue, and holiness. I want to be like you, St. Joseph. I want to be pure, humble, loving, and merciful.

Now that I am yours and you are mine, I promise never to forget you. I know that you will never forget me, and this gives me boundless joy! I am loved by St. Joseph! I belong to St. Joseph!

Praise to the Holy Trinity who has blessed you and raised you to be the greatest saint after Mary. Praise to the Virgin who loves you and wants souls to love you. Praise to you, St. Joseph, my father, my guardian, and my all! Amen!

Act of Consecration to St. Joseph
by St. Peter Julian Eymard

I consecrate myself to you, good St. Joseph, as my spiritual father. I choose you to rule my soul and to teach me the interior life, the life hidden away with Jesus, Mary, and yourself.

Above all, I want to imitate the humble silence with which you shrouded Jesus and Mary. For me everything lies in that — self-abnegation like our Lord in his hidden life, making the world forget me by my silence and my practice of virtue.

I consecrate myself to you as my guide and model in all my

duties so that I may learn to fulfill them with meekness and humility: with meekness toward my brethren, my neighbor, and all with whom I come in contact; with humility toward myself and simplicity before God.

I choose you, good saint, as my counselor, my confidant, my protector in all my difficulties and trials. I do not ask to be spared crosses and sufferings, but only from self-love which might take away their value by making me vain about them.

I choose you as my protector. Be my father as you were the father of the Holy Family at Nazareth. Be my guide; be my protector. I do not ask for temporal goods, greatness, or power. I ask only that I serve with fidelity and devotedness my divine King.

I shall honor, love, and serve you with Mary, my mother, and never shall I separate her name from yours.

O Jesus, give me Joseph for a father as you have given me Mary as a mother. Fill me with devotion, confidence, and filial love. Listen to my prayer. I know that you will. Already I feel more devout, more full of hope and confidence in good St. Joseph, your foster father and my spiritual father. Amen.

Act of Consecration to St. Joseph
by St. Alphonsus Liguori

O Holy Patriarch, I rejoice with you at the exalted dignity by which you were deemed worthy to act as father to Jesus, to give him orders and to be obeyed by him whom heaven and earth obey.

O great saint, as you were served by God, I too wish to be taken into your service. I choose you, after Mary, to be my chief advocate and protector.

I promise to honor you every day by some special act of devotion and by placing myself under your daily protection.

By that sweet company which Jesus and Mary gave you in your lifetime, protect me all through life, so that I may never separate myself from my God by losing his grace.

My dear St. Joseph, pray to Jesus for me. Certainly, he can never refuse you anything, as he obeyed all your orders while on earth. Tell him to detach me from all creatures and from myself, to inflame me with his holy love, and then to do with me what he pleases.

By that assistance which Jesus and Mary gave you at death, I beg of you to protect me in a special way at the hour of my death, so that dying assisted by you, in the company of Jesus and Mary, I may go to thank you in paradise and, in your company, to praise my God for all eternity. Amen.

Act of Consecration to St. Joseph
by St. Bernardine of Siena

O my beloved St. Joseph, adopt me as thy child. Take charge of my salvation; watch over me day and night; preserve me from the occasions of sin; obtain for me purity of body. Through thy intercession with Jesus, grant me a spirit of sacrifice, humility, self-denial, burning love for Jesus in the Blessed Sacrament, and a sweet and tender love for Mary, my mother. Saint Joseph, be with me living, be with me dying, and obtain for me a favorable judgment from Jesus, my merciful Savior. Amen.

Daily Acts of Consecration to St. Joseph

Daily Act of Consecration to St. Joseph

My Father and my Guardian, I give myself entirely to you, and to show my devotion to you, I consecrate to you this day my eyes, my ears, my mouth, my heart, my whole being without reserve. Wherefore, O good Father, since I am your own, keep me and guard me as your property and possession. Amen.

Daily Act of Consecration to St. Joseph

O dearest St. Joseph, I consecrate myself to your honor and give myself to you, that you may always be my father, my protector, and my guide in the way of salvation. Obtain for me a greater purity of heart and fervent love of the interior life. After your example, may I do all my actions for the greater glory of God, in union with the Sacred Heart of Jesus and the Immaculate Heart of Mary. O Blessed St. Joseph, pray for me, that I may share in the peace and joy of your holy death. Amen.

Daily Act of Consecration to St. Joseph
by Fr. Donald Calloway, MIC

Saint Joseph, spouse of Mary, virginal father of Jesus, and my spiritual father, I consecrate myself entirely to you. I lovingly embrace your fatherhood and take refuge under your paternal cloak. Help me to pray and be virtuous today. Instruct me in the wisdom of the saints, protect me from the snares of the enemy, and keep me from sinning. Should I take my last breath today, be by my side, and take me to heaven to be with Jesus and Mary. Amen.

Prayers to St. Joseph

Memorare to St. Joseph

Remember, O Most Chaste Spouse of the Virgin Mary, that never was it known that anyone who fled to thy protection, implored thy help, or sought thy intercession was left unaided.

Inspired by this confidence, I fly unto you, my spiritual father, and beg your protection. O Foster Father of the Redeemer, despise not my petitions, but in your goodness hear and answer me. Amen.

Prayer of St. Louis de Montfort

Hail Joseph the just, wisdom is with you; blessed are you among all men and blessed is Jesus, the fruit of Mary, your faithful spouse.

Holy Joseph, worthy foster-father of Jesus Christ, pray for us sinners and obtain divine wisdom for us from God, now and at the hour of our death. Amen.

Prayer of Blessed William Joseph Chaminade

O chaste spouse of the most pure and most holy of creatures, how happy you must be for having found such favor and grace before the Eternal Father, who gave his Son; before the Son who made you the tutor of his sacred humanity; before the Holy Spirit who entrusted his spouse to you so that you could be like the cherubim who guarded the fruit of life in the garden of Eden. How happy and blessed are they whom you love and whom you take under your protection!

O faithful guardian of the Mother of God, keep those who honor you amid the trials and joys of this life. Lovable tutor of Jesus, help your servants in the dangers and difficulties of their exile; may they feel the effects of your love. Obtain for them devotion to your spouse, fidelity to your Son, unfailing respect for the Eternal Father who reigns with the Holy Spirit through endless ages. Amen.

Prayer of Pope Leo XIII
(to be prayed after the rosary in October)

To you, O Blessed Joseph, we have recourse in our affliction, and having implored the help of your most holy spouse, we now, with hearts filled with confidence, earnestly beg you to take us under your protection. Through that sacred bond of charity which united you to the Immaculate Virgin Mother of God, and by that fatherly love with which you embraced the Child Jesus, we humbly beg you to look graciously upon the beloved inheritance which Jesus Christ purchased by his blood, and to aid us in our necessities with your power and strength.

Defend, O most watchful guardian of the Holy Family, the chosen children of Jesus Christ. Keep from us, O most loving father, all blight of error and corruption. Aid us from on high, most valiant defender, in this conflict with the powers of darkness. And just as you once saved the Child Jesus from mortal danger, so now defend God's Holy Church from the snares of the enemy and from all adversity. Shield us by your constant protection, so that, supported by your example and strengthened by your help, we may be able to live a virtuous life, die a happy death, and obtain everlasting bliss in heaven. Amen.

Prayer of St. Pope Pius X to St. Joseph the Worker

O glorious St. Joseph, model of all who labor, obtain for me the grace to work in the spirit of penance in expiation for my numberless sins; preferring devotion to duty to my inclinations; to work with joy and gratitude, regarding it as an honor to develop and employ by work the gifts which I have received from God; to work with order, peace, patience, and moderation, without ever recoiling before weariness and difficulties; to work, especially, with a pure intention and detached from myself, ever having death before my eyes and the account which I must give for time lost, for talents unused, for good omitted, and for vain satisfaction in success, so fatal to the work of God. Amen.

Prayer of St. Pope John XXIII

O St. Joseph, guardian of Jesus, chaste spouse of Mary, you who passed your life in the perfect fulfillment of duty, sustaining the Holy Family of Nazareth with the work of your hands, kindly keep those who with total trust now come to you. You know their aspirations, their miseries, and their hopes. They come to you because they know that you understand and protect them. You, too, have known trial, toil, and weariness. But even in the midst of worries about the material life, your soul was filled with profound peace, and it exulted in unerring joy through intimacy with the Son of God Who was entrusted to you, and with Mary, his most sweet mother. May those whom you protect understand they are not alone in their toil, but show them how to discover Jesus at their side, to receive him with grace, to guard him faithfully, as you have done. And with your prayers obtain that in every family, in every factory, in every workshop, wherever a Christian works, all may be satisfied in charity, in patience, in justice, in seeking righteousness, so that abundant gifts may shower upon them from heaven. Amen.

Prayer of St. Francis de Sales

Glorious St. Joseph, spouse of the Virgin Mary, we beseech you through the Heart of Jesus Christ, grant to us your fatherly protection.

O you whose power reaches all our necessities and who knows how to make possible the most impossible things, open your fatherly eyes to the needs of your children. In the confusion and pain which press upon us, we have recourse to you with confidence.

Deign to take beneath your charitable guidance this important and difficult affair, the cause of our worries, and make that its happy outcome serve for the glory of God and the good of his devoted servants. Amen.

Prayer of St. John Paul II for the Solemnity of St. Joseph (March 19)

St. Joseph, Spouse of the Virgin Mother of God, teach us unceasingly all the divine truth and all the human dignity contained in the vocation of spouses and parents!

St. Joseph, obtain from God that we may cooperate, with constancy, with the grace of the great sacrament in which man and woman promise each other love, fidelity, and conjugal integrity till death!

St. Joseph, man of justice, teach us responsible love towards those whom God entrusts to us in a special way: love between spouses and love between parents and those to whom they give life! Teach us responsibility towards every life, from the first moment of its conception to its last instant on this earth. Teach us a great respect for the gift of life. Teach us to adore deeply the Creator, Father, and Giver of life.

St. Joseph, Patron of human work, assist us in all work, in that vocation of man on earth. Teach us to resolve the difficult problems connected with work in the life of each generation, beginning with the young, and in the life of society.

St. Joseph, Protector of the Church, today, on your solemnity, we pray to God with these words: "Almighty God, who chose to entrust the beginnings of our redemption to the loving care of St. Joseph, by his intercession grant that your Church may cooperate faithfully in the fulfillment of the work of salvation." Amen.

Prayer of St. Bernardine of Siena

Remember us, St. Joseph, and plead for us to your foster-child. Ask your most holy bride, the Virgin Mary, to look kindly upon us, since she is the mother of him who with the Father and the Holy Spirit lives and reigns eternally. Amen.

Prayer of St. Peter Julian Eymard

O glorious St. Joseph, you who did faithfully obey the law of God, your heart was pierced at the sight of the Precious Blood that was shed by the infant Savior during his circumcision, but the name of Jesus gave you new life and filled you with quiet joy.

By this sorrow and this joy, obtain for us the grace to be freed from all sin during life, and to die rejoicing, with the holy name of Jesus in our hearts and on our lips. Amen.

Prayer of Blessed Bartolo Longo

Prostrate at your feet, O great saint, I venerate you as the Father of my Lord and my God. You are the Head of the Holy Family, and a cause of joy and delight to the Holy Trinity. What a glory for you to be the Father of a Son who is the Only Begotten of God! What a blessing to know that you are a father to us and that we are your children. Yes, we are your children because we are brothers and sisters of Jesus Christ, who wanted to be called your Son.

As your children, we have a right to the tenderness and goodness of your paternal heart. Accept us therefore! Take us under your protection! Teach us to love patience, prudence, kindness, modesty, and purity. Be our refuge and solace in all our pains, in all our needs, both now and at the hour of our death. Amen.

Prayer of Blessed Bartolo Longo

Saint Joseph, Vicar of the Holy Spirit in fulfilling the duties of your wonderful marriage with Mary, introduce the Holy Spirit to my will in order to ignite it with God's holy love. Present my will to the Most Holy Trinity so that my desires may always be at God's disposal. Offer my heart to God so that He may dwell it in as on a throne of love and mercy. Present the movements of my soul and all the affections of my heart to God so that through your intercession I will always be faithful to the grace and inspirations of the Holy Spirit. Amen.

Prayer of St. Alphonsus Liguori for a Happy Death

St. Joseph, by that assistance which Jesus and Mary gave you at death, I beg you to protect me in a special way at the hour of my death, so that dying assisted by you, in the company of Jesus and Mary, I may go to thank you in heaven, and in your company sing God's praises for all eternity. Amen.

Praises of St. Joseph by St. John Eudes

Hail Joseph, image of God the Father.
Hail Joseph, father of God the Son.
Hail Joseph, temple of the Holy Spirit.
Hail Joseph, beloved of the Most Holy Trinity.
Hail Joseph, most faithful coadjutor of the great counsel.
Hail Joseph, most worthy spouse of the Virgin Mary.
Hail Joseph, father of all the faithful.
Hail Joseph, guardian of all those who have embraced holy virginity.
Hail Joseph, faithful observer of holy silence.
Hail Joseph, lover of holy poverty.
Hail Joseph, model of meekness and patience.
Hail Joseph, mirror of humility and obedience.
Blessed art thou above all men.
Blessed thine eyes, which have seen the things which thou hast seen.
Blessed thine ears, which have heard the things which thou hast heard.
Blessed thy hands, which have touched and handled the Incarnate Word.
Blessed thine arms, which have borne him who bears all things.
Blessed thy bosom, on which the Son of God fondly rested.
Blessed thy heart, inflamed with burning love.
Blessed be the Eternal Father, who chose thee.

Blessed be the Son, who loved thee.

Blessed be the Holy Spirit, who sanctified thee

Blessed be Mary, thy spouse, who cherished thee as her spouse and
brother.

Blessed be the angel who served thee as a guardian,

And blessed forever be all who love and bless thee. Amen.

Prayer of the Holy Cloak Novena

O Glorious Patriarch St. Joseph, you who were chosen by God above all men to be the earthly head of the most holy of families, I beseech you to accept me within the folds of your holy cloak, that you may become the guardian and custodian of my soul.

From this moment on, I choose you as my father, my protector, my counselor, my patron, and I beseech you to place in your custody my body, my soul, all that I am, all that I possess, my life, and my death.

Look upon me as one of your children; defend me from the treachery of my enemies, invisible or otherwise, assist me at all times in all my necessities; console me in the bitterness of my life, and especially at the hour of my death. Say but one word for me to the Divine Redeemer whom you were deemed worthy to hold in your arms, and to the Blessed Virgin Mary, your most chaste spouse. Request for me those blessings which will lead me to salvation. Include me amongst those who are most dear to you and I shall set forth to prove myself worthy of your special patronage. Amen.

Prayer to St. Joseph, Terror of Demons

Saint Joseph, Terror of Demons, cast your solemn gaze upon the devil and all his minions, and protect us with your mighty staff. You fled through the night to avoid the devil's wicked designs; now with the power of God, smite the demons as they flee from you! Grant special protection, we pray, for children, fathers, families, and the dying. By God's grace, no demon dares approach while you are near, so we beg of you, always be near to us! Amen.

Prayer to St. Joseph for the Salvation of a Soul
by Fr. Donald Calloway, MIC

O wonderful St. Joseph, I earnestly recommend to your care the salvation of _____. Jesus shed his blood for this person; let not the precious blood of our Savior have been shed in vain. Deliver _____ from the snares of the devil, heal _____ from the poison of the world, and, I beg you, do not stop interceding for _____ until the gates of heaven are opened to their soul. Beg your spouse to place _____ under her maternal mantle. While this soul lives on earth, grant them conversion, love of Jesus, Mary, and the Catholic Church, and a return to full participation in the Sacraments. Where else can I turn but to you, my spiritual father? In you I have confidence. In you I have hope. Hear my prayer, my spiritual father, and take away my fears. God will listen to you. Ask him for me for the sake of the love you have for all of us. Amen.

Prayer to St. Joseph for a Soul in Purgatory
by Fr. Donald Calloway, MIC

Saint Joseph, reigning in heaven with Jesus and Mary, intercede for the souls in purgatory. Today, in particular, I ask you to turn your gaze to the soul who is most forgotten in purgatory. This soul longs to see the face of God, O good father. Ask the Holy Trinity to take this soul to the glory of heaven today. Remember me, St. Joseph, when I die. I beg you to be prompt in delivering me from purgatory so that I can see you, Jesus, and Mary face to face. Amen.

Prayer to St. Joseph for Purity
by Fr. Donald Calloway, MIC

Saint Joseph, strong spiritual father, defend me against sins of the flesh. Jesus said: "Blessed are the pure of heart, for they shall see God." Saint Joseph, Terror of Demons, protect me from lust, immoral desires in my heart, and impure actions in my body. Help me not to offend God. Here and now, I chain myself to you and sacrifice everything for the good, the true, and the beautiful. I love you, St. Joseph, and I thank you for being my spiritual father. Amen.

Prayer to the Sleeping St. Joseph

O St. Joseph, you are a man greatly favored by the Most High. The angel of the Lord appeared to you in dreams, while you slept, to warn you and guide you as you cared for the Holy Family. You were both silent and strong, a loyal and courageous protector. Dear St. Joseph, as you rest in the Lord, confident in his absolute power and goodness, look upon me. Please take my need into your heart, dream of it, and present it to your Son *(mention your request)*. Help me then, good St. Joseph, to hear the voice of God, to arise, and to act with love. I praise and thank God with joy. Saint Joseph, I love you. Amen.

Veni, Sancte Spiritus
(Come, Holy Spirit)

Come, Holy Spirit,
send down those beams,
which sweetly flow in silent streams
from Thy bright throne above.

O come, Thou Father of the poor;
O come, Thou source of all our store,
come, fill our hearts with love.

O Thou, of comforters the best,
O Thou, the soul's delightful guest,
the pilgrim's sweet relief.

Rest art Thou in our toil, most sweet
refreshment in the noonday heat;
and solace in our grief.

O blessed Light of life Thou art;
fill with Thy light the inmost heart
of those who hope in Thee.

Without Thy Godhead nothing can,
have any price or worth in man,
nothing can harmless be.

Lord, wash our sinful stains away,
refresh from heaven our barren clay,
our wounds and bruises heal.

To Thy sweet yoke our stiff necks bow,
warm with Thy fire our hearts of snow,
our wandering feet recall.

Grant to Thy faithful, dearest Lord,
whose only hope is Thy sure word,
the sevenfold gifts of grace.

Grant us in life Thy grace that we,
in peace may die and ever be,
in joy before Thy face.
Amen. Alleluia.

APPENDICES

APPENDIX A

How to Make the 33-Day Preparation and Consecration to St. Joseph as a Group

To do the 33-day preparation and consecration as a group, there must be an organizer/leader who sets up six meetings over a period of five to six weeks.

The first thing the organizer/leader must do is pick a consecration date (Day 33). It is highly recommended that the consecration date be a feast day associated with St. Joseph, or a Wednesday, the day traditionally assigned for devotion to St. Joseph. It is very important for you to remember that the consecration date is Day 33. Once the consecration date is selected, the organizer/leader needs to establish the five dates that the group will meet prior to the consecration day (six meetings total).

Here is an example:

CONSECRATION DAY: MARCH 19
(Solemnity of St. Joseph).

1. First group meeting: February 15*
2. Second group meeting: February 22**
3. Third group meeting: March 1
4. Fourth group meeting: March 8
5. Fifth group meeting: March 15
6. Sixth group meeting and Consecration Day: March 19
   *In a leap year, this particular schedule begins on February 16.
   **In a leap year, this particular meeting would be February 23.

Refer to the chart on page 10 to establish a 33-day preparation schedule. You are not limited to the chart, however. Feel free to select any end date that works for your group and schedule your meetings and consecration day accordingly.

Once the dates have been set, the organizer/leader should invite people to participate in the preparation and consecration to

St. Joseph through word-of-mouth, church bulletins, or other ways. People should be given enough time to purchase their own copy of *Consecration to St. Joseph.*

Each participant in the group will need their own copy of *Consecration to St. Joseph.* Everything that is needed for the organizer/leader and the participants is in one book.

It is suggested that each group meeting last between 90-120 minutes. It is recommended that an image or statue of St. Joseph be present at the meetings. The image or statue should be beautiful and not one that depicts St. Joseph as an old man.

Below are the sections of the book that need to be covered in each meeting:

1. First group meeting: Introduction and Day 1.
2. Second group meeting: Days 2-8
3. Third group meeting: Days 9-15
4. Fourth group meeting: Days 16-22
5. Fifth group meeting: Days 23-29
6. Sixth group meeting: Days 30-33 and the Consecration Day

Below is the format to follow for each weekly meeting, as well as discussion questions:

FIRST GROUP MEETING
(Introduction and Day 1)

- The leader welcomes the participants, thanks them for participating in the 33-day preparation and consecration to St. Joseph, and opens by asking everyone to pray together the *Veni, Sancte Spiritus* prayer (page 247) followed by the *Memorare* to St. Joseph (page 240).

- The leader reads aloud pages 1 to 6 from the **Introduction** to *Consecration to St. Joseph.*

- The leader presents the following format to be followed for the group meetings: *Veni, Sancte Spiritus;* **Readings; Discussion Questions; Litany of St. Joseph.**

- The leader reads aloud **Day 1** (page 13).

- The leader reads aloud the following **discussion questions** one at a time and allows the group to share their responses after each:

  1. What has drawn you to participate in this 33-day preparation and consecration to St. Joseph? How did you hear about it?

2. Before reading the *Introduction*, were you aware of the many things God has been doing to draw our attention to St. Joseph? Do you know of any others that were not mentioned?

3. Father Calloway mentioned a few reasons why the Church and the world need St. Joseph today, namely, that the Church and families are under attack, and the world needs to be re-evangelized. Can you think of any other reasons why we need St. Joseph today?

4. What has been your experience of St. Joseph? Has he been a part of your faith journey? Do you believe, as Fr. Calloway states, that now is the time of St. Joseph?

5. Joseph's name means "increase." What do you expect to increase in your life as a result of consecrating yourself to St. Joseph? Are you asking for a particular favor or grace from St. Joseph?

6. The idea of becoming "another Joseph" for Jesus and Mary is fascinating. Do you have any thoughts on this concept?

7. Does anyone have a story about how St. Joseph has helped you, a family member, or a friend?

8. Does anyone have any questions about the format, or anything else, before we pray the Litany of St. Joseph together?

• The leader leads the group in the **Litany of St. Joseph** (page 233).

• The leader closes the meeting and reminds everyone to do the daily readings and prayers in preparation for the next meeting.

SECOND GROUP MEETING
(Days 2-8)

• The leader welcomes the participants and opens by asking everyone to pray the *Veni, Sancte Spiritus* prayer (page 247) followed by the **Prayer of St. Bernardine of Siena** (page 243)

• The leader reminds the participants of some of the topics that they've read since the first group meeting (for example: the Litany of St. Joseph; St. Joseph in relation to each Person of the Holy Trinity; the spiritual fatherhood of St. Joseph; St.

André Bessette and St. Joseph's Oratory in Montreal, Canada; and how St. Joseph is the First Knight of Our Lady).

- The leader reads the following discussion questions aloud and allows the group to share:
  1. Do you like praying the Litany of St. Joseph? Do any of the titles really stand out for you?
  2. Prior to this week's readings, had you ever heard of Fr. Joseph Kentenich and the Schoenstatt Movement? What are your thoughts on the idea of becoming an "apparition of St. Joseph" in the world?
  3. Mary is your spiritual mother, Jesus is your brother, and St. Joseph is your spiritual father. Have you ever thought of St. Joseph as your spiritual father? What appeals to you about relating to St. Joseph as his son/daughter?
  4. Saint Joseph is a representative of the Heavenly Father for us and a model to imitate in our quest for holiness. How do you think St. Joseph is an image of God the Father to us? How is he a model that we can imitate?
  5. When the Second Person of the Holy Trinity took on human nature, he had to learn things from his father, St. Joseph, according to the normal process of human development. Can you think of anything that St. Joseph would have taught Jesus? Why is it important for all children to have a father?
  6. In what ways does St. Joseph spiritually feed, clothe, educate, protect, and correct us?
  7. Do you have a statue or painting of St. Joseph in your home? Have you ever seen an image of St. Joseph that depicts his cloak as a protective shield?
  8. Has anyone ever been to St. Joseph's Oratory in Montreal? If so, tell us about your time there. If not, has anyone visited another shrine or church dedicated to St. Joseph?
  9. Saint Joseph is the First Knight of Our Lady. Have you ever thought of St. Joseph as a knight or a warrior? How would you describe St. Joseph?
  10. The reading from Venerable Mary of Ágreda on the privileges of devotion to St. Joseph is very powerful. Are you experiencing an increase in your relationship to Jesus, Mary, and Joseph after this week's readings?

11. Are there other things from the readings that you want to mention or discuss further?

- The leader reads **Day 8** (page 27) out loud.

- The leader (or multiple people) reads **Delight of Saints** (page 85) out loud.

- The leader reads the following **discussion questions** out loud and allows the group to share in response to each:

    1. Many saints have been devoted to St. Joseph. Are there any names that you were not familiar with in today's reading (see pages 90-91)? Do you know of other saints or blesseds who were devoted to St. Joseph?

    2. Were you aware of the categories of *latria, hyper-dulia, protodulia,* and *dulia* (see page 89)? Why is it important to make such theological distinctions?

    3. Saint Teresa of Avila had great confidence in St. Joseph's intercession. She challenged people to test for themselves the efficacy of St. Joseph's intercession. Saint are bold! Are you willing to give St. Teresa's "challenge" a try?

    4 In recent centuries, many popes have expressed tremendous love for St. Joseph. Of those listed on page 91, do you have a favorite? Do you know any other popes who were devoted to St. Joseph?

    5. Does anyone have any other questions or comments?

- The leader leads the group in the **Litany of St. Joseph** (page 233).

- The leader closes the meeting and reminds everyone to do the daily readings and prayers in preparation for the next meeting.

THIRD GROUP MEETING
(Days 9-15)

- The leader welcomes the participants and opens by asking everyone to pray the *Veni, Sancte Spiritus* prayer (page 247) followed by the **Prayer of Pope Leo XIII** (page 241).

- The leader reminds the participants of some of the topics that were covered since the last meeting (for example: the nobility of St. Joseph; the similarities between the Joseph of the Old Testament and our St. Joseph; the love that Joseph and Mary had for each other in their marriage; the age of St. Joseph; the unique dignity of being the father of Jesus; the virginity of St.

Joseph; and St. Joseph's title "Savior of the Savior.")
- The leader reads the following **discussion questions** aloud and allows the group to share responses to each:
  1. As a descendant of King David, St. Joseph is a member of a royal bloodline. Saint Joseph is greater than all the Old Testament Patriarchs. Is there a person in your life or family history that reflects the goodness and virtues of St. Joseph?
  2. Saints and popes have drawn our attention to the parallels between the Joseph of the Old Testament and the New Testament St. Joseph. What parallels particularly struck you? Can you think of any others?
  3. What are your thoughts on the age of St. Joseph? Do you think St. Joseph was old or young? Have you ever seen an image or statue of St. Joseph that depicts him as young, strong, and full of life? What are your thoughts on the image of St. Joseph on the cover of the book, as well as the commissioned artwork in the book (see pages 311-320).
  4. Did you know about the Feast of the Holy Spouses? Were you aware of the tradition in the Church that posits that St. Joseph was a virgin?
  5. There are many ways to describe the type of fatherhood St. Joseph exercised toward Jesus (for example, foster father, putative father, legal, spiritual, and virgin father). Which is your favorite, and why?
  6. Blessed William Joseph Chaminade described St. Joseph as the "Savior of the Savior." It's a bold title and one only given to St. Joseph. Do you have a story of how St. Joseph came to your aid at a very critical moment in your life? If not, has someone you know related such a story to you?
  7. Were there other things in the readings that you want to mention or discuss?
- The leader reads **Day 15** (page 41) aloud.
- The leader (or multiple people) reads **The Holy House of Loreto** (page 180) aloud.
- The leader reads the following **discussion questions** aloud and allows the group to share responses to each:
  1. What are your thoughts about a husband/father being the head of the family? It's a touchy subject today. However, if a man imitates the example of St.

Joseph, his headship can be a tremendous blessing to the family, as well as society. In what ways do you think men today can be more like St. Joseph in their families?

2. A husband and wife each have unique roles in a family. Can you think of anything that a man, as the head of a family, should do? What should he not do?

3. Serving as head of a family is a role of service and self-sacrifice for the good of others. How might a husband and father be of greater service in a marriage, to his children, and in his role as head of the household?

4. The Holy House of Loreto is one of the most visited places of pilgrimage in the world. Had you ever heard of it? Has anyone in the group ever been to Loreto or known someone who has?

5. The number of saints who have visited the Holy House is impressive. If you were to visit Loreto, is there anything in particular that would be on your mind as you visited and prayed inside the Holy House?

6. Saint Thérèse of Lisieux wrote down her experience of visiting the Holy House, stating that she found it enchanting. In a childlike manner, she touched her rosary to the Holy House as a sign of reverence and devotion. Pilgrims often touch their rosary to holy things associated with Jesus, Mary, and the saints. Have you ever done something similar in another holy place?

7. Does anyone have any other questions or comments?

- The leader leads the group in the **Litany of St. Joseph** (page 233).

- The leader closes the meeting and reminds everyone to do the daily readings and prayers in preparation for the next meeting.

FOURTH GROUP MEETING
(Days 16-22)

- The leader welcomes the participants and opens by asking everyone to pray the *Veni, Sancte Spiritus* prayer (page 247), followed by the **Prayer of Blessed William Joseph Chaminade** (page 240).

- The leader reminds the participants of some of the topics

that were covered since the last meeting (for example: the justice and reverence of St. Joseph; the Santo Anello; the Seven Sorrows and Seven Joys of St. Joseph; Mother Angelica's statement that "Old men don't walk to Egypt"; the obedience of St. Joseph; and St. Joseph's adoration.

- The leader reads the following **discussion questions** aloud and allows the group to share:

    1. The New Testament calls St. Joseph a "just man." Had you ever heard of the three theories regarding St. Joseph's response to Mary's pregnancy? (see pages 142-143). Do you have a favorite?

    2. It's amazing that the holy wedding ring (Santo Anello) still exists! Has anyone in the group ever seen it? If you went on pilgrimage to Italy and were able to see the Santo Anello, what grace would you ask of St. Joseph and Mary? Are there any couples that you would pray for?

    3. The Seven Sorrows and Seven Joys of St. Joseph is a wonderful devotion. Do any of the Seven Sorrows or Seven Joys resonate with you more than the others? Can you think of any other sorrows or joys that St. Joseph might have experienced during his life with Jesus and Mary?

    4. Mother Angelica believed that St. Joseph was young rather than an elderly man. Her pithy statement "Old men don't walk to Egypt" makes a lot of sense. What are your thoughts on Mother Angelica's statement?

    5. God often spoke to St. Joseph in his sleep. Had you ever heard before of the devotion to the "Sleeping St. Joseph"? Do you think you will obtain a "Sleeping St. Joseph" statue and entrust your intentions to the dreams (prayers) of St. Joseph? Do you have any thoughts on the selection from the poem by Charles Péguy (see page 201)?

    6. Saint Joseph never received Holy Communion or worshipped Jesus in the Blessed Sacrament. Yet, with Mary, he was the first adorer of the physical presence of the Son of God. What are your thoughts on this amazing reality?

    7. Do you think St. Joseph accompanied Mary to Elizabeth's house? If so, might he have heard Elizabeth's greeting to Mary and Mary's *Magnificat*? Do you think he stayed with Mary for three months, or do

you think he returned to Nazareth?

8. Had you ever heard of fetal microchimerism? What are your thoughts on this incredible scientific discovery?

9. Were there other things in the readings that you want to mention or discuss?

- The leader reads **Day 22** (page 55) aloud.

- The leader (or multiple people) reads **The Roman Canon** (page 94) aloud.

- The leader reads the following **discussion questions** aloud and allows the group to share:

    1. Blessed Gabriele Allegra stated that St. Joseph had a patience more heroic than Job's. That's quite the statement. In what circumstances or events do you see the virtue of patience in St. Joseph's life?

    2. Do you struggle with the virtue of patience? Many people do. If there is a particular situation or person that constantly causes you to lose your patience, how can imitating St. Joseph and invoking his intercession help you? Are you willing to turn to St. Joseph for help?

    3. Did you know that the Church has four Eucharistic Prayers? Do you know them well enough to have a favorite? Prior to today, do you remember hearing St. Joseph's name during the Mass?

    4. Does your parish have a statue of St. Joseph? What does it look like? How does it depict St. Joseph's age?

    5. It wasn't until 1962 that St. Joseph's name was placed into the prayers of the Mass (the Roman Canon). In 2013, St. Joseph's name was placed in the other Eucharistic Prayers as well. Besides the Mass, are you aware of any cultural traditions that exist in which people honor St. Joseph in a particular way?

    6. Bishop Peter Cule attributed his survival in a Yugoslavian concentration camp to the intercession of St. Joseph. Are you familiar with any other instances in which people have called upon the aid of St. Joseph and received miracles?

    7. Does anyone have any other questions or comments?

- The leader leads the group in the **Litany of St. Joseph** (see page 233).

- The leader closes the meeting and reminds everyone to do the daily readings and prayers in preparation for the next meeting.

FIFTH GROUP MEETING
(Days 23-29)

- The leader welcomes the participants and opens by asking everyone to pray the *Veni, Sancte Spiritus* prayer (page 247), followed by the **Prayer of St. Pope John XXIII** (page 241).

- The leader reminds the participants of some of the topics that were covered in the reading since the last meeting (for example: the poverty of St. Joseph; St. Joseph's Perpetual Adoration; the feast of St. Joseph the Worker; the Miraculous Staircase in New Mexico; the silence of St. Joseph; apparitions of St. Joseph; and the Pious Union of St. Joseph).

- The leader reads the following **discussion questions** aloud and allows the group to share:

  1. Saint Joseph was materially poor, but he had stewardship of the greatest treasure known to man: Jesus. Saint Peter Julian Eymard offers many insights into how St. Joseph, though poor, lived in a state of Perpetual Adoration. Had you ever heard of St. Peter Julian Eymard? What do you think about his statements on St. Joseph's adoration of Jesus?

  2. Work is a way of glorifying God and helping others. Venerable Pope Pius XII established the Feast of St. Joseph the Worker as a response to communism's threat. Can you think of any moral or social issues that St. Joseph, the Model of Workmen, can protect workers and families from today?

  3. We learned that neither St. Teresa of Avila nor St. André Bessette ever buried a statue of St. Joseph to sell a house. Have you ever done this? If so, what happened? Without judging others or being insensitive, what does the group think about such a practice?

  4. Did you know that St. Thérèse of Lisieux and St. Faustina were so devoted to St. Joseph? Both of these holy women placed themselves under the protection of St. Joseph and became great saints. Have you read any of their spiritual writings? Which of these great saints do you have a greater devotion to, or is there another modern saint that you are particularly devoted to?

  5. Saint Joseph came to the aid of religious sisters in New Mexico when they needed a staircase. Had

you heard of the Miraculous Staircase before? Has anyone in the group ever seen it?

6. Venerable Mary of Ágreda, Blessed Anne Catherine Emmerich, and other mystics were given tremendous insights into the life of St. Joseph. In modern times, St. Joseph himself has come in apparitions, such as at Cotignac, France; Knock, Ireland; Zeitoun, Egypt; and Fatima, Portugal. Do you have any thoughts on these apparitions? Is there anything from the alleged apparitions of Our Lady of America, especially regarding St. Joseph's words to Sr. Mary Ephrem, that stands out to you?

7. Were there other things in the readings that you want to mention or discuss?

- The leader reads **Day 29** (page 69) out loud.

- The leader (or multiple people) reads **Votive Masses** (page 203) aloud.

- The leader reads the following **discussion questions** and allows the group to share:

1. When she was pregnant with St. Thérèse, St. Zélie was certain that the child in her womb was a boy. She and her husband intended to name the child after Joseph. Your spiritual father's name is one of the most popular names for boys in the world. Are any of you named Joseph or the female equivalents? Do you have family members with this name?

2. Did you know that St. Joseph saved the life of little Thérèse when she was an infant? The testimony of St. Zélie Martin is incredible and shows the importance of asking St. Joseph for help. Have you or someone you know ever asked St. Joseph to come to the assistance of someone who is very sick or dying?

3. Many people are not aware of it, but Wednesday is the day the Church sets aside to honor St. Joseph. Did you know this? Were you aware of all the other designations for the days of the week listed on page 203. Saint Joseph not only has a day of the week dedicated to him, but he also has his own month: March. Does anyone in the group have a birthday in March? An anniversary?

4. In light of St. Joseph's day of the week being Wednesday, would you consider going to Mass or having a

votive Mass said on a Wednesday in his honor? If you are unable to attend Mass during the week, is there another form of devotion to St. Joseph you might be willing to do on a Wednesday to honor St. Joseph (for example, praying the Litany of St. Joseph, the Seven Sorrows and Seven Joys of St. Joseph, or the Joyful Mysteries of the rosary)?

5. The souls in purgatory are very special to St. Joseph. Have you ever had Masses said for the poor souls, or prayed rosaries to gain indulgences for them? The witness of Blessed Mary of Providence shows us that St. Joseph wants to help the souls in purgatory. Did you know that every hour, at least 6,000 people around the world die? Every day, at least 150,000 people die. Every year, at least 55 million people die. Might you call upon the intercession of St. Joseph more fervently in order to help the souls in purgatory?

6. Does anyone have any other questions or comments?

- The leader leads the group in the **Litany of St. Joseph** (page 233).

- If the group is in agreement, it would be nice to have a celebration at the next meeting after the group consecration prayer is recited. Volunteers who will bring a cake, drinks, and other treats can be assigned.

- The leader closes the meeting, announces that the next meeting will be sooner than all the others, and reminds everyone to do the daily readings and prayers in preparation for the next meeting. The next meeting is in four days, and is also the Consecration Day!

SIXTH GROUP MEETING
(Days 30-33) and Consecration Day

- The leader welcomes the participants and opens by asking everyone to pray the *Veni, Sancte Spiritus* prayer (page 247), followed by the **Prayer of the Holy Cloak Novena** (page 245).

- The leader reminds the participants of some of the topics that were covered since the last meeting (for example: St. Joseph as the Patron of the Dying; the possibility of St. Joseph being sanctified in the womb; his assumption/ascension into heaven; his unique titles "Terror of Demons" and "Patron of the Universal Church").

- The leader reads the following **discussion questions** and allows the group to share:

    1. Have you ever heard of the phrase "memento mori"? Without being morbid, do you think about your own death? Are you ready for death?

    2. Saint Joseph died in the arms of Jesus and Mary. Some saints believe that he was assumed into heaven after the Resurrection of Christ. Do you think he was assumed into heaven? What about that interesting passage from Matthew 27 that states that after the Crucifixion of Jesus many people rose from their tombs and appeared in Jerusalem (see page 210)? Blessed Anne Catherine Emmerich seemed to think that St. Joseph's body was incorrupt and in an undisclosed location in the Holy Land. Do you have any thoughts on this?

    3. Saint Joseph suffered much for Jesus and Mary. What are your thoughts on love being a reason for St. Joseph's death? Do you think God spared St. Joseph from witnessing the Crucifixion because it would have been too much for him to bear?

    4. The title "Terror of Demons" is unique. In what ways do you think St. Joseph frightens demons? In addition to purity and the humble use of authority, what other ways might men imitate St. Joseph and be terrors of demons today?

    5. Had you ever heard of the Dominican Blessed Jean-Joseph Lataste? Blessed Pope Pius IX declared St. Joseph the Patron of the Universal Church due to Blessed Jean-Joseph's sacrificial offering. Do you see St. Joseph as your personal patron?

    6. Today there is great confusion, scandal, and lukewarmness in the Church. How can St. Joseph help us overcome these difficulties? Is there anything in particular that you would like to ask St. Joseph to do for the Church?

    7. Are there other things in the readings that you would like to mention or discuss?

- The leader reads **Day 33** (page 77) aloud.

- The leader reads the following **discussion questions** aloud and allows the group to share responses to each question:

1. Saint Joseph is the "lord of God's household and prince over all His possessions." As the preparation for consecration nears its end, do you have a renewed understanding of the greatness of St. Joseph? Has the 33-day preparation helped you to understand St. Joseph's importance and why you need him in your life?

2. As you prepare to consecrate yourself to St. Joseph, is there anything in particular that you want to ask St. Joseph for? Do you feel closer to St. Joseph now than when you started the 33-day preparation? Has anything changed in your spiritual life since you began the 33-day preparation?

3. Are you ready to become another St. Joseph for Jesus and Mary? Do you think you can put forth your best effort at being an apparition of St. Joseph for the world? Is there anything that you need to re-think in your life that would prohibit you from being more like St. Joseph?

4. How has this small group preparation been for you? Is there anything you would do differently?

5. Are you ready to consecrate yourself to St. Joseph?

6. Does anyone have any other questions or comments?

- The leader leads the group in the **Litany of St. Joseph** (page 233).

- The leader reads **Consecration Day** (page 79) aloud.

- The group should take a look at the various consecration formulas offered on pages 235-239 and agree upon a formula to recite together. If the communal consecration is done in a church, the group should recite the consecration prayer before the tabernacle or in front of a statue/image of St. Joseph. If the consecration is done in another location, it should be recited before a statue/image of St. Joseph as well.

- Everyone together recites an **Act of Consecration to St. Joseph.**

- Congratulations! You are now consecrated to St. Joseph! It is time for you to be an apparition of St. Joseph for the world!

- The leader recommends that everyone read **"After the Con-secration"** on their own at a later time.

Ite ad Ioseph!

APPENDIX B

After the Consecration

I promise to honor thee [St. Joseph] every day by some special act of devotion and by placing myself under thy daily protection.[1]

— St. Alphonsus Liguori

The fruit of consecration to St. Joseph is for you to resemble your spiritual father and become Joseph-like in virtue. The purpose of *Consecration to St. Joseph* is to make you an "apparition of St. Joseph" in the world. People need to see the virtues of St. Joseph in you. Your words and actions should reflect his holiness, purity, love, humility, prayerfulness, and sacrificial spirit.

Additionally, those who have consecrated themselves to St. Joseph are not required to wear an external sign of consecration. You may choose to wear a scapular or a medal, or some other sacramental in honor of St. Joseph, but it is not required. The most important thing to remember is that *you* are the sign.

Now, to prevent the initial fervor of having consecrated yourself to St. Joseph from wearing off, I suggest you do one or all of the items listed below.

1. Recite a daily act of consecration to St. Joseph. (See page 239)
2. Pray to St. Joseph every day. For example, St. Faustina recited an Our Father, Hail Mary, Glory Be, and a *Memorare* to St. Joseph every day.
3. Continue to pray the Litany of St. Joseph on a regular basis. Try to memorize it.
4. On Wednesdays, spend a little more time with St. Joseph than on other days of the week.
5. Practice the Seven Sundays Devotion to St. Joseph. (See pages 157-159)
6. Frequently pray the Joyful Mysteries of the rosary in honor of St. Joseph.
7. Make a pilgrimage to a church or a shrine dedicated to St. Joseph. (See page 283 for some options.) If possible, join me on a pilgrimage. I lead 3-4 pilgrimages a year. You can view my pilgrimages at: www.fathercalloway.com

8. Annually renew your long-form consecration prayer to St. Joseph. You don't necessarily have to re-do the 33-day preparation (though that's not a bad idea).

9. Start a consecration group in your parish, family, diocese, convent, seminary, or religious community. (See page 249 for how to conduct a group program.) It requires little effort and is easy to do. Jesus and Mary will greatly bless you for spreading devotion to St. Joseph. Consecration to St. Joseph launches the first worldwide movement spreading consecration to St. Joseph in the 2,000-year history of Christianity! Be a part of the movement!

10. Pray for the pope to declare a Year of St. Joseph.

11. Pray for the Church to establish a feast in honor of St. Joseph's fatherhood.

Join the Association of Marian Helpers. This is an apostolate of my religious community, the Marian Fathers of the Immaculate Conception. The Marian Fathers were founded in Poland in 1670 by St. Stanislaus Papczyński. Our Founder was very devoted to Our Lady and St. Joseph. Part of the charism of the Marian Fathers is to spread devotion to Our Lady, pray for the souls in purgatory, and be apostles of Divine Mercy. After the Immaculate Conception, St. Joseph is our primary patron. By joining the Association of Marian Helpers, you can help the Marian Fathers spread these devotions and save souls. You will receive many spiritual benefits when you join the Association. To join the Association of Marian Helpers, write, call, or sign up on our website. Below is the information you need in order to become a member:

Phone: 1-800-462-7426
Website: www.marian.org
Mailing address:
Marian Helpers Center
2 Prospect Hill Rd.
Stockbridge, MA 01263

Every day, pray to St. Joseph and seek his protection.[2]

— Blessed Marie-Léonie Paradis

ADDENDUM I

A Meditation for the Solemnity of St. Joseph
Blessed William Joseph Chaminade

The glory of St. Joseph is incomparable; he has no equal in the services he has rendered and in the virtues he has practiced.

Consider that we must not be satisfied merely with receiving the gifts of God; we must make the most of them. For the saints, perfection does not consist in receiving great favors from his goodness but in being faithful to him.

If the glory of the saints is due to their virtue, then Joseph's glory is incomparable, for in his life you will find no virtue that has not some rare quality not found in others but that is his alone.

Picture to yourself the sanctity of all the patriarchs of old, that long line of successive generations which is the mysterious ladder of Jacob, culminating in the person of the Son of God. See how great was the faith of Abraham, the obedience of Isaac, the courage of David, the wisdom of Solomon. After you have formed the highest opinion of these saints, remember that Joseph is at the top of the ladder, at the head of the saints, the kings, the prophets, the patriarchs, that he is more faithful than Abraham, more obedient than Isaac, more generous than David, wiser than Solomon, in a word, as superior in grace as he is close to the source, Jesus, sleeping in his arms. Our Lord Jesus Christ, having come into this world an orphan, that is without a father in the flesh, wanted Joseph to be his foster father in all things. In the genealogical ladder of the patriarchs drawn up by St. Matthew, he wants his sacred humanity, which had no human roots, to rest on the great saint as on the topmost rung.

Leave the Old Testament, look at the New Testament and consider the most dazzling virtues of the saints; he far surpasses them, says St. Bernardine of Siena. To the Doctors he gave the form and model of their preaching, said St. Hilary. He was the first to suffer from the persecution of the martyrs. He was sanctified while in his mother's womb before St. John the Baptist. He was confirmed in grace before all the apostles. He surpassed the virgins in purity. To the anchorites he opened up the deserts of Egypt. He entered into the world in shining innocence like the dawn and he left it like the sun, rising to heaven in body and soul to accompany the triumph of Jesus Christ and to forestall that of Mary.

Now consider the celestial hierarchies; he raises himself above all the blessed spirits. By his integrity, he is an angel; by his office he is an Archangel; by his actions he is a Virtue; by his vocation he is a Domination; by his service he is a Throne; by his knowledge he is a Cherubim; by his love, a Seraphim.

Do not be surprised. He who exercised the authority of the Eternal Father over Jesus Christ, and that of the Holy Spirit over the Blessed Virgin, had to be this holy. His was the power to command the Son and the Mother, that is, this miracle of nature, grace, and glory, who shares with God the government of the world, who sees all creatures subject to her rule, who projects the terror of her name even to the abyss, who is Daughter of the Father, Mother of the Son, Spouse of the Holy Spirit, the honor of heaven, the hope of the earth, the terror of hell. What saint, what angel, what seraph ever had such a holy task, such a glorious empire?

Let us now consider more particularly the virtues he practiced; you will be completely convinced of their excellence.

In the first place, did his purity not have a marvelous and special bearing on the Incarnation of the Word? Did not Joseph's virginity remain sterile so that Mary's might be fruitful? The purity of the virgins in heaven is so eminent that it gives them the right to chant a special canticle, and to follow the Lamb wherever he goes. Yet this virtue merely considers the external glory of Jesus Christ. But the purity of St. Joseph has for immediate object the mystery of the Incarnation. Here is the reason. It was fitting that the Blessed Virgin be married when she became a mother in order to protect her reputation. Now to be Mother of God she had to be a virgin. To be both mother and virgin, her husband also had to be a virgin. Draw the conclusion. The life of Joseph depends on the maternity of the Virgin; the maternity of the Virgin depends on her virginity; her virginity depends on that of Joseph. Therefore, if we link the first to the last, we see that virginity has a special relation to the life of Jesus. So that Jesus can say: "There are only two virgins in the world to whom I owe my life: my mother from whom I was born pure and divine, and Joseph, who remained a virgin so as not to prevent this miracle of grace." The Blessed Virgin can say: "There is only one God and one man to whom I owe the honor of my maternity: my Son who chose me as his mother; my husband, the guardian of my virginity, without whom I should never have been Mother of God." Finally, the world can say: "There are only two persons to whom I owe the birth of my Savior: Mary, who gave the purest blood of her heart to fashion his body; Joseph, who gave up his flesh and blood for the benefit of this holy enterprise."

If we mix roses with lilies, his charity is just as pronounced as his virginity.

Love takes on many aspects depending on the diversity of the subject. A servant's love is inferior to that of a friend; a friend's to that of a child. The love of a father and husband ranks above these. Now what is the love of the saints for the Son of God? Nothing more than the love of servants, of friends, of children, and of adopted brothers. But St. Joseph was given the heart of a father toward Jesus Christ, the heart of a husband towards the mother. The Holy Spirit, who guided Mary and Joseph, entrusted the Blessed Virgin to the fidelity of Joseph. Then he formed the sacred humanity of the Son of God from Mary's flesh and planted in Joseph's heart a fatherly love toward the child that was to be born. He did this because Joseph was to discharge all the duties of a father towards him; he would raise him and care for him during his childhood. Joseph's love for Jesus must have been that of a father. Supernatural? No, for the love of a father for his son is natural. It is best to call it both natural and supernatural. It is natural if I consider the person. An instinctive love, for fathers instinctively love their children. An instinct not guided by nature but by grace; a very special grace, very much akin to the maternal love which the holy Fathers praise so highly in the Blessed Virgin.

If we wish to combine the ardor of his love to the insights of his wisdom, we can simply say that St. Joseph governed not the mystical body of the Church as did St. Peter, but rather its Head; not the heavens, as do the wise heavenly spirits, but the God of heaven and earth. With the Holy Spirit, he was charged with the guidance of the Incarnate Word; the Holy Spirit took charge of the interior direction and St. Joseph of the external. Saint Joseph's leadership therefore, had to conform itself to that of the Holy Spirit. It had to be perfect and to harmonize with a rare and extraordinary wisdom. What a wonderful situation! Of course God took extraordinary care of his Son and watched over him through a decree of his Providence that was very much out of the ordinary. Yet this Father, who was so zealously protective of his Son, is convinced that he has provided sufficiently for his safety by confiding him to St. Joseph, and relying on his solicitude. He who appoints ten angels to be the guardians of men wants one man to be the guardian angel of the Word. Must this divine Child be taken to Egypt? He will go in the arms of Joseph. Must he be brought back from exile? He will be led back by Joseph. Must he go to the Temple of Jerusalem? He will be accompanied by Joseph. Must he dwell in Nazareth? He will live in Joseph's house and under his authority. Must he be clothed, fed and given all the necessities? All this will be provided by Joseph. We admire the wisdom of the Creator who provides food for the smallest creatures. When we see the fields covered with crops and refreshed by the springs of the earth, we cannot thank sufficiently the Providence of this good head of the family who gives such delicious food to his children. Why do we not admire St. Joseph who feeds the Creator of men and angels? Is it less honorable to nourish the Son of God than the children of men? To command the Creator than to command creatures? O loving Providence, it is evident that you take pleasure in yielding to your friends, and to do through them more than you do on your own.

If the wisdom of St. Joseph was put to such good use in directing the Incarnate Word, the patience he displayed in vexing situations is no less glorious. For every step he took, every attention he lavished, every drop of sweat he shed, all the sufferings he endured and all the pains he took were directed solely to the life of Jesus on which the fate of all men depended. If there are men who suffered more than he, none did so for such a worthy cause.

The anchorites practiced great abstinence to safeguard the life of their souls. But Joseph took the bread from his own mouth to give it to Jesus and Mary. The martyrs suffered greatly for the name of Jesus; but Joseph exposed his life for Jesus' sake. To give life to someone is the greatest of all gifts. To save a life is the next. Who gave life to Jesus? It was Mary. Who saved his life? It was Joseph. We can find an infinite number of murderers who are guilty of his death; there is no need to descend to hell to find them. Ask St. Paul who persecuted him. Saint Peter who denied him. Ask all the saints who put him to death. It is I; it is you who are telling me this, we have all dipped our hands into the blood of this Lamb.

But if we ask, who saved his life? Be silent, patriarchs, be silent, prophets, be silent apostles, confessors, and martyrs. Let St. Joseph speak, for this honor is his alone; he alone is the savior of his Savior.

If he sought so zealously to preserve his life, he was no less eager to promote his glory. If we forget for the moment everything that he has in common with the others, St. Joseph had the honor of making the name of Jesus known, of manifesting it to men. The Eternal Father had chosen this name from all eternity, the angel had revealed it to the Virgin, but St. Joseph was the first to reveal it. It is in his capacity as father that he first pronounces the adorable name of Jesus, this name which the Son of God prized more than his life, which he bought at the price of his blood, which he made an object of fear to the devils, of adoration to the angels, of love and salvation to all mortals.

> O great saint, whatever honor we may give this holy name, we are but the echo of your own voice. We learned it from you. If the apostles spread its sound throughout the world, you gave them the example. Joseph carried Jesus Christ first to Egypt, then to Judea and so traced for us the path of the apostles who preached his name to the Jews and to the Gentiles.[1]

— St. Hilary of Poitiers

Saint Paulinus of Nola would have considered it a happy privilege to kiss the dust under the feet of Jesus Christ:

> Oh, who will give me, a puny creature, the grace to purify my lips with chaste fire, to touch my tongue to the burning coal of the seraphim, and so to make me worthy to kiss but the heel of Jesus Christ, respectfully to bow my head till it touch his feet.[2]

But how much happier was St. Joseph who bore him in his arms and pressed him to his heart? Can we imagine a more excellent prayer than that of this great saint who was always at the feet of the ark of the covenant and before the substantial image of the Eternal Father? What a sublime vision to have the Son of God ever before his eyes! Ecstasy most rare! Rapture most marvelous! O most intimate familiarity to be always with God, to speak only to God, to work, to rest, to converse in the company and presence of God! How many times did the happy tutor of the Child Jesus, like a chaste bee, gather the nectar of pure devotion from this beautiful flower of Jesse? How many times did he, like the dove, hide in the heart of this rock? How many times did he, like the lone sparrow, nestle on the roof of that holy temple of the Divinity, contemplating this divine Child sleeping in his arms, and thinking of his eternal repose in the bosom of the heavenly Father? "Rest, O Incarnate Word," he said, "you who give

---

[1] St. Hilary of Poitiers, Commentarius in Matthacum, Chapter 2. Patrologia Latina 9, 924.
[2] St. Paulinus of Nola, *Epistula* 23, No. 38. *Patrologia Latina* 61, 282a.

sleep to all creatures, who cause joy and the sweetness of peace to flow like an abundant stream into the hearts of men." He gazed on his adorable leader who encompassed all the heavenly treasures. He took his little hands and, raising them to heaven, he said: "Stars of heaven, behold the hands which created you; O Sun, behold the arm that drew you out of nothingness." Pondering the divine perfections, he exclaimed: "How lovable you are O Son of the living God! If only men could know you! O you mortals! Open your eyes; behold your treasure, your salvation, your ransom, your life, and your all!"

How can we not admire the happiness of this great saint? How can we not admit that he is incomparable in his virtues, that he has not his equal? When he suffers it is to save the life of Jesus. When he works it is to sustain the life of Jesus. When he talks, it is with Jesus. When Moses spoke with the angel, his forehead shone so brilliantly that he blinded those that looked on him. A single vision made St. Paul into an apostle. A single word of the Gospel carried the Hilarions and the Anthonys to the highest perfection. What of Joseph, then, who spent his life with Jesus, who deserved to die in the arms of his Savior and to be buried by him whose cradle he had made?

You can now form some idea of the respect which you owe this admirable saint and the confidence you should have in his protection. For if he has uncommon merit, he will also have uncommon power and influence with God. Some saints, say the angelic Doctor [St. Thomas Aquinas], have received from God the power to help us in some specific need. But the influence of St. Joseph knows no limit. His power is universal and extends to all sorts of needs and to all kinds of circumstances. All who have recourse to him with holy dispositions can be sure of his assistance and paternal protection. All men, whatever be their state, find in him a motive for personal trust: the highborn, because he is the grandson of Patriarchs and Kings; the workers and the poor, because he did not despise their condition nor did he refuse to work; the virgins, because he is the guardian of the Blessed Virgin; married couples, because he is the head of the most holy and happy family that ever was; children, because he guided the childhood of Jesus.

Prepare yourself to reap the fruits of this intercession. Take him for your special protector, if you have not already done so. Ask him to number you among his children, since he is the adoptive father of Jesus. Let him explain the running of his household, he who is the head of the Holy Family of the Son of God. Make him responsible for the protection of your person, he who saved the life of his Savior. May he take charge of the affair of your salvation. Just as he led the Son of God in his travels, may he be your guide on the voyage of this life until you arrive at the haven of eternal happiness.

Taken, with slight editing, from William Joseph Chaminade, *Marian Writings*, vol. 1, ed. J.B. Armbruster, SM, trans. Henry Bradly, SM, and Joseph H. Roy, SM (Dayton, OH: Marianist Resources Commission, 1980), 229-236. Used with permission.

The Predestination of St. Joseph and His Eminent Sanctity

Fr. Reginald Garrigou-Lagrange, OP

"He that is lesser among you all, he is the greater."

— Lk 9:48

Saint Joseph's Preeminence Over the Other Saints

The opinion that St. Joseph is the greatest of the saints after Our Lady is one which is becoming daily more commonly held in the Church. We do not hesitate to look on the humble carpenter as higher in grace and eternal glory than the patriarchs and the greatest of the prophets — than St. John the Baptist, the apostles, the martyrs, and the great doctors of the Church. He who is least in the depth of his humility is, because of the interconnection of the virtues, the greatest in the height of his charity: "He that is lesser among you all, he is the greater."

Saint Joseph's pre-eminence was taught by Jean Gerson[3] and St. Bernardine of Siena.[4] It became more and more common in the course of the 16th century. It was admitted by St. Teresa of Avila, by the Dominican Isidore de Isolanis, who appears to have written the first treatise on St. Joseph,[5] by St. Francis de Sales, by Francisco

---

[3] Gerson, *Sermo in Nativitatem Virginis Mariae*, IVa consideration.
[4] St. Bernardine of Siena, *Sermo I de S. Joseph*, c. iii, *Opera*, (Lyon, France: 1960), t. IV, 254.
[5] Isidore de Isolanis, *Summa de donis S. Joseph*, ann. 1522. There is a new edition by Fr. Berthier (Rome, 1897).

Suarez, SJ,[6] and later by St. Alphonsus Liguori,[7] Sauve,[8] Cardinal Lepicier,[9] and Msgr. Sinibaldi;[10] it is very ably treated of in the article "Joseph" in the Dict. de Theol. Cath. by M.A. Michel.

The doctrine of St. Joseph's pre-eminence received the approval of Leo XIII in his encyclical *Quamquam pluries* (August 15, 1889).

> The dignity of the Mother of God is so elevated that there can be no higher created one. But since St. Joseph was united to the Blessed Virgin by the conjugal bond, there is no doubt that he approached nearer than any other to that super-eminent dignity of hers by which the Mother of God surpasses all created natures. Conjugal union is the greatest of all; by its very nature it is accompanied by a reciprocal communication of the goods of the spouses. If then God gave St. Joseph to Mary to be her spouse he certainly did not give him merely as a companion in life, a witness of her virginity, a guardian of her honor, but he made him also participate by the conjugal bond in the eminent dignity which was hers.[11]

The multitude of Christians in all succeeding generations are committed to him in a real though hidden manner. This idea is expressed in the litany approved by the Church:

St. Joseph, illustrious descendant of David
Light of the Patriarchs
Spouse of the Mother of God
Guardian of the Virgin
Foster-father of the Son of God
Vigilant defender of Christ
Head of the Holy Family
Joseph most just
Joseph most chaste
Joseph most prudent
Joseph most strong
Joseph most obedient
Joseph most faithful
Mirror of patience
Lover of poverty
Model of workers

---

[6] Francisco Suarez, *In Summam S. Thomae*, IIIa, q. 29, disp. 8, sect. 1.
[7] St. Alphonsus Liguori, *Sermone di S. Giuseppe*, Discorsi Morali (Naples, 1841).
[8] Sauve, *Saint Joseph Intime* (Paris, 1920).
[9] Cardinal Lepicier, *Tractatus de Sancto Joseph* (Paris, 1908).
[10] Msgr. Sinibaldi, *La Grandezza di San Giuseppe* (Rome, 1927), 36ff.
[11] Pope Leo XIII, *Quamquam Pluries* (August 15, 1889).

Glory of domestic life
Guardian of virgins
Support of families
Consolation of the afflicted
Hope of the sick
Patron of the dying
Terror of demons
Protector of the Holy Church

He is the greatest after Mary!

The Reason for St. Joseph's Preeminence

What is the justification of this doctrine which has been more and more accepted in the course of five centuries? The principle invoked more or less explicitly by St. Bernard, St. Bernardine of Siena, Isidore de Isolanis, Francisco Suarez, and more recent authors is the one, simple and sublime, formulated by St. Thomas when treating of the fullness of grace in Jesus and of holiness in Mary: "An exceptional divine mission calls for a corresponding degree of grace."

This principle explains why the holy soul of Jesus, being united personally to the Word, the source of all grace, received the absolute fullness of grace. It explains also why Mary, called to be the Mother of God, received from the instant of her conception an initial fullness of grace which was greater than the initial fullness of all the saints together; since she was nearer than any other to the source of grace she drew grace more abundantly. It explains also why the apostles who were nearer to Our Blessed Lord than the saints who followed them had more perfect knowledge of the mysteries of faith. To preach the Gospel infallibly to the world they received at Pentecost the gift of a most eminent, most enlightened, and most firm faith as the principle of their apostolate.

The same truth explains St. Joseph's pre-eminence. To understand it we must add one remark: all works which are to be referred immediately to God himself are perfect. The work of creation, for example, which proceeded entirely and directly from the hand of God was perfect. The same must be said of his great servants, whom he has chosen exceptionally and immediately — not through a human instrument — to restore the order disturbed by sin. God does not choose as men do. Men often choose incompetent officials for the highest posts. But those whom God himself chooses directly and immediately to be his exceptional ministers in the work of redemption receive from him grace proportionate to their vocation. This was the case with St. Joseph. He must have received a relative fullness of grace proportionate to his mission since he was chosen not by men nor by any creature but by God himself and by God alone to fulfill a mission unique in the world. We cannot say at what precise moment St. Joseph's sanctification took place. But we can say that, from the time of his marriage to Our Lady, he was confirmed in grace, because of his special mission.[12]

To What Order Does St. Joseph's Exceptional Mission Belong?

Saint Joseph's mission is evidently higher than the order of nature — even by angelic nature. But is it simply of the order of grace, as were that of St. John the Baptist who prepared the way of salvation, and that the apostles had in the Church for the sanctification of souls, and that more particular mission of the founders of religious orders? If we examine the question carefully we shall see that St. Joseph's mission surpassed the order of grace. It borders, by its term, on the hypostatic order, which is constituted by the mystery of the Incarnation. But it is necessary to avoid both exaggeration and understatement in this matter.

Mary's unique mission, her divine motherhood, has its term in the hypostatic order. So also, in a sense, St. Joseph's hidden mission. This is the teaching of many saints and other writers. Saint Bernard says of St. Joseph: "He is the faithful and prudent servant whom the Lord made the support of his mother, the foster-father of his flesh, and the sole most faithful co-operator on earth in his great design."[13]

Saint Bernardine of Siena writes: "When God chooses a person by grace for a very elevated mission, he gives all the graces required for it. This is verified in a specially outstanding manner in the case of St. Joseph, foster-father of Our Lord Jesus Christ and spouse of Mary."[14] Isidore de Isolanis places St. Joseph's vocation above that of the apostles. He remarks that the vocation of the apostles is to preach the gospel, to enlighten souls, to reconcile them with God, but that the vocation of St. Joseph is more immediately in relation with Christ himself since he is the Spouse of the Mother of God, the

---

[12] Cf. *Dict. Theol. Cath.*, art. *Joseph*, col. 1518.
[13] St. Bernard, *Homil. II super Missus est.*
[14] St. Bernardine of Siena, *Sermo I de S. Joseph.*

Foster Father and protector of the Savior.[15] Suarez teaches to the same effect: "Certain offices pertain to the order of sanctifying grace, and among them that of the apostles holds the highest place; thus they have need of more gratuitous gifts than other souls, especially gratuitous gifts of wisdom. But there are other offices which touch upon or border on the order of the hypostatic union, as can be seen clearly in the case of the divine maternity of the Blessed Virgin, and it is to that order that the ministry of St. Joseph pertains.[16]

Some years ago Msgr. Sinibaldi, titular bishop of Tiberias and secretary of the Sacred Congregation of Studies, treated the question very ably. He pointed out that the ministry of St. Joseph belonged, in a sense, because of its term, to the hypostatic order: not that St. Joseph co-operated intrinsically as physical instrument of the Holy Spirit in the realization of the mystery of the Incarnation — for under that respect his role is very much inferior to that of Mary — but that he was predestined to be, in the order of moral causes, the protector of the virginity and the honor of Mary at the same time as foster-father and protector of the Word made flesh. "His mission pertains by its term to the hypostatic order, not through intrinsic physical and immediate co-operation, but through extrinsic moral and mediate (through Mary) co-operation, which is, however, really and truly co-operation."[17]

Saint Joseph's Predestination is One with the Decree of the Incarnation

Saint Joseph's pre-eminence becomes all the clearer if we consider that the eternal decree of the Incarnation covered not merely the Incarnation in abstraction from circumstances of time and place but the Incarnation here and now — that is to say, the Incarnation of the Son of God who by the operation of the Holy Spirit was to be conceived at a certain moment of time by the Virgin Mary, espoused to a man of the family of David whose name was Joseph: "The angel Gabriel was sent from God into a city of Galilee, called Nazareth, to a virgin espoused to a man whose name was Joseph, of the house of David" (Lk 1:26-27).

---

[15] Isidore de Isolanis, *Summa de donis sancti Joseph,* Pars IIIa, c. xviii. This work was very highly praised by Pope Benedict XIV.

[16] Suarez, *In Summam S. Thomae,* IIIa, q. 29, disp. 8, sect. I.

[17] Sinibaldi, *La Grandezza di San Giuseppe.* (Rome, 1927), especially pages 36 and following.

All the indications are therefore that St. Joseph was predestined to be foster-father of the Incarnate Word before being predestined to glory; the ultimate reason being that Christ's predestination as man to the natural divine sonship precedes the predestination of all the elect, since Christ is the first of the predestined.[18] The predestination of Christ to the natural divine sonship is simply the decree of the Incarnation, which, as we have seen, includes Mary's predestination to the divine motherhood and Joseph's to be foster-father and protector of the Incarnate Son of God.

As the predestination of Christ to the natural divine sonship is superior to his predestination to glory and precedes it, and as the predestination of Mary to the divine motherhood precedes (*in signo priori*) her predestination to glory, so also the predestination of St. Joseph to be foster-father of the Incarnate Word precedes his predestination to glory and to grace. In other words, the reason why he was predestined to the highest degree of glory after Mary, and in consequence to the highest degree of grace and of charity, is that he was called to be the worthy foster-father and protector of the Man-God.

The fact that St. Joseph's first predestination was one with the decree of the Incarnation shows how elevated his unique mission was. This is what people mean when they say that St. Joseph was made and put into the world to be the foster-father of the Incarnate Word and that God willed for him a high degree of glory and grace to fit him for his task.

The Special Character of St. Joseph's Mission

This point is explained admirably by Bossuet in his first panegyric of the saint:

> Among the different vocations, I notice two in the scriptures which seem directly opposed to each other: the first is that of the apostles, the second that of St. Joseph. Jesus was revealed to the apostles that they might announce him throughout the world; He was revealed to St. Joseph who was to remain silent and keep him hidden. The apostles are lights to make the world see Jesus. Joseph is a veil to cover him; and under that mysterious veil are hidden from us the virginity of Mary and the greatness of the Savior of souls. He who makes the apostles glorious with the glory of preaching, glorifies Joseph by the humility of silence.[19]

---

[18] St. Thomas Aquinas, *Summa Theologica*, IIIa, q. 24, a. I, 2-4.
[19] Jacques-Bénigne Bossuet, *First Panegyric of St. Joseph*, ed. Lebarcq, t. II, pp. 135.

The hour for the manifestations of the mystery of the Incarnation had not yet struck: it was to be preceded by the thirty years of the hidden life.

Perfection consists in doing God's will, each one according to his vocation: St. Joseph's vocation of silence and obscurity surpassed that of the apostles because it bordered more nearly on the redemptive Incarnation. After Mary, Joseph was nearest to the author of grace, and in the silence of Bethlehem, during the exile in Egypt, and in the little home of Nazareth he received more grace than any other saint.

His mission was a dual one.

As regards Mary, he preserved her virginity by contracting with her a true but altogether holy marriage. The angel of the Lord said to him: "Joseph, son of David, fear not to take unto thee Mary thy wife, for that which is conceived of her is of the Holy Spirit" (Mt 1:20; Lk 2:5). Mary is truly his wife. The marriage was a true one, as St. Thomas explains when showing its appropriateness. There should be no room for doubt, however light, regarding the honor of the Son and the mother: if ever doubt did arise, Joseph, the most informed and the least suspect witness, would be there to defend it. Besides, Mary would find help and protection in St. Joseph. He loved her with a pure and devoted love, in God and for God. Their union was stainless, and most respectful on the side of St. Joseph. Thus he was nearer than any other saint to the Mother of God and the spiritual mother of men — and he too was a man. The beauty of the whole universe was nothing compared with that of the union of Mary and Joseph, a union created by the Most High, which ravished the angels and gave joy to the Lord.

As regards the Incarnate Word, Joseph watched over him, protected him, and contributed to his human education. He is called his foster-father, but the term does not express fully the mysterious supernatural relation between the two. A man becomes foster-father of a child normally as a result of an accident. But it was no accident in the case of St. Joseph: he had been created and put into the world for that purpose: it was the primary reason of his predestination and the reason for all the graces he received. Bossuet expresses this well:

> If nature does not give a father's heart, where will it be found? In other words, since Joseph was not Jesus' father, how could he have a father's heart in his [Jesus'] regard? Here we must recognize the action of God. It is by the power of God that Joseph has a father's heart, and if nature fails, God gives one with

his own hand; for it is of God that it is written that he directs our inclinations where he wills. He gives some a heart of flesh when he softens their nature by charity. Does he not give all the faithful the hearts of children when he sends to them the Spirit of his son? The apostles feared the least danger, but God gave them a new heart and their courage became undaunted. The same hand gave Joseph the heart of a father and Jesus the heart of a son. That is why Jesus obeys and Joseph does not fear to command. How has he the courage to command his Creator? Because the true Father of Jesus Christ, the God who gives him birth from all eternity, having chosen Joseph to be the father of his only son in time, sent down into his bosom some ray or some spark of his own infinite love for his son; that is what changed his heart, that is what gave him a father's love, and Joseph the just man who feels that father's heart within him feels also that God wishes him to use his paternal authority, so that he dares to command him who he knows is his Master.[20]

That is equivalent to saying that Joseph was predestined first to take the place of a father in regard to the Savior who could have no earthly father,[21] and in consequence to have all the gifts which were given him that he might be a worthy protector of the Incarnate Word.

Is it necessary to say with what fidelity St. Joseph guarded the triple deposit confided to him: the virginity of Mary, the person of Jesus Christ, and the secret of the Eternal Father, that of the Incarnation of his Son, a secret to be guarded faithfully till the hour appointed for its revelation?

In a discourse delivered in the Constitutional Hall on March 19, 1928, Pope Pius XI said, after having spoken on the missions of St. John the Baptist and St. Peter:

> Between these two missions there appears that of St. Joseph, one of recollection and silence, one almost unnoticed and destined to be lit up only many centuries afterwards, a silence which would become a resounding hymn of glory, but only after many years. But where the mystery is deepest it is there precisely that the mission is highest and that a more brilliant cortege of virtues is required with their corresponding echo of merits. It was a unique and sublime mission, that of guarding the Son of God, the king of the world, that of protecting the virginity of Mary, that of entering into participation in the mystery hidden from the eyes of ages and so to co-operate in the Incarnation and the redemption.

---

[20] Bossuet, *First Panegyric of St. Joseph*, ed. Lebarcq, t. II, pp. 135ff.

[21] We read that Jesus was subjected to Mary and Joseph. Joseph in this humility must have been confounded that he, the least of the three, should be the head of the Holy Family.

That is equivalently to state that Divine Providence conferred on St. Joseph all the graces he received in view of his special mission: in other words, St. Joseph was predestined first of all to be as a father to the Savior, and was then predestined to the glory and the grace which were becoming in one favored with so exceptional a vocation.

The Virtues and Gifts of St. Joseph

St. Joseph's virtues are those especially of the hidden life, in a degree proportioned to that of his sanctifying grace: virginity, humility, poverty, patience, prudence, fidelity, simplicity, faith enlightened by the gifts of the Holy Spirit, confidence in God and perfect charity. He preserved what had been confided to him with a fidelity proportioned to its inestimable value.

Bossuet makes this general observation about the virtues of the hidden life:

> It is a common failing of men to give themselves entirely to what is outside and to neglect what is within; to work for mere appearances and to neglect what is solid and lasting; to think often of the impression they make and little of what they ought to be. That is why the most highly esteemed virtues are those which concern the conduct and direction of affairs. The hidden virtues, on the contrary, which are practiced away from the public view and under the eye of God alone, are not only neglected but hardly even heard of. And yet this is the secret of true virtue. A man must be built up interiorly in himself before he deserves to be given rank among others; and if this foundation is lacking, all the other virtues, however brilliant, will be mere display. They will not make the man according to God's heart. Joseph sought God in simplicity; Joseph found God in detachment; Joseph enjoyed God's company in obscurity.[22]

Saint Joseph's humility must have been increased by the thought of the gratuity of his exceptional vocation. He must have said to himself: "Why has the Most High given me, rather than any other man, his Son to watch over?" Only because that was his good pleasure. Joseph was freely preferred from all eternity to all other men to whom the Lord could have given the same gifts and the same fidelity to prepare them for so exceptional a vocation. We see in St. Joseph's predestination a reflection of the gratuitous predestination of Jesus and Mary. The knowledge of the value of the grace he received and

---

[22] Bossuet, *Second Panegyric on St. Joseph.*

of its absolute gratuitousness, far from injuring his humility, would strengthen it. He would think in his heart: "What have you that you have not received?"

Joseph appears the most humble of the saints after Mary — more humble than any of the angels. If he is the most humble, he is by that fact the greatest, for the virtues are all connected and a person's charity is as elevated as his humility is profound. "He that is lesser among you all, he is the greater" (Lk 9:48).

Bossuet says well:

> Though by an extraordinary grace of the Eternal Father he possessed the greatest treasure, it was far from Joseph's thought to pride himself on his gifts or to make them known, but he hid himself as far as possible from mortal eyes, enjoying with God alone the mystery revealed to him and the infinite riches of which he was the custodian. Joseph has in his house what could attract the eyes of the whole world, and the world does not know him; he guards a God-Man, and breathes not a word of it; he is the witness of so great a mystery, and he tastes it in secret without divulging it abroad.[23]

His faith cannot be shaken in spite of the darkness of the unexpected mystery. The word of God communicated to him by the angel throws light on the virginal conception of the Savior: Joseph might have hesitated to believe a thing so wonderful, but he believes it firmly in the simplicity of his heart. By his simplicity and his humility, he reaches up to divine heights.

Obscurity follows once more. Joseph was poor before receiving the secret of the Most High. He becomes still poorer when Jesus is born, for Jesus comes to separate men from everything so as to unite them to God. There is no room for the Savior in the last of the inns of Bethlehem. Joseph must have suffered from having nothing to offer to Mary and her Son.

His confidence in God was made manifest in trials. Persecution came soon after Jesus' birth. Herod tried to put him to death, and the head of the Holy Family was forced to conceal the Child, to take refuge in a distant country where he was unknown and where he did not know how he could earn a living. But he set out on the journey relying on Divine Providence.

His love of God and of souls did not cease to increase during the hidden life of Nazareth; the Incarnate Word is an unfailing source

---

[23] Bossuet, *Second Panegryic on St. Joseph.*

of graces, ever newer and more choice, for docile souls who oppose no obstacle to his action. We have said already, when speaking of Mary, that the progress of such docile souls is one of uniform acceleration, that is to say, they are carried all the more powerfully to God the nearer they approach him. This law of spiritual gravitation was realized in Joseph; his charity grew up to the time of his death, and the progress of his latter years was more rapid then that of his earlier years, for finding himself nearer to God he was more powerfully drawn by him.

Along with the theological virtues the gifts of the Holy Spirit, which are connected with charity, grew continuously. Those of understanding and of wisdom made his living faith more penetrating and more attuned to the divine. In a simple but most elevated way his contemplation rose to the infinite goodness of God. In its simplicity his contemplation was the most perfect after Mary's.

His loving contemplation was sweet, but it demanded of him the most perfect spirit of abnegation and sacrifice when he recalled the words of Simeon: "This child will be a sign that will be contradicted" and "thy own soul a sword shall pierce." He needed all his generosity to offer to God the Infant Jesus and his Mother Mary whom he loved incomparably more than himself.

Saint Joseph's death was a privileged one. Saint Francis de Sales writes that it was a death of love.[24] The same holy doctor teaches with Suarez that St. Joseph was one of the saints who rose after the Resurrection of the Lord (see Mt 27:52ff) and appeared in the city of Jerusalem; he holds also that these resurrections were definitive and that Joseph entered heaven then, body and soul. Saint Thomas Aquinas is much more reserved regarding this point.

Saint Joseph's Role in the Sanctification of Souls

The humble carpenter is glorified in heaven to the extent to which he was hidden on earth. He to whom the Incarnate Word was subject has now an incomparable power of intercession. Pope Leo XIII, in his encyclical *Quamquam Pluries*, finds in St. Joseph's mission in regard to the Holy Family the reasons why he is Patron and Protector of the Universal Church:

> Just as Mary, mother of the Savior, is spiritual mother of all Christians, Joseph looks on all Christians as having been confided to

---

[24] St. Francis de Sales, *Treatise on the Love of God*, Bk. VII, Ch. 13.

himself. He is the defender of the Holy Church which is truly the house of God and the kingdom of God on earth.[25]

What strikes us most in St. Joseph's role till the end of time is that there are united in it in an admirable way apparently opposed prerogatives. His influence is universal over the whole Church, and yet, like Divine Providence, it descends to the least details: "model and workman," he takes an interest in everyone who turns to him. He is the most universal of the saints, and yet he helps a poor man in his ordinary daily needs. His action is primarily of the spiritual order, and yet it extends to temporal affairs; he is the support of families and of communities, the hope of the sick. He watches over Christians of all conditions, of all countries, over fathers of families, husbands and wives, consecrated virgins; over the rich to inspire them to distribute their possessions charitably, and over the poor so as to help them. He is attentive to the needs of great sinners and of souls advanced in virtue. He is the patron of a happy death, of lost causes; he is terrible to the demons, and St. Teresa of Avila tells us that he is the guide of interior souls in the ways of prayer. His influence is a wonderful reflection of that of Divine Wisdom which "reacheth from end to end mightily, and ordereth all things sweetly" (Wisdom 8:1).

He has been clothed and will remain clothed in divine splendor. Grace has become fruitful in him and he will share its fruit with all who strive to attain to the life which is "hid with Christ in God" (Col 3:3).

Taken from Fr. Reginald Garrigou-Lagrange, OP, *The Mother of the Savior and Our Interior Life* (Charlotte, NC: TAN Books, 1993), 277-290. Used with permission.

---

[25] Pope Leo XIII, *Quamquam pluries.*

ADDENDUM II

Churches and Shrines of St. Joseph

There are many places around the world that are dedicated to St. Joseph. Entire countries have him as their patron and there are many cathedrals and parishes that are named after him. Listed below are a few of the more well-known locations of devotion to St. Joseph.

NAZARETH, ISRAEL

Church of St. Joseph. Also known as the Church of the Nutrition and/or St. Joseph's Workshop. Some traditions claim that this was St. Joseph's childhood home and the place of his workshop once he was espoused to the Virgin Mary

LORETO, ITALY

The Holy House of Loreto. This is the home where the Holy Family lived in Nazareth. It was miraculously transported to Italy by angels in the 13th century.

VATICAN CITY

Altar of St. Joseph (located inside St. Peter's Basilica). This side chapel is where daily Masses are celebrated in St. Peter's Basilica. In 1963, St. Pope John XXIII commissioned an image of St. Joseph and the Baby Jesus to be placed above the altar.

ROME, ITALY

Basilica di San Giuseppe al Trionfale. This minor basilica was founded by St. Luigi Guanella with the encouragement of St. Pope Pius X. It was consecrated in 1912. It is the international headquarters of the Pious Union of St. Joseph.

San Giuseppe a Capo le Case ("St. Joseph at the End of the Houses"). This small convent parish was established in the 17th century.

San Giuseppe alla Lungara. A small convent church located in the north end of the Trastevere region of Rome. It was established in the 18th century and is a hidden gem.

San Giuseppe dei Falegnami (St. Joseph of the Carpenters). Located in the Roman Forum area, this titular church was established in the 16th century. It is located above the Mamertine Prison, where Sts. Peter and Paul were imprisoned.

Chapel of St. Joseph. Located in the Basilica Church of Sant' Andrea delle Fratte is a side chapel containing an exquisitely beautiful painting of St. Joseph. It was painted by Francesco Cozza in 1732. Next to the Chapel of St. Joseph is the famous Chapel of the "Madonna del Miracolo," where in 1842 the Virgin Mary appeared to the Jewish banker, Alphonse Ratisbonne. He later converted to Catholicism and became a priest. Saint Maximilian Kolbe celebrated his first Mass at the altar of the "Madonna del Miracolo."

ASTI, ITALY

Sanctuary of St. Joseph. This Romanesque style church was dedicated in 1931 and is the motherhouse for the Oblates of St. Joseph. The Oblates were founded by St. Joseph Marello and it is in this church that his tomb is located.

MONTRÉAL, CANADA

St. Joseph's Oratory. Initiated by St. André Bessette in 1904, the Oratory was dedicated as a Basilica in 1967. It is the largest shrine in the world dedicated to St. Joseph and is considered by many to be the preeminent international center of devotion to St. Joseph.

KNOCK, IRELAND

National Marian Shrine. Primarily dedicated to the Mother of God, the shrine also honors St. Joseph and his appearance in the Knock apparitions that took place here in 1879.

RABAT, MALTA

National Sanctuary of St. Joseph. Located inside the Church of St. Mary of Jesus is the most famous statue of St. Joseph in Malta. The sanctuary is also the headquarters for the Archconfraternity of St. Joseph. The church and sanctuary are operated by Franciscans. The staff attached to the statue of St. Joseph is said to be miraculous and is often brought to the bedside of the sick as they ask for St. Joseph's intercession.

COTIGNAC, FRANCE

Monastery of St. Joseph. Located in southeastern France, the monastery is located at the site of the 17th-century apparition of St. Joseph to a shepherd in which a miraculous spring was revealed.

LE PUY-EN-VELAY, FRANCE

Sanctuary of Saint Joseph de Bon Espoir (St. Joseph of Good Hope). Featuring a 48-foot high statue of St. Joseph and a grotto dedicated to St. Joseph, this sanctuary is a delightful place to visit.

SMAKT, NETHERLANDS

St. Joseph Chapel. Approximately a two-hour drive from Amsterdam, St. Joseph Chapel dates back to 1699 and is a frequent place of pilgrimage for people from the Netherlands. There are special devotions to St. Joseph on the First Wednesday of each month, and the chapel contains a beautiful and unique statue of St. Joseph.

BARCELONA, SPAIN

Real Santuario de San José de la Montaña (Royal Sanctuary of St. Joseph of the Mountain). An incredible place of devotion to St. Joseph, the sanctuary was founded by Blessed Petra of St. Joseph in the late 19ᵗʰ century.

KALISZ, POLAND

Sanctuary of St. Joseph. A minor basilica, the sanctuary has been in existence for centuries. The first confirmed miraculous healing through the image of St. Joseph housed here was recorded in 1673. The sanctuary is Poland's most well-known place of devotion to St. Joseph.

KRAKOW, POLAND

Church of St. Joseph and Convent of the Bernardine Sisters. Housed within the convent chapel of the Bernardine Sisters is a beautiful image of St. Joseph, said to be miraculous.

FARNBOROUGH, ENGLAND

National Shrine to St. Joseph. With a fascinating history going back to the 19ᵗʰ century, the current location for England's devotion to St. Joseph is at St. Michael's Abbey. The Abbey was declared the National Shrine of St. Joseph in 2008. The statue of St. Joseph at the Shrine is a site to see.

SAN LUIS POTOSÍ, MEXICO

Santuario de San José. Dedicated to St. Joseph the Worker, the shrine is very popular and a major location of devotion to St. Joseph in Mexico. It was declared a shrine in 1985.

MEXICO CITY, MEXICO

Basilica de San Jose y Nuestra Señora del Sagrado Corazón. The basilica is a World Heritage Site and a hidden gem in the midst of busy Mexico City. It has a beautiful statue of St. Joseph, with which there are frequent processions.

SAN JOSÉ, URUGUAY

Santuario Nacional de San José. This beautiful shrine also functions as the Cathedral Basilica of the Diocese of San José de Mayo. It was designated as the National Sanctuary of St. Joseph by the bishops of Uruguay in 1957.

CEBU, PHILIPPINES

National Shrine of St. Joseph. The Philippines have many shrines dedicated to St. Joseph. The one in Cebu is recognized as the official national shrine of St. Joseph, being declared as such in 2001.

SANTA FE, NEW MEXICO (United States)

Miraculous Staircase of Loretto Chapel. In the late 19th century, St. Joseph mysteriously appeared to a group of nuns and constructed a staircase for them that continues to baffle architects and carpenters.

DE PERE, WISCONSIN (United States)

National Shrine of St. Joseph. Located at St. Norbert College inside Old St. Joseph Church, the center of devotion at the shrine is the beautiful statue of St. Joseph. A perpetual novena to St. Joseph has been prayed there since 1888. It was recognized as the National Shrine of St. Joseph by Pope Leo XIII in 1892.

ST. LOUIS, MISSOURI (United States)

Shrine of St. Joseph. Established as a parish church by the Jesuits in the 19th century, the parish quickly became a center of devotion when prayers to St. Joseph spared the locals from a cholera outbreak in 1866.

SANTA CRUZ, CALIFORNIA (United States)

Shrine of St. Joseph — Guardian of the Redeemer. Operated by the Oblates of St. Joseph, the shrine is located directly across from Steamer Lane, one of the best surf breaks in central California! A delightful St. Joseph art exhibit is also located at the shrine.

GRASS LAKE, MICHIGAN (United States)

Shrine of St. Joseph. Located 20 miles west of Ann Arbor, the shrine is the location for the United States branch of the Pious Union of St. Joseph, Patron for the Suffering and Dying.

DETROIT, MICHIGAN (United States)

St. Joseph Oratory. A magnificent Victorian Gothic edifice, St. Joseph Oratory is a parish operated by the Canons of the Institute of Christ the King Sovereign Priest. The priests offer the Tridentine Latin Mass. The parish has a Confraternity of St. Joseph and every Wednesday are novena prayers to St. Joseph.

STIRLING, NEW JERSEY (United States)

Shrine of St. Joseph. Founded in 1924 by Fr. Thomas A. Judge, CM, the shrine continues to be operated by the religious community he founded, the Missionary Servants of the Most Holy Trinity. The shrine offers many different cultural events.

YARNELL, ARIZONA (United States)

Shrine of St. Joseph of the Mountains. An outdoor shrine established in 1939. It has beautiful Stations of the Cross and statues of St. Joseph. It is open 24 hours a day.

LOWELL, MASSACHUSETTS (United States)

St. Joseph the Worker Shrine. Dedicated in 1956 as a place of devotion to St. Joseph by the Missionary Oblates of Mary Immaculate, the shrine continues to attract many people in New England.

STOCKBRIDGE, MASSACHUSETTS (United States)

St. Joseph Chapel at The National Shrine of The Divine Mercy. Located inside the National Shrine, on the left side of the main altar, is a lovely chapel dedicated to St. Joseph.

References

• Initial quote at the beginning of the book:
St. Peter Julian Eymard, *Month of St. Joseph* (Cleveland, OH: Emmanuel Publications, 1948), 41.

~ Image of St. Joseph on the page before the introduction is from a mosaic in the Cappella delle Reliquie (Chapel of the Relics) in St. Peter's Basilica in Vatican City. The mosaic was done by Francesco Grandi in 1888. Unfortunately, the chapel where the mosaic is housed is no longer accessible to the public. A large tapestry of the mosaic was made by the Vatican and is occasionally displayed outside St. Peter's Basilica for public veneration. The image of the mosaic is made available here courtesy of the Fabbrica di San Pietro in Vaticano, and through the generosity of Fr. Tarcisio Giuseppe Stramare, OSJ.

Introduction

[1] St. John of the Cross, as quoted in Stratford Caldecott, *The Chivalry of St. Joseph* (a talk given to the Knights of Our Lady on October 19, 2002), available at https://www.catholicculture.org/culture/library.
[2] St. José Manyanet, as quoted by Sergio Cimignoli, SF, in "José de Nazaret y Josep Manyanet," available at http://profetadelafamilia.blogspot.com/2017/03/jose-de-nazaret-y-josep-manyanet-por.html. English translation courtesy of Miss Ileana E. Salazar, MA.
[3] St. Pope John XXIII, *Le Voci* (For the Protection of St. Joseph on the Second Vatican Council), March 19, 1961.
[4] Sr. Lucia dos Santos, "Letter to Cardinal Carlo Caffarra," *Voce di Padre Pio Magazine* (2008).
[5] St. John Paul II, Apostolic Exhortation *Redemptoris Custos* (*On the Person and Mission of St. Joseph in the Life of Christ and of the Church*), no. 29, available at www.vatican.va.
[6] St. Josemaría Escrivá, "A Homily: In Joseph's Workshop," as quoted in Michael D. Griffin, OCD, ed., *Saint Joseph and the Third Millennium* (Hubertus, WI: Teresian Charism Press, 1999), 356.

PART I: 33-Day Preparation

DAY 1

[1] St. Peter Julian Eymard, Month of St. Joseph (Cleveland, OH: Emmanuel Publications, 1948), 41.
[2] St. Bernard of Clairvaux, as quoted in Rosalie Marie Levy, *Joseph the Just Man* (Derby, NY: Daughters of St. Paul, 1955), 27-28.
[3] Blessed William Joseph Chaminade, *Marian Writings*, vol. 1, ed. J.B. Armbruster, SM (Dayton, OH: Marianist Press, 1980), 121.
[4] St. Peter Julian Eymard, *Month of St. Joseph*, 60.

DAY 2

[1] St. Teresa of Avila, as quoted in Rosalie Marie Levy, *Joseph the Just Man* (Derby, NY: Daughters of St. Paul, 1955), 146.

[2] St. Clement Mary Hofbauer, as quoted in Levy, *Joseph the Just Man*, 250.

[3] Blessed William Joseph Chaminade, *Marian Writings*, vol. 1, ed. J.B. Armbruster, SM (Dayton, OH: Marianist Press, 1980), 116.

[4] St. Peter Julian Eymard, *Month of St. Joseph* (Cleveland, OH: Emmanuel Publications, 1948), 94.

[5] St. Madeleine Sophie Barat, as quoted in Levy, *Joseph the Just Man*, 147-148.

DAY 3

[1] St. Peter Julian Eymard, *Month of St. Joseph* (Cleveland, OH: Emmanuel Publications, 1948), 12.

[2] Blessed William Joseph Chaminade, *Marian Writings*, vol. 1, ed. J.B. Armbruster, SM (Dayton, OH: Marianist Press, 1980), 223-224.

[3] St. Bernardine of Siena, as quoted in Francis L. Filas, SJ, *Joseph and Jesus: A Theological Study of Their Relationship* (Milwaukee, WI: Bruce Publishing Co., 1952), 79.

DAY 4

[1] St. Alphonsus Liguori, as quoted in Rosalie Marie Levy, *Joseph the Just Man* (Derby, NY: Daughters of St. Paul, 1955), 143.

[2] Venerable Francis Xavier Nguyễn Văn Thuận, as quoted in *Magnificat* (December 2019). Vol. 21, No. 10: 436.

[3] Blessed Januarius Maria Sarnelli, as quoted in *Favorite Prayers to St. Joseph* (Charlotte, NC: TAN Books, 1997), 20.

[4] St. Hilary of Poitiers, as quoted in Blessed William Joseph Chaminade, *Marian Writings*, vol. 1, ed. J.B. Armbruster, SM (Dayton, OH: Marianist Press, 1980), 234.

[5] Blessed Jean Joseph Latate, OP, as quoted in Jean-Marie Gueullette, OP, *My Dear Sisters: Life of Bl. Jean-Joseph Lataste, OP, Apostle to Prisoners*, trans. George G. Christian, OP. (New Hope, Kentucky: New Hope Publications, 2018), 219.

DAY 5

[1] Blessed William Joseph Chaminade, *Marian Writings*, vol. 1, ed. J.B. Armbruster, SM (Dayton, OH: Marianist Press, 1980), 112.

[2] St. Joseph Sebastian Pelczar, as quoted in the unpublished manuscript, "*Meditation 48: The Imitation of Saint Joseph in the Interior Life*," trans. Mother Agnieszka Kijowska, SSCJ. Courtesy of Sr. Mary Joseph Calore, SSCJ, and Mother Klara Slonina, SSCJ.

[3] St. John Paul II, Apostolic Exhortation *Redemptoris Custos* (*On the Person and Mission of St. Joseph in the Life of Christ and of the Church*), no. 27, available at www.vatican.va.

DAY 6

[1] St. Peter Julian Eymard, *Month of St. Joseph* (Cleveland, OII: Emmanuel Publications, 1948), 5.

[2] St. Francis de Sales, as quoted in Rosalie Marie Levy, *Joseph the Just Man* (Derby, NY: Daughters of St. Paul, 1955), 130-131.

[3] Blessed William Joseph Chaminade, *Marian Writings*, vol. 1, ed. J.B. Armbruster, SM (Dayton, OH: Marianist Press, 1980), 112.

DAY 7

[1] St. Leonard of Port Maurice, as quoted in Andrew Doze, *Saint Joseph: Shadow of the Father*, trans. Florestine Audett, RJM (Staten Island, NY: Alba House, 1992), 18.

[2] Blessed William Joseph Chaminade, as quoted in *From a Full Heart: Thoughts from Father Chaminade* (North American Center for Marianist Studies, NACMS), compiled by Francis J. Greiner, SM (St. Meinard, IN: The Grail Press, 1949), entry for March 12.

[3] Blessed Bartolo Longo, *Il Mese di Marzo: In Onore di San Giuseppe*, 15th ed., (Pompei, Italy: Pontificio Santuario di Pompei, 2001), 123. English translation courtesy of Miss Ileana E. Salazar, MA.

DAY 8

[1] St. Pope Paul VI, "Discourse to the *Equipes Notre Dame* Movement (May 4, 1970)," as quoted in St. John Paul II, Apostolic Exhortation *Redemptoris Custos* (*On the Person and Mission of St. Joseph in the Life of Christ and of the Church*), 7, available at www.vatican.va.

DAY 9

[1] St. Peter Julian Eymard, *Month of St. Joseph* (Cleveland, OH: Emmanuel Publications, 1948), 16.

[2] Pope Benedict XVI, *Address of July 5, 2010*, as quoted in Jose A. Rodrigues, *The Book of Joseph: God's Chosen Father* (Toronto, ON: Ave Maria Centre of Peace, 2017), 28.

[3] St. Alphonsus Liguori, as quoted in Andrew Doze, *Saint Joseph: Shadow of the Father*, trans. Florestine Audett, RJM (Staten Island, NY: Alba House, 1992), 19-20.

[4] St. Josemaría Escrivá, *Christ is Passing By* (New York, NY: Scepter, 1973), 93.

[5] St. Alphonsus Liguori, as quoted in Doze, *Saint Joseph: Shadow of the Father*, 19-20.

DAY 10

[1] Blessed William Joseph Chaminade, *The Chaminade Legacy*, vol. 2, *Notes for Conferences and Sermons*, trans. Joseph Stefanelli, SM (Dayton, OH: North American Center for Marianist Studies, 2008), 416.

[2] Blessed William Joseph Chaminade, *Marian Writings*, vol. 1, ed. J.B. Armbruster, SM (Dayton, OH: Marianist Press, 1980), 230.

[3] Pope Benedict XVI, *Address in Yaounde, Cameroon (March 19, 2009)*, as quoted in Jose A. Rodrigues, *The Book of Joseph: God's Chosen Father* (Toronto, ON: Ave Maria Centre of Peace, 2017), 110.

DAY 11

[1] Blessed Gabriele Allegra, *Mary's Immaculate Heart: A Way to God* (Chicago, IL: Franciscan Herald Press, 1983), 55.

[2] Pope Benedict XVI, *Address in Yaounde, Cameroon (March 19, 2009)*, as quoted in Jose A. Rodrigues, *The Book of Joseph: God's Chosen Father* (Toronto, ON: Ave Maria Centre of Peace, 2017), 110.

[3] Pope Leo XIII, as quoted in Larry Toschi, OSJ, *Husband, Father, Worker: Questions and Answers about St. Joseph* (Liguori, MO: Liguori, 2012), 107.

DAY 12

[1] St. Francis de Sales, as quoted in Francis L. Filas, SJ, *Joseph and Jesus: A Theological Study of Their Relationship* (Milwaukee, WI: Bruce Publishing Co., 1952), 99.

[2] Pope Benedict XVI (Joseph Cardinal Ratzinger) and Hans Urs von Balthasar, *Mary: The Church at the Source*, trans. Adrian Walker (San Francisco, CA: Ignatius Press, 2005), 88.

DAY 13

[1] Venerable Joseph Mindszenty, *The Mother*, trans. Rev. Benedict P. Lenz, CSsR (St. Paul, MN: Radio Replies Press, 1949), 49.

[2] St. Albert the Great, as quoted in Francis L. Filas, SJ, *Joseph and Jesus: A Theological Study of Their Relationship* (Milwaukee, WI: Bruce Publishing Co.), 63.

[3] St. Peter Julian Eymard, *Month of St. Joseph* (Cleveland, OH: Emmanuel Publications, 1948), 8.

[4] St. Ephrem the Syrian, as quoted in Rosalie Marie Levy, *Joseph the Just Man* (Derby, NY: Daughters of St. Paul, 1955), 152.

DAY 14

[1] St. Josemaría Escrivá, *Christ is Passing By* (New York, NY: Scepter, 1973), 93.

[2] Blessed William Joseph Chaminade, *Marian Writings. Volume 2* (Dayton, OH: Marianist Press, 1980), 52.

[3] Blessed William Joseph Chaminade, *The Chaminade Legacy*, vol. 2, *Notes for Conferences and Sermons*, trans. Joseph Stefanelli, SM (Dayton, OH: North American Center for Marianist Studies, 2008), 416.

[4] Blessed William Joseph Chaminade, *Marian Writings*, vol. 1 (Dayton, OH: Marianist Press, 1980), 229.

DAY 15

[1] St. Peter Julian Eymard, *Month of St. Joseph* (Cleveland, OH: Emmanuel Publications, 1948), 6-7.

[2] Pope Leo XIII, Apostolic Letter *Neminem Fugit* (*On the Institution of the Association of the Holy Family*), as quoted in Francis L. Filas, SJ, *St. Joseph & Daily Christian Living* (New York, NY: Macmillan Co., 1959), 188.

[3] St. John Paul II, *Homily at the Shrine of St. Joseph in Kalisz, Poland*, June 4, 1997.

DAY 16

[1] Pope Pius XI, Encyclical Letter *Divini Redemptoris* (*On Atheistic Communism*), March 19, 1937, no. 81.

[2] St. Josemaría Escrivá, *Christ is Passing By* (New York, NY: Scepter, 1973), 40.

[3] St. Maximus of Turin, as quoted in *The Glories of Saint Joseph* (Flavigny-sur-Ozerain, France: Traditions Monastiques Press, 2009), 57.

[4] St. Pope Paul VI, *Homily on the Solemnity of St. Joseph*, March 19, 1969.

DAY 17

[1] St. Francis de Sales, as quoted in Rev. Nicholas O'Rafferty, *Discourses on St. Joseph*. (Milwaukee, WI: Bruce Publishing Co., 1951), 38.

[2] Pope Leo XIII, Encyclical Letter *Quamquam Pluries* (*On Devotion to St. Joseph*), August 15, 1889, no. 2.

DAY 18

[1] Blessed William Joseph Chaminade, *Marian Writings*, vol. 1, ed. J.B. Armbruster, SM (Dayton, OH: Marianist Press, 1980), 112.

[2] *Catechism of the Catholic Church*, no. 1806.

[3] Blessed William Joseph Chaminade, *Marian Writings*, vol. 1, ed. J.B. Armbruster, SM (Dayton, OH: Marianist Press, 1980), 112.

[4] Servant of God John A. Hardon, *St. Joseph: Foster Father of Jesus*, as quoted at www.therealpresence.org.

[5] Blessed William Joseph Chaminade, *The Chaminade Legacy*, vol. 2, *Notes for Conferences and Sermons*, trans. Joseph Stefanelli, SM (Dayton, OH: North American Center for Marianist Studies, 2008), 412.

DAY 19

[1] St. Bridget of Sweden, as quoted in Antony J. Patrignani, SJ, *A Manual of Practical Devotion to St. Joseph* (Rockford, IL: TAN Books, 1982), 206.

[2] St. Bernardine of Siena, as quoted in Rosalie Marie Levy, *Joseph the Just Man* (Derby, NY: Daughters of St. Paul, 1955), 245.

DAY 20

[1] St. Joseph Sebastian Pelczar, as quoted in the unpublished manuscript "*Meditation 48: The Imitation of Saint Joseph in the Interior Life*," trans. Mother Agnieszka Kijowska, SSCJ. Courtesy of Sr. Mary Joseph Calore, SSCJ and Mother Klara Slonina, SSCJ.

[2] Pope Benedict XVI, as quoted in Fr. Richard W. Gilsdorf, *Go to Joseph* (Green Bay, WI: Star of the Bay Press, 2009), 122

[3] St. John Paul II, Apostolic Exhortation *Redemptoris Custos* (*On the Person and Mission of St. Joseph in the Life of Christ and of the Church*), August 15, 1989, no. 19, available at www.vatican.va.

DAY 21

[1] St. John Paul II, *Homily for the Solemnity of St. Joseph*, March 19, 1987. English translation courtesy of Miss Ileana E. Salazar, MA.

[2] Blessed Anne Catherine Emmerich, as quoted in Rosalie A. Turton, ed., *St. Joseph as Seen by Mystics and Historians* (Asbury, NJ: 101 Foundation, Inc., 2000), 12.

[3] St. John Paul II, *Letter to Cardinal Angelo Sodano for the 6th International Symposium on St. Joseph*, August 21, 1993. English translation courtesy of Miss Ileana E. Salazar, MA.

DAY 22

[1] Blessed Gabriele Allegra, *Mary's Immaculate Heart: A Way to God* (Chicago, IL: Franciscan Herald Press, 1983), 55.
[2] St. Joseph Marello, as quoted in Larry Toschi, OSJ, *St. Joseph in the Lives of Two Blesseds of the Church: Blessed Junipero Serra and Blessed Joseph Marello* (Santa Cruz, CA: Guardian of the Redeemer Books, 1994), 75.

DAY 23

[1] St. Francis de Sales, as quoted in Rosalie Marie Levy, *Joseph the Just Man* (Derby, NY: Daughters of St. Paul, 1955), 129-130.
[2] St. Bonaventure, as quoted in Fr. Antony-Joseph Patrignani, SJ, *A Manual of Devotion to St. Joseph* (Charlotte, NC: TAN Books, 2012), 206.

DAY 24

[1] St. John Paul II, Apostolic Exhortation *Redemptoris Custos* (*On the Person and Mission of St. Joseph in the Life of Christ and of the Church*), no. 22, available at www.vatican.va.
[2] Pope Pius XI, Encyclical Letter *Divini Redemptoris* (*On Atheistic Communism*), March 19, 1937, no. 81.
[3] St. Peter Julian Eymard, *Month of St. Joseph* (Cleveland, OH: Emmanuel Publications, 1948), 2.

DAY 25

[1] St. Josemaría Escrivá, *Christ is Passing By* (New York, NY: Scepter, 1973), 119.
[2] Pope Pius XI, as quoted in Francis L. Filas, SJ, *St. Joseph & Daily Christian Living* (New York, NY: Macmillan Co., 1959), 195.

DAY 26

[1] St. Thérèse of Lisieux, *Story of a Soul* (New York, NY: Image Books, 1957), 77.
[2] St. Faustina Kowalska, *Diary, Divine Mercy in My Soul* (Stockbridge, MA: Marian Press, 1998), par. 1203.
[3] St. Teresa of Avila, as quoted in Rev. Nicholas O'Rafferty, *Discourses on St. Joseph* (Milwaukee, WI: Bruce Publishing Co., 1951), 209.
[4] St. Elizabeth of the Trinity, *Elizabeth of the Trinity: A Thought a Day*, trans. Fr. Donald Kinney, OCD (Trivandrum, India: St. Joseph's Press, 2018), 37.

DAY 27

[1] St. Teresa of Avila, as quoted in Rosalie Marie Levy, *Joseph the Just Man* (Derby, NY: Daughters of St. Paul, 1955), 146.
[2] St. John Paul II, *Letter to Families*, February 2, 1994, no. 5.
[3] Blessed Anne Catherine Emmerich, *The Complete Visions of Anne Catherine Emmerich* (San Bernardino, CA: Catholic Book Club, 2013), 127. NB: The private revelations of Bl. Anne Catherine Emmerich, in which she claims to

have seen or been present at certain events in the life of Jesus, Mary, and the saints, have not been authenticated by the Catholic Church. Most of her mystical experiences were written down and filtered through her friend, the poet Clemens Brentano, and historians often have questioned the accuracy of his accounts, arguing that they appear at times to be colored by his own ideas or poetic exaggerations. Nevertheless, it is likely that in the main these accounts give us at least the gist of what she experienced, though not accurate in every detail. This means that although they cannot be relied upon for their doctrinal or historical details, they do at least, by and large, reflect the pious meditations of Blessed Anne.

DAY 28

[1] St. Francis de Sales, as quoted in Andrew Doze, *Saint Joseph: Shadow of the Father,* trans. Florestine Audett, RJM (Staten Island, NY: Alba House, 1992), 56.

[2] St. Joseph Marello, as quoted by the Oblates of St. Joseph website for the Shrine of St. Joseph — Guardian of the Redeemer, available at https://www.shrinestjoseph.com/seven-sorrows-joys-old-2.

[3] Pope Benedict XVI, *Address in Yaounde, Cameroon (March 19, 2009),* as quoted in Jose A. Rodrigues, *The Book of Joseph: God's Chosen Father* (Toronto, ON: Ave Maria Centre of Peace, 2017), 119.

DAY 29

[1] St. John Paul II, Apostolic Exhortation *Redemptoris Custos (On the Person and Mission of St. Joseph in the Life of Christ and of the Church),* no. 8, available at www.vatican.va.

[2] St. Zélie Martin, as quoted in Helene Mongin, *The Extraordinary Parents of St. Thérèse of Lisieux* (Huntington, IN: Our Sunday Visitor, 2015), 105-106.

[3] St. Joseph Marello, as quoted in John Baptist Cortona, OSJ, *Brief Memories of the Life of Joseph Marello, Bishop of Acqui* (Santa Cruz, CA: Guardian of the Redeemer Books, 1993), 26.

DAY 30

[1] Blessed William Joseph Chaminade, as quoted in Maria Cecilia Baij, OSB, *The Life of St. Joseph* (Asbury, NJ: 101 Foundation, Inc., 1996), 421.

[2] St. Alphonsus Liguori, as quoted in Maria Cecilia Baij, OSB, *The Life of St. Joseph* (Asbury, NJ: 101 Foundation, Inc., 1996), 416.

[3] *Catechism of the Catholic Church,* no. 1014.

[4] Blessed William Joseph Chaminade, as quoted in *From a Full Heart: Thoughts from Father Chaminade* (North American Center for Marianist Studies, NACMS), compiled by Francis J. Greiner, SM (St. Meinard, IN: The Grail Press, 1949), entry for March 12.

[5] Venerable Nelson Baker, as quoted in Richard Gribble, CSC, *Father of the Fatherless: The Authorized Biography of Father Nelson Baker* (Mahwah, NJ: Paulist Press, 2011), 282.

DAY 31

[1] Venerable Mary of Agreda, *The Mystical City of God*, vol. 2, *The Incarnation* (Charlotte, NC: TAN Books, 2013), 552.

[2] St. John Neumann, as quoted in Joseph F. Chorpenning, OSFS, "St. Joseph's Presence in the Life and Ministry of John N. Neumann, CSsR," in *St. Joseph Studies: Papers in English from the Seventh and Eighth International St. Joseph Symposia: Malta 1997 and El Salvador 2001,* ed. Larry Toschi, OSJ (Santa Cruz, CA: Guardian of the Redeemer Books, 2002), 135.

DAY 32

[1] St. Pope Paul VI, "Homily on the Solemnity of St. Joseph," March 19, 1969, as quoted in Jose A. Rodrigues, *The Book of Joseph: God's Chosen Father* (Toronto, ON: Ave Maria Centre of Peace, 2017), 120.

[2] St. Pope John XXIII, as quoted in Tarcisio Stramare, OSJ, *Saint Joseph, Guardian of the Redeemer: Text and Reflections,* trans. Paul J. Pavese, OSJ (Santa Cruz, CA: Guardian of the Redeemer Books, 1997), 145.

[3] St. Joseph Marello, as quoted in John Baptist Cortona, OSJ, *Brief Memories of the Life of Joseph Marello, Bishop of Acqui* (Santa Cruz, CA: Guardian of the Redeemer Books, 1993), 79.

[4] Blessed Miguel Pro, as quoted in Gerald Muller, CSC, *Father Miguel Pro: A Modern Mexican Martyr* (San Francisco, CA: Ignatius Press, 2018), 127.

DAY 33

[1] Blessed Pope Pius IX, Decree *Quemadmodum Deus* (*St. Joseph as the Patron of the Universal Church*), December 8, 1870.

[2] Blessed William Joseph Chaminade, *Marian Writings,* vol. 1, ed. J.B. Armbruster, SM (Dayton, OH: Marianist Press, 1980), 227.

[3] St. Peter Julian Eymard, *Month of St. Joseph* (Cleveland, OH: Emmanuel Publications, 1948), 41.

[4] St. Peter Julian Eymard, *Month of St. Joseph*, 105.

CONSECRATION DAY

[1] St. Joseph Sebastian Pelczar, as quoted in the unpublished manuscript "*Meditation 48: The Imitation of Saint Joseph in the Interior Life*," trans. Mother Agnieszka Kijowska, SSCJ. Courtesy of Sr. Mary Joseph Calore, SSCJ and Mother Klara Slonina, SSCJ.

[2] St. Peter Julian Eymard, as quoted in Rosalie Marie Levy, *Joseph the Just Man* (Derby, NY: Daughters of St. Paul, 1955), 150.

PART II: The Wonders of Our Spiritual Father

WONDER 1: Delight of Saints

• Quote on page 83, St. Gertrude the Great, as quoted in *Favorite Prayers to St. Joseph* (Charlotte, NC: TAN Books, 1997), 52.

St. Joseph's Oratory

[1] St. André Bessette, as quoted in Henri-Paul Bergeron, CSC, *Brother André:*

The Wonder Man of Mount Royal, trans. Rev. Real Boudreau, CSC (Montreal, QC: Saint Joseph Oratory, 1997), 72.

[2] St. André Bessette, as quoted in Jose A. Rodrigues, *The Book of Joseph: God's Chosen Father* (Toronto, ON: Ave Maria Centre of Peace, 2017), 125.

[3] St. John Paul II, *Preghiera del Santo Padre Giovanni Paolo II presso la tomba di Fratel André Bessette*, September 11, 1984. Available at www.vatican.va. English translation courtesy of Miss Ileana E. Salazar, MA.

Delight of Saints

[1] St. Maximilian Kolbe, *The Writings of St. Maximilian Kolbe*, vol. 2 (Lugano, CH: Nerbini International, 2016), 1624.

[2] St. Gregory Nazianzen, as quoted in Antony J. Patrignani, SJ, *A Manual of Practical Devotion to St. Joseph* (Rockford, IL: TAN Books, 1982), 72.

[3] St. Lawrence of Brindisi, *Opera Omnia: Feastday Sermons*, trans. Vernon Wagner, OFM Cap (Delhi, India: Media House, 2007), 538.

[4] St. Lawrence of Brindisi, *Opera Omnia*, 535.

[5] St. Lawrence of Brindisi, *Opera Omnia*, 539.

[6] St. Leonard of Port Maurice, as quoted in Andrew Doze, *Saint Joseph: Shadow of the Father*, trans. Florestine Audett, RJM (Staten Island, NY: Alba House, 1992), 18-19.

[7] St. Alphonsus Liguori, *The Glories of Mary* (Charlotte, NC: TAN Books, 2012), 589.

[8] St. Teresa of Avila, as quoted in Mark Miravalle, *Meet Your Spiritual Father: A Brief Introduction to St. Joseph* (Stockbridge, MA: Marian Press, 2015), 11-12.

[9] St. Thomas Aquinas, as quoted in Rev. Nicholas O'Rafferty, *Discourses on St. Joseph* (Milwaukee, WI: Bruce Publishing Co., 1951), 208.

[10] Pope Leo XIII, Encyclical Letter *Quamquam Pluries* (*On Devotion to St. Joseph*), August 15, 1889

[11] Blessed Bartolo Longo, *Il Mese di Marzo: In Onore di San Giuseppe*, 15th ed., (Pompei, Italy: Pontificio Santuario di Pompei, 2001), 136. English translation courtesy of Miss Ileana E. Salazar, MA.

[12] St. George Preca, *San Guzepp* (Societas Doctrinae Christianae: Zabbar, Malta, 1997), 40.

[13] Pius XI, *Allocution to Married Couples*, March 19, 1938.

[14] St. Pope John XXIII, *Allocution (March 19, 1959)*, as quoted in Jose A. Rodrigues, *The Book of Joseph: God's Chosen Father* (Toronto, ON: Ave Maria Centre of Peace, 2017), 121.

[15] Blessed Bartolo Longo, *Il Mese di Marzo: In Onore di San Giuseppe*, 15th ed., (Pompei, Italy: Pontificio Santuario di Pompei, 2001), 134. English translation courtesy of Miss Ileana E. Salazar, MA.

The Roman Canon

[1] St. John Paul II, Apostolic Exhortation *Redemptoris Custos* (*On the Person and Mission of St. Joseph in the Life of Christ and of the Church*), no. 6, available at www.vatican.va.

[2] St. Josemaría Escrivá, *Christ is Passing By* (New York, NY: Scepter, 1973), 103-104.

WONDER 2: Our Spiritual Father

• Quote on page 97, St. Joseph Marello, as quoted in Larry Toschi, OSJ, *St. Joseph in the Lives of Two Blesseds of the Church: Blessed Junipero Serra and Blessed Joseph Marello* (Santa Cruz, CA: Guardian of the Redeemer Books, 1994), 173.

Patron of the Universal Church

[1] Pope Leo XIII, as quoted in Francis L. Filas, SJ, *Joseph and Jesus: A Theological Study of Their Relationship* (Milwaukee, WI: Bruce Publishing Co., 1952), 117.

[2] Blessed Pope Pius IX, as quoted in Jean-Marie Gueullette, OP, *My Dear Sisters: Life of Bl. Jean-Joseph Lataste, OP, Apostle to Prisoners,* trans. George G. Christian, OP (New Hope, Kentucky: New Hope Publications, 2018), 194.

[3] St. Pope John XXIII, *Le Voci Che Da Tutti (For the Protection of St. Joseph on the Second Vatican Council),* March 19, 1961.

[4] Sacred Congregation of Rites, *Quemadmodum Deus,* December 8, 1870

Our Spiritual Father

[1] St. John Paul II, Apostolic Exhortation *Redemptoris Custos (On the Person and Mission of St. Joseph in the Life of Christ and of the Church),* no. 1, available at www.vatican.va.

[2] Jesus' words to Servant of God Sr. Mary Martha Chambon, as quoted in Visitation Sisters of Chambery, France, *Mystic of the Holy Wounds: The Life and Revelations of Sister Mary Martha Chambon,* trans. Ryan P. Plummer (St. Louis, MO: Lambfount, 2019), 98.

[3] St. Josemaría Escrivá, "A Homily: In Joseph's Workshop," as quoted in Michael D. Griffin, OCD, ed., *Saint Joseph and the Third Millennium* (Hubertus, WI: Teresian Charism Press, 1999), 356.

[4] Pope Benedict XVI, *Address in Yaounde, Cameroon (March 19, 2009),* as quoted in Jose A. Rodrigues, *The Book of Joseph: God's Chosen Father* (Toronto, ON: Ave Maria Centre of Peace, 2017), 77.

[5] St. John Paul II, *Redemptoris Custos,* no. 16.

[6] Venerable Fulton J. Sheen, *The World's First Love: Mary, Mother of God* (San Francisco, CA: Ignatius Press, 1996), 103.

[7] Pope Benedict XVI, *General Audience,* December 28, 2011.

[8] Blessed William Joseph Chaminade, *Letters of Father Chaminade,* 674 (March 19, 1833).

[9] Blessed William Joseph Chaminade, *Marian Writings,* vol. 1, ed. J.B. Armbruster, SM (Dayton, OH: Marianist Press, 1980), 114.

[10] Venerable Pope Pius XII, as quoted in Francis L. Filas, SJ, *St. Joseph & Daily Christian Living* (New York, NY: Macmillan Co., 1959), 202.

[11] Pope Leo XIII, Encyclical Letter *Quamquam Pluries* (On Devotion to St. Joseph), August 15, 1889, no. 3.

[12] St. Bernadette Soubirous, as quoted in Andrew Doze, *Saint Joseph: Shadow of the Father,* trans. Florestine Audett, RJM (Staten Island, NY: Alba House, 1992), 68.

[13] Pope Leo XIII, *Quamquam Pluries,* no. 3.

[14] St. Francis de Sales, as quoted in Fr. Marie-Dominique Philippe, OP, *The Mystery of Joseph* (Bethesda, Maryland: Zaccheus Press, 2009), 153.

Ite ad Ioseph!
[1] Venerable Pope Pius XII, as quoted in Francis L. Filas, SJ, *St. Joseph & Daily Christian Living* (New York, NY: Macmillan Co., 1959), 196.
[2] St. Lawrence of Brindisi, *Opera Omnia: Feastday Sermons*, trans. Vernon Wagner, OFM Cap (Delhi, India: Media House, 2007), 535.
[3] St. Lawrence of Brindisi, *Opera Omnia: Feastday Sermons*, trans. Vernon Wagner, OFM Cap (Delhi, India: Media House, 2007), 539.
[4] Blessed Pope Pius IX, *Quemadmodum Deus* (December 8, 1870).
[5] St. Bernard of Clairvaux, as quoted in St. Peter Julian Eymard, *Month of St. Joseph* (Cleveland, OH: Emmanuel Publications, 1948), 7.
[6] Ven. Fulton J. Sheen, *The World's First Love: Mary, Mother of God* (San Francisco, CA: Ignatius Press, 1996), 245.

WONDER 3: Young Husband of Mary

• Quote on page 113, St. Josemaría Escrivá, "A Homily: In Joseph's Workshop," as quoted in Michael D. Griffin, OCD, ed., *Saint Joseph and the Third Millennium* (Hubertus, WI: Teresian Charism Press, 1999), 341-342.

Old Men Don't Walk to Egypt
[1] Blessed William Joseph Chaminade, *Marian Writings*, vol. 1, ed. J.B. Armbruster, SM (Dayton, OH: Marianist Press, 1980), 112.
[2] Servant of God Sr. Mary Martha Chambon, as quoted in Visitation Sisters of Chambery, France, *Mystic of the Holy Wounds: The Life and Revelations of Sister Mary Martha Chambon*, trans. Ryan P. Plummer (St. Louis, MO: Lambfount, 2019), 99.

Young Husband of Mary
[1] St. Josemaría Escrivá, "A Homily: In Joseph's Workshop," as quoted in Michael D. Griffin, OCD, ed., *Saint Joseph and the Third Millennium* (Hubertus, WI: Teresian Charism Press, 1999), 341-342.
[2] Ven. Fulton J. Sheen, *The World's First Love: Mary, Mother of God* (San Francisco, CA: Ignatius Press, 1996), 91-95.
[3] St. Francis de Sales, as quoted in Rosalie Marie Levy, *Joseph the Just Man* (Derby, NY: Daughters of St. Paul, 1955), 130.
[4] Blessed William Joseph Chaminade, *Marian Writings. Vol. 1*, ed. J.B. Armbruster, SM (Dayton, OH: Marianist Press, 1980), 228.
[5] St. John Henry Newman, as quoted in Maria Cecilia Baij, OSB, *The Life of St. Joseph* (Asbury, NJ: 101 Foundation, Inc., 1996), 422.
[6] Blessed William Joseph Chaminade, *The Chaminade Legacy*, Monograph Series, Document no. 53, vol. 2, trans. Joseph Stefanelli, SM (Dayton, OH: NACMS, 2008), 411.
[7] St. Josemaría Escrivá, "A Homily: In Joseph's Workshop," as quoted in Griffin, *Saint Joseph and the Third Millennium*, 342.
[8] St. Lawrence of Brindisi, *Opera Omnia: Feastday Sermons*, trans. Vernon Wagner, OFM Cap (Delhi, India: Media House, 2007), 539.

[9] Blessed Gabriele Allegra, *Mary's Immaculate Heart: A Way to God* (Chicago, IL: Franciscan Herald Press, 1983), 56.

The Consecrated Knight
[1] Blessed Gabriele Allegra, *Mary's Immaculate Heart: A Way to God* (Chicago, IL: Franciscan Herald Press, 1983), 55.
[2] Pope Benedict XVI, as quoted in Fr. Richard W. Gilsdorf, *Go to Joseph* (Green Bay, WI: Star of the Bay Press, 2009), 127-128.
[3] Venerable Francis Xavier Nguyễn Văn Thuận, as quoted in *Magnificat* (December 2019). Vol. 21, No. 10: 436-437.
[4] St. Mary Magdalen de Pazzi, as quoted in Antony J. Patrignani, SJ, *A Manual of Practical Devotion to St. Joseph* (Rockford, IL: TAN Books, 1982), 179.
[5] St. André Bessette, as quoted in *Une pensee par jour: Saints et Bienheureux de la Nouvelle-France* (Montreal, Quebec: Mediaspaul, 2009), 20. English translation courtesy of Miss Ileana E. Salazar, MA.
[6] Venerable Pope Pius XII, as quoted in Francis L. Filas, SJ, *St. Joseph & Daily Christian Living* (New York, NY: Macmillan Co., 1959), 200.

WONDER 4: Virginal Father of Jesus

• Quote on page 125, St. Jerome, as quoted in Rev. Nicholas O'Rafferty, *Discourses on St. Joseph.* (Milwaukee, WI: Bruce Publishing Co., 1951), 37.

Feast of the Holy Spouses
[1] Ven. Fulton J. Sheen, *The World's First Love: Mary, Mother of God* (San Francisco, CA: Ignatius Press, 1996), 93.
[2] Blessed Anne Catherine Emmerich, *The Complete Visions of Anne Catherine Emmerich* (San Bernardino, CA: Catholic Book Club, 2013), 73-74.
[3] Venerable Mary of Agreda, *The Mystical City of God*, vol. 1, *The Conception* (Charlotte, NC: TAN Books, 2013), 581.
[4] St. Bonaventure, as quoted in Tarcisio Stramare, OSJ, *Saint Joseph, Guardian of the Redeemer: Text and Reflections*, trans. Paul J. Pavese, OSJ (Santa Cruz, CA: Guardian of the Redeemer Books, 1997), 95.

Virginal Father of Jesus
[1] St. Peter Damian, as quoted in Antony J. Patrignani, SJ, *A Manual of Practical Devotion to St. Joseph* (Rockford, IL: TAN Books, 1982), 193.
[2] St. Pope Siricius, *Letter to Bishop Anysius of Thessalonica*, in *The Church Teaches: Documents of the Church in English Translation* (Charlotte, NC: TAN Books, 2009).
[3] *Catechism of the Catholic Church*, no. 500.
[4] St. Jerome, as quoted in Francis L. Filas, SJ, *St. Joseph & Daily Christian Living* (New York, NY: Macmillan Co., 1959), 71.
[5] St. Bede the Venerable, as quoted in Florent Raymond Bilodeau, "The Virginity of Saint Joseph in the Latin Fathers and Medieval Ecclesiastical Writers," STL Dissertation (Baltimore, Maryland: St Mary's University, 1957), available at www.osjusa.org
[6] St. Jerome, as quoted in Mark Miravalle, *Meet Your Spiritual Father: A Brief Introduction to St. Joseph* (Stockbridge, MA: Marian Press, 2015), 39.

[7] St. Thomas Aquinas, as quoted in Fr. Marie-Dominique Philippe, OP, *The Mystery of Joseph* (Bethesda, MD: Zaccheus Press, 2010), 166.

[8] St. Francis de Sales, as quoted in Rev. Nicholas O'Rafferty, *Discourses on St. Joseph* (Milwaukee, WI: Bruce Publishing Co., 1951), 38.

[9] St. Peter Julian Eymard, as quoted in Rosalie A. Turton (ed.), *St. Joseph As Seen by Mystics and Historians* (Asbury, NJ: 101 Foundation, Inc., 2000), 107.

[10] Servant of God John A. Hardon, *St. Joseph: Foster Father of Jesus,* as quoted on www.therealpresence.org

[11] St. Pope Pius X, as quoted in O'Rafferty, *Discourses on St. Joseph,* 49.

[12] St. Pope Paul VI, "Discourse to the *Equipes Notre Dame* Movement (May 4, 1970)," as quoted in St. John Paul II, Apostolic Exhortation *Redemptoris Custos* (*On the Person and Mission of St. Joseph in the Life of Christ and of the Church*), no. 7, available at www.vatican.va.

[13] St. Stanislaus Papczyński, *St. Stanislaus Papczyński: The Life and Writings of the Marians' Founder* (Stockbridge, MA: Marian Press, 2016), 85-86.

[14] St. Augustine, as quoted in Miravalle, *Meet Your Spiritual Father,* 55-56

[15] St. Jerome, as quoted in Francis L. Filas, SJ, *Joseph and Jesus: A Theological Study of Their Relationship* (Milwaukee, WI: Bruce Publishing Co.), 34-35.

[16] St. Bernardine of Siena, as quoted in Rosalie Marie Levy, *Joseph the Just Man* (Derby, NY: Daughters of St. Paul, 1955), 39.

[17] St. Francis de Sales, as quoted in Maria Cecilia Baij, OSB, *The Life of St. Joseph* (Asbury, NJ: 101 Foundation, Inc., 1996), 388.

[18] St. John Henry Newman, as quoted in Baij, *The Life of St. Joseph,* 422.

[19] St. Thomas Aquinas, as quoted in Francis L. Filas, *Joseph: The Man Closest to Jesus* (Boston, MA: Daughters of St. Paul, 1962), 101.

[20] St. Albert the Great, as quoted in Filas, *Joseph and Jesus: A Theological Study of Their Relationship,* 62.

[21] Venerable Mary of Agreda, *The Mystical City of God,* vol. 1, *The Conception,* trans. Fiscar Marison (Charlotte, NC: TAN books, 2013), 581.

Santo Anello

[1] St. Francis de Sales, as quoted in Joseph F. Chorpenning, OSFS, ed., *Patron Saint of the New World: Spanish American Colonial Images of St. Joseph* (Philadelphia, PA: St. Joseph's University Press, 1992), 22.

[2] Blessed Anne Catherine Emmerich, *The Life of the Blessed Virgin Mary,* trans. Michael Palairet (Charlotte, NC: TAN Books, 2013), 137-138.

[3] Blessed Bartolo Longo, *Il Mese di Marzo: In Onore di San Giuseppe.* 15th ed., (Pompei, Italy: Pontificio Santuario di Pompei, 2001), 27-28. English translation courtesy of Miss Ileana E. Salazar, MA.

WONDER 5: Just and Reverent Man

• Quote on page 139, St. John Paul II, as quoted in Domenic de Domenico, OP, *True Devotion to St. Joseph and the Church* (New Hope, KY: New Hope Publications, 2003), 167.

Son of David
[1] Blessed Gabriele Allegra, *Mary's Immaculate Heart: A Way to God* (Chicago, IL: Franciscan Herald Press, 1983), 55.
[2] St. Bernardine of Siena, *St. Bernardine's Sermon on St. Joseph*, trans. Eric May, OFM, Cap (Paterson, NJ: St. Anthony Guild, 1947), 9.
[3] St. Peter Chrysologus, *Selected Sermons and St. Valerian Homilies*, trans. George E. Ganss, SJ (New York, NY: Fathers of the Church, Inc., 1953), 235.

Just and Reverent Man
[1] St. Francis de Sales, as quoted in Rosalie Marie Levy, *Joseph the Just Man* (Derby, NY: Daughters of St. Paul, 1955), 140.   .
[2] Blessed Jean Joseph Lataste, OP, as quoted in Jean-Marie Gueullette, OP, *My Dear Sisters: Life of Bl. Jean-Joseph Lataste, OP, Apostle to Prisoners*, trans. George G. Christian, OP (New Hope, Kentucky: New Hope Publications, 2018), 219.
[3] Ignace de la Potterie, SJ, *Mary in the Mystery of the Covenant*, trans. Bertrand Buby, SM (Staten Island, NY: Alba House, 1992), 37.
[4] Origen, as quoted in Francis Filas, SJ., *Joseph: The Man Closest to Jesus* (Boston, MA: Daughters of St. Paul, 1962), 145-146.
[5] St. Basil the Great, as quoted in Filas, *Joseph: The Man Closest to Jesus*, 145.
[6] St. Ephrem the Syrian, as quoted in Michael O'Carroll, CSSp, *Theotokos: A Theological Encyclopedia of the Blessed Virgin Mary* (Collegeville, MN: Liturgical Press, 1990), 123-124.
[7] St. John Chrysostom, as quoted in Fr. Richard W. Gilsdorf, *Go to Joseph* (Green Bay, WI: Star of the Bay Press, 2009), 21-22.
[8] St. Romanus the Melodist, as quoted in John Saward, *Redeemer in the Womb: Jesus Living in Mary* (San Francisco, CA: Ignatius Press, 1993), 41.
[9] St. Bernard of Clairvaux, *In Laud. Virg. Matr., Hom. 2,*. ed, J. Leclercq, OSB (Rome, 1966), 31-32.
[10] St. Thomas Aquinas, *Commentary on Matthew, I, no. 117,* as quoted in Fr. Marie-Dominique Philippe, OP, *The Mystery of Joseph* (Bethesda, MD: Zaccheus Press, 2010), 169.
[11] St. Thomas Aquinas, as quoted in Devin Schadt, *Joseph's Way: The Call to Fatherly Greatness* (San Francisco, CA: Ignatius Press, 2013), 267.
[12] St. Bridget of Sweden, as quoted in Joseph Chorpenning, OSFS, *Just Man, Husband of Mary, Guardian of Christ: An Anthology of Readings from Jeronimo Gracian's Summary of the Excellencies of St. Joseph (1597)* (Philadelphia, PA: St. Joseph's University Press, 1993), 86.
[13] St. John Paul II, Apostolic Exhortation *Redemptoris Custos* (*On the Person and Mission of St. Joseph in the Life of Christ and of the Church*), no. 20, available at www.vatican.va.
[14] St. Francis de Sales, as quoted in Levy, *Joseph the Just Man*, 137.
[15] St. Stanislaus Papczyński, *St. Stanislaus Papczyński: The Life and Writings of the Marians' Founder* (Stockbridge, MA: Marian Press, 2016), 87.

Gifts of the Holy Spirit
[1] St. Bernardine of Siena, *Sermo 2*, as quoted in *The Liturgy of the Hours*, vol.

2, *Lenten and Easter Season* (New York, NY: Catholic Book Publishing Co., 1976), 1722.
² Blessed William Joseph Chaminade, *Marian Writings*, vol. 1, ed. J.B. Armbruster, SM (Dayton, OH: Marianist Press, 1980), 226.

WONDER 6: Savior of the Savior

• Quote on page 157, Pope Leo XIII, Encyclical Letter *Quamquam Pluries* (*On Devotion to St. Joseph*), August 15, 1889, no. 3.

Seven Sorrows and Seven Joys
¹ St. Peter Julian Eymard, *Month of St. Joseph* (Cleveland, OH: Emmanuel Publications, 1948), 77.
² St. Joseph Sebastian Pelczar, as quoted in the unpublished manuscript "*Meditation 48: The Imitation of Saint Joseph in the Interior Life*," trans. Mother Agnieszka Kijowska, SSCJ. Courtesy of Sr. Mary Joseph Calore, SSCJ, and Mother Klara Slonina, SSCJ.
³ Blessed Januarius Maria Sarnelli, as quoted in *Favorite Prayers to St. Joseph* (Charlotte, NC: TAN Books, 1997), 19.
⁴ Blessed William Joseph Chaminade, *Marian Writings*, vol. 1, ed. J.B. Armbruster, SM (Dayton, OH: Marianist Press, 1980), 236.

Savior of the Savior
¹ Blessed William Joseph Chaminade, *Marian Writings*, vol. 1, ed. J.B. Armbruster, SM (Dayton, OH: Marianist Press, 1980), 234.
² Blessed William Joseph Chaminade, *Marian Writings*, vol. 1, 236.
³ Pope Pius XI, Encyclical Letter *Divini Redemptoris* (*On Atheistic Communism*), March 19, 1937, no. 81
⁴ St. Madeleine Sophie Barat, as quoted in Rosalie Marie Levy, *Joseph the Just Man* (Derby, NY: Daughters of St. Paul, 1955), 147-148.
⁵ St. Alphonsus Liguori, *The Glories of Mary* (Charlotte, NC: TAN Books, 2012), 596-597.
⁶ St. Mary Magdalen de Pazzi, as quoted in Fr. Antony-Joseph Patrignani, SJ, *A Manual of Practical Devotion to St. Joseph* (Charlotte, NC: TAN Books, 2012), 179.
⁷ Blessed Bartolo Longo, *Il Mese di Marzo: In Onore di San Giuseppe*, 15ᵗʰ ed., (Pompei, Italy: Pontificio Santuario di Pompei, 2001), 42-43. English translation courtesy of Miss Ileana E. Salazar, MA.
⁸ Blessed Concepción Cabrera de Armida, *Roses and Thorns*, ed. Ron Leonardo (Staten Island, NY: Society of St. Paul, 2007), 53.
⁹ Blessed Bartolo Longo, *Il Mese di Marzo: In Onore di San Giuseppe*, 15ᵗʰ ed., (Pompei, Italy: Pontificio Santuario di Pompei, 2001), 50. English translation courtesy of Miss Ileana E. Salazar, MA.
¹⁰ St. Francis de Sales, as quoted in Joseph Chorpenning, OSFS, ed., *The Holy Family as Prototype of the Civilization of Love: Images from the Viceregal Americas* (Philadelphia, PA: St. Joseph's University Press, 1996), 53.
¹¹ St. John Paul II, *Homily at the Shrine of St. Joseph in Kalisz, Poland*, June 4, 1997.

[12] St. Pio of Pietrelcina, as quoted in Jose A. Rodrigues, *The Book of Joseph: God's Chosen Father* (Toronto, ON: Ave Maria Centre of Peace, 2017), 126.

[13] St. Peter Julian Eymard, *Month of St. Joseph* (Cleveland, OH: Emmanuel Publications, 1948), 105.

[14] St. Joseph Marello, as quoted in Fr. Mario Pascolo, OSJ, "Memories of St. Joseph Marello," trans. Fr. John Warburton, OSJ, *Custos* (Summer 2017): 10.

Saint Joseph's Workshop

[1] St. Josemaría Escrivá, *Christ is Passing By* (New York, NY: Scepter, 1973), 119-121.

WONDER 7: Adorer of Christ

• Quote of page 171, Blessed William Joseph Chaminade, *Marian Writings*, vol. 1, ed. J.B. Armbruster, SM (Dayton, OH: Marianist Press, 1980), 235.

Perpetual Adoration

[1] St. Peter Julian Eymard, *Month of St. Joseph* (Cleveland, OH: Emmanuel Publications, 1948), 32.

[2] St. Peter Julian Eymard, *Month of St. Joseph*, 23-25, 32-33.

[3] St. Joseph Marello, as quoted in Larry Toschi, OSJ, *St. Joseph in the Lives of Two Blesseds of the Church: Blessed Junipero Serra and Blessed Joseph Marello* (Santa Cruz, CA: Guardian of the Redeemer Books, 1994), 78.

Adorer of Christ

[1] Blessed William Joseph Chaminade, *Marian Writings*, vol. 1, ed. J.B. Armbruster, SM (Dayton, OH: Marianist Press, 1980), 235.

[2] St. Peter Julian Eymard, *Month of St. Joseph* (Cleveland, OH: Emmanuel Publications, 1948), 51.

[3] Venerable Mary of Agreda, as quoted in Sandro Barbagallo, *St. Joseph in Art: Iconology and Iconography of the Redeemer's Silent Guardian* (Citta del Vaticano: Edizioni Musei Vaticani, 2014), 33.

[4] Venerable Joseph Mindszenty, *The Mother*, trans. Rev. Benedict P. Lenz, CSsR (St. Paul, MN: Radio Replies Press, 1949), 42.

[5] Blessed William Joseph Chaminade, *Marian Writings*, vol. 1, ed. J.B. Armbruster, SM (Dayton, OH: Marianist Press, 1980), 235.

[6] St. Alphonsus Liguori, *The Glories of Mary* (Charlotte, NC: TAN Books, 2012), 596.

[7] St. Francis de Sales, as quoted in Rev. Nicholas O'Rafferty, *Discourses on St. Joseph* (Milwaukee, WI: Bruce Publishing Co., 1951), 203.

[8] Blessed Concepción Cabrera de Armida, *Roses and Thorns*, ed. Ron Leonardo (Staten Island, NY: Society of St. Paul, 2007), 53.

[9] Venerable Fulton J. Sheen, *The World's First Love: Mary, Mother of God* (San Francisco, CA: Ignatius Press, 1996), 211.

[10] St. Peter Julian Eymard, *Month of St. Joseph*, 2.

[11] St. John Paul II, *Homily at the Shrine of St. Joseph in Kalisz, Poland*, June 4, 1997.

[12] St. Joseph Sebastian Pelczar, "Thoughts of St. Joseph Sebastian Pelczar for Every Day of the Year," as quoted at www.sacredheartsisters.org.

[13] Blessed Bartolo Longo, *Il Mese di Marzo: In Onore di San Giuseppe*. 15th

Edition (Pompei, Italy: Pontificio Santuario di Pompei, 2001), 63. English translation courtesy of Miss Ileana E. Salazar, MA.

The Holy House of Loreto
[1] St. Peter Canisius, as quoted in Godfrey E. Phillips, *The House of the Virgin Mary* (Manchester, NH: Sophia Institute Press, 2017), 155.
[2] Blessed Anne Catherine Emmerich, *The Complete Visons of Anne Catherine Emmerich* (San Bernardino, CA: Catholic Book Club, 2018), 76.
[3] St. John Henry Newman, as quoted in Phillips, *House of the Virgin Mary*, 3-4.
[4] St. Alphonsus Liguori, *The Glories of Mary* (Brooklyn, NY: Redemptorist Fathers, 1931), 696.
[5] St. Jerome, as quoted in Phillips, *House of the Virgin Mary*, 26.
[6] Blessed Pope Pius IX, as quoted in Phillips, *House of the Virgin Mary*, 142.
[7] St. Thérèse of Lisieux, *The Story of a Soul* (New York, NY: Cosimo Classics, 2007), 86.
[8] Blessed Baptist Spagnoli of Mantua, as quoted in Phillips, *House of the Virgin Mary*, 108.
[9] Pope Leo XIII, as quoted in Phillips, *House of the Virgin Mary*, 142.
[10] Blessed Pope Pius IX, as quoted in Phillips, *House of the Virgin Mary*, 141.
[11] Pope Benedict XIV, as quoted in St. Alphonsus Liguori, *The Glories of Mary*, 696.

WONDER 8: Silent Witness

• Quote on page 189, Blessed Gabriele Allegra, *Mary's Immaculate Heart: A Way to God* (Chicago, IL: Franciscan Herald Press, 1983), 55.

A Miraculous Staircase in New Mexico
[1] Blessed William Joseph Chaminade, *Marian Writings*, vol. 1, ed. J.B. Armbruster, SM (Dayton, OH: Marianist Press, 1980), 235.

Silent Witness
[1] St. Pope Paul VI, *Homily for the Feast of St. Joseph*, March 27, 1969.
[2] St. Peter Julian Eymard, *Month of St. Joseph* (Cleveland, OH: Emmanuel Publications, 1948), 20.
[3] Blessed William Joseph Chaminade, *Marian Writings*, vol. 1, ed. J.B. Armbruster, SM (Dayton, OH: Marianist Press, 1980), 224.
[4] Jacques-Bénigne Bossuet, as quoted in Fr. Reginald Garrigou-Lagrange, OP, *The Mother of the Savior and Our Interior Life* (Charlotte, NC: TAN Books, 1993), 283.
[5] Jacques-Bénigne Bossuet, *Oeuvres de Bossuet*, ed. Lebarcq (Paris, 1890), 3:429.
[6] Our Lady's words to St. Bridget of Sweden, as quoted in *Favorite Prayers to St. Joseph* (Charlotte, NC: TAN Books, 2009), 50.
[7] Blessed Gabriele Allegra, *Mary's Immaculate Heart: A Way to God* (Chicago, IL: Franciscan Herald Press, 1983), 55.
[8] Sr. Mary Ephrem, as quoted in Mark Miravalle, *Meet Your Spiritual Father: A Brief Introduction to St. Joseph* (Stockbridge, MA: Marian Press, 2014),

94-98. Although the Church in the United States has generally looked positively on the supernatural authenticity of these revelations, and they have been judged not to contradict the Catholic Faith, *all by themselves* they cannot form the basis for new doctrines or dogmas. They are just one important witness in an ongoing process of the whole Church in unfolding the mysteries of St. Joseph.
[9] Pope Benedict XVI, *Angelus,* December 18, 2005.

Sleeping St. Joseph
[1] Charles Péguy, *The Portal of the Mystery of Hope*, trans. David Louis Schindler, Jr. (Grand Rapids, MI: Eerdmans Publishing Company, 1996), 124-125.

WONDER 9: Patron of a Happy Death

• Quote on page 203, St. Peter Julian Eymard, *Month of St. Joseph* (Cleveland, OH: Emmanuel Publications, 1948), 101.

Votive Masses
[1] St. Francis de Sales, as quoted in Rosalie Marie Levy, *Joseph the Just Man* (Derby, NY: Daughters of St. Paul, 1955), 141.
[2] Monks of St. Joseph Abbey, *The Glories of St. Joseph* (France: Traditions Monastiques, 2009), 205.
[3] St. Joseph's words to Servant of God Sr. Mary Martha Chambon, as quoted in Visitation Sisters of Chambery, France, *Mystic of the Holy Wounds: The Life and Revelations of Sister Mary Martha Chambon*, trans. Ryan P. Plummer (St. Louis, MO: Lambfount, 2019), 98.
[4] St Bernardine of Siena, *Sermo 2*, as quoted in *The Liturgy of the Hours*, vol. 2, *Lenten and Easter Season* (New York, NY: Catholic Book Publishing Co., 1976), 1722.

Patron of a Happy Death
[1] St. Alphonsus Liguori, as quoted in Rosalie Marie Levy, *Joseph the Just Man* (Derby, NY: Daughters of St. Paul, 1955), 144.
[2] St. Bernardine of Siena, *St. Bernardine's Sermon on St. Joseph*, trans. Eric May, OFM, Cap (Paterson, NJ: St. Anthony Guild, 1947), 37.
[3] St. Bernardine of Siena, as quoted in Blessed William Joseph Chaminade, *The Chaminade Legacy*, Monograph Series, Document no. 53, vol. 2, trans. Joseph Stefanelli, SM (Dayton, OH: NACMS, 2008), 414-415.
[4] St. Peter Julian Eymard, *Month of St. Joseph* (Cleveland, OH: Emmanuel Publications, 1948), 101.
[5] Blessed Anne Catherine Emmerich, as quoted in Rosalie A. Turton, ed., *St. Joseph as Seen by Mystics and Historians* (Asbury, NJ: 101 Foundation, Inc., 2000), 344.
[6] Blessed Anne Catherine Emmerich, *The Complete Visions of Anne Catherine Emmerich* (San Bernardino, CA: Catholic Book Club, 2013), 130.
[7] St. Bernardine of Siena, *St. Bernardine's Sermon on St. Joseph*, 40.
[8] St. Francis de Sales, as quoted in Joseph F. Chorpenning, OSFS, ed., *Patron Saint of the New World: Spanish American Colonial Images of St. Joseph* (Philadelphia, PA: St. Joseph's University Press, 1992), 26.

[9] St. Francis de Sales, as quoted in Levy, *Joseph the Just Man*, 142.

[10] St. Pope John XXIII, *Homily for the Canonization of Gregorio Barbarigo* (May 26, 1960). English translation courtesy of Miss Ileana E. Salazar, MA.

[11] St. George Preca, *San Guzepp* (Societas Doctrinae Christianae: Zabbar, Malta, 1997), 26.

[12] St. Lawrence of Brindisi, *Opera Omnia: Feastday Sermons*, trans. Vernon Wagner, OFM Cap (Delhi, India: Media House, 2007), 538.

[13] Blessed Bartolo Longo, *Il Mese di Marzo: In Onore di San Giuseppe*. 15th ed., (Pompei, Italy: Pontificio Santuario di Pompei, 2001), 269. English translation courtesy of Miss Ileana E. Salazar, MA.

[14] Venerable Mary of Ágreda, *The Mystical City of God*, vol. 3, *The Transfixion*, trans. Fiscar Marison (Charlotte, NC: TAN Books, 2013), 154.

[15] St. Peter Julian Eymard, *Month of St. Joseph*, 90-91.

[16] St. Peter Julian Eymard, *Month of St. Joseph*, 84.

[17] St. Bernardine of Siena, as quoted in Antony J. Patrignani, SJ, *A Manual of Practical Devotion to St. Joseph* (Rockford, IL: TAN Books, 1982), 226.

[18] Blessed Anne Catherine Emmerich, as quoted in Turton, *St. Joseph as Seen by Mystics and Historians*, 344.

[19] St. Peter Julian Eymard, *Month of St. Joseph*, 84.

[20] Venerable Mary of Ágreda, as quoted in Jose A. Rodrigues, *The Book of Joseph: God's Chosen Father* (Toronto, ON: Ave Maria Centre of Peace, 2017), 91.

Pious Union of St. Joseph

[1] St. Luigi Guanella, as quoted in *L'Osservatore Romano* (March 16, 2011), 9.

[2] Pope Leo XIII, as quoted in Rev. Nicholas O'Rafferty, *Discourses on St. Joseph* (Milwaukee, WI: Bruce Publishing Co., 1951), 169.

[3] Blessed Bartolo Longo, *Il Mese di Marzo: In Onore di San Giuseppe*. 15th ed. (Pompei, Italy: Pontificio Santuario di Pompei, 2001), 175. English translation courtesy of Miss Ileana E. Salazar, MA.

WONDER 10: Terror of Demons

• Quote on page 217, St. Alphonsus Liguori, as quoted in Maria Cecilia Baij, OSB, *The Life of St. Joseph* (Asbury, NJ: 101 Foundation, Inc., 1996), 416.

Saint Joseph the Worker

[1] St. Josemaría Escrivá, *Christ is Passing By* (New York, NY: Scepter, 1973), 115.

[2] Pope Pius XI, Encyclical Letter *Divini Redemptoris* (*On Atheistic Communism*), March 19, 1937.

[3] Ven. Pope Pius XII, *Allocution to the Christian Association of Italian Workers*, (May 1, 1955.

Terror of Demons

[1] St. Anthony Mary Claret, *The Golden Key to Heaven* (Buffalo, NY: Immaculate Heart Publications, 1955), 132.

[2] Blessed William Joseph Chaminade, *Marian Writings*, vol. 1, ed. J.B. Armbruster, SM (Dayton, OH: Marianist Press, 1980), 118.

[3] Blessed Bartolo Longo, *Il Mese di Marzo: In Onore di San Giuseppe*. 15th

ed., (Pompei, Italy: Pontificio Santuario di Pompei, 2001), 156. English translation courtesy of Miss Ileana E. Salazar, MA.

[4] Blessed Bartolo Longo, *Il Mese di Marzo: In Onore di San Giuseppe*. 15th ed. (Pompei, Italy: Pontificio Santuario di Pompei, 2001), 87-88. English translation courtesy of Miss Ileana E. Salazar, MA.

[5] Blessed William Joseph Chaminade, *Marian Writings*, vol. 1, ed. J.B. Armbruster, SM (Dayton, OH: Marianist Press, 1980), 117.

[6] Blessed James Alberione, *Mary, Queen of Apostles* (Boston, MA: Daughters of St. Paul, 1976), 142.

[7] St. Madeleine Sophie Barat, as quoted in Rosalie Marie Levy, *Joseph the Just Man* (Derby, NY: Daughters of St. Paul, 1955), 147-148.

[8] St. John Paul II, Apostolic Exhortation *Redemptoris Custos* (*On the Person and Mission of St. Joseph in the Life of Christ and of the Church*), no. 8, available at www.vatican.va.

[9] St. Alphonsus LIguori, *The Glories of Mary* (Charlotte, NC: TAN Books, 2012), 592.

[10] St. Francis de Sales, as quoted in Levy, *Joseph the Just Man*, 138.

[11] Pope Leo XIII, *Quamquam Pluries* (*On Devotion to St. Joseph*), August 15, 1889.

[12] St. Thomas Aquinas, as quoted in Rev. Nicholas O'Rafferty, *Discourses on St. Joseph* (Milwaukee, WI: Bruce Publishing Co., 1951), 208.

[13] St. Augustine, as quoted in Rev. Nicholas O'Rafferty, *Discourses on St. Joseph*, 208.

[14] St. Teresa of Avila, as quoted in Joseph F. Chorpenning, OSFS, *Just Man, Husband of Mary, Guardian of Christ: An Anthology of Readings from Jeronimo Gracian's Summary of the Excellencies of St. Joseph (1597)* (Philadelphia, PA: St. Joseph's University Press, 1993), 166.

[15] St. Ambrose, as quoted in Rev. Nicholas O'Rafferty, *Discourses on St. Joseph*, 206.

[16] St. Alphonsus Liguori, as quoted in Rev. Nicholas O'Rafferty, *Discourses on St. Joseph*, 207.

[17] St. Bernardine of Siena, as quoted in Mark Miravalle, *Meet Your Spiritual Father: A Brief Introduction to St. Joseph* (Stockbridge, MA: Marian Press, 2015), 62-63.

[18] St. Pio of Pietrelcina, as quoted in Jose A. Rodrigues, *The Book of Joseph: God's Chosen Father* (Toronto, ON: Ave Maria Centre of Peace, 2017), 126.

[19] Blessed Bartolo Longo, *Il Mese di Marzo: In Onore di San Giuseppe*. 15th Edition (Pompei, Italy: Pontificio Santuario di Pompei, 2001), 13. English translation courtesy of Miss Ileana E. Salazar, MA.

Privileges of Devotion to St. Joseph

[1] St. Josemaría Escrivá, *The Forge* (London, UK: Scepter, 1987), par. 554.

[2] St. George Preca, *San Guzepp* (Societas Doctrinae Christianae: Zabbar, Malta, 1997), 6.

[3] Blessed Maria Teresa of St. Joseph, *Mother Mary Teresa of St. Joseph: An Autobiography* (Wauwatosa, WI: Carmelite Convent, 1953), 25-26.

[4] Blessed Maria Teresa of St. Joseph, *Mother Mary Teresa of St. Joseph: An*

Autobiography, 34.

[5] Venerable Mary of Agreda, *The Mystical City of God*, vol. 3, *The Transfixion*, trans. Fiscar Marison (Charlotte, NC: TAN Books, 2013), 166-168.

[6] Our Lady's words to Venerable Mary of Agreda, as quoted in *The Mystical City of God*, vol. 3, *The Transfixion*, 166-168.

[7] Blessed Concepción Cabrera de Armida, *Roses and Thorns*, ed. Ron Leonardo (Staten Island, NY: Society of St. Paul, 2007), 52.

APPENDIX B

AFTER THE CONSECRATION

[1] St. Alphonsus Liguori, as quoted in Rev. Nicholas O'Rafferty, *Discourses on St. Joseph* (Milwaukee, WI: Bruce Publishing Co., 1951), 236.

[2] Blessed Marie-Léonie Paradis, as quoted in *Une pensee par jour: Saints et Bienheureux de la Nouvelle-France* (Montreal, QC: Mediaspaul, 2009), 25. English translation courtesy of Miss Ileana E. Salazar, MA.

COMMISSIONED ART
ON ST. JOSEPH

St. Joseph and the Christ Child by Jacob Zumo (2019). Commissioned by Fr. Donald H. Calloway, MIC.

St. Joseph, Patron of the Universal Church by Gabrielle Schadt (2019). Commissioned by Fr. Donald H. Calloway, MIC.

St. Joseph Assumed into Heaven by Adonai Camilleri Cauchi (Malta-Gozo, 2019). Commissioned by Fr. Donald H. Calloway, MIC.

St. Joseph and Saints by Cecilia Lawrence (2018). Saints on left (from top to bottom): St. Stanislaus Papczyński, St. Dominic, St. John Paul II. Saints on right (from top to bottom): St. Philomena, St. Andreas Wouters, Blessed Bartolo Longo. Commissioned by Fr. Donald H. Calloway, MIC.

St. Joseph by Manuel Farrugia (2019). With St. George Preca (upper right) and Blessed Nazju Falzon (lower right). Commissioned by Fr. Donald H. Calloway, MIC.

The Crowning of St. Joseph by Manuel Farrugia (2019). Commissioned by Fr. Donald H. Calloway, MIC.

St. Joseph, Terror of Demons by Bernadette Carstensen (2019). Commissioned by Fr. Donald H. Calloway, MIC.

1. St. Joseph Marello
2. St. Bernardine of Siena
3. St. Francis de Sales
4. St. Teresa of Avila
5. Venerable Fulton Sheen
6. Blessed Petra of St. Joseph
7. Pope Leo XIII
8. St. Peter Julian Eymard
9. St. Lawrence of Brindisi
10. St. Leonardo Murialdo
11. Blessed Pope Pius IX
12. Venerable Mary of Ágreda
13. Blessed Anne Catherine Emmerich

14. St. André Bessette
15. Venerable Pope Pius XII
16. Blessed Jean-Joseph Lataste
17. St. Luigi Guanella
18. Blessed Maria Teresa of St. Joseph
19. Blessed Maria Repetto
20. Blessed William Joseph Chaminade
21. St. Josemaría Escrivá
22. Pope Benedict XV
23. St. Pope John XXIII
24. St. Alphonsus Liguori
25. Blessed Gabriele Allegra
26. St. John Paul II

Matthew 20:23 by Blair Piras (2019). From left to right: Mary, Jesus, St. Joseph. Commissioned by Fr. Donald H. Calloway, MIC.

ABOUT THE AUTHOR

Father Donald Calloway, MIC, a convert to Catholicism, is a member of the Congregation of Marian Fathers of the Immaculate Conception. Before his conversion, he was a high school dropout who had been kicked out of a foreign country, institutionalized twice, and thrown in jail multiple times. After his radical conversion, he earned a BA in philosophy and theology from the Franciscan University of Steubenville, Ohio; MDiv and STB degrees from the Dominican House of Studies in Washington, D.C.; and an STL in Mariology from the International Marian Research Institute in Dayton, Ohio.

In addition to *Consecration to St. Joseph*, he has also written *10 Wonders of the Rosary* (Marian Press, 2019), *26 Champions of the Rosary* (Marian Press, 2017), *How to Pray the Rosary* (Marian Press, 2017), the best-selling books *Champions of the Rosary: The History and Heroes of a Spiritual Weapon* (Marian Press, 2016); *Under the Mantle: Marian Thoughts from a 21ˢᵗ Century Priest* (Marian Press, 2013); and *No Turning Back: A Witness to Mercy* (Marian Press, 2010), a bestseller that recounts his dramatic conversion story. He also is the author of the book *Purest of All Lilies: The Virgin Mary in the Spirituality of St. Faustina* (Marian Press, 2008). He introduced and arranged *Marian Gems: Daily Wisdom on Our Lady* (Marian Press, 2014); *Rosary Gems: Daily Wisdom on the Holy Rosary* (Marian Press, 2015); and *St. Joseph Gems: Daily Wisdom on Our Spiritual Father* (Marian Press, 2018). Further, he has written many academic articles and is the editor of a number of books, including: *The Immaculate Conception in the Life of the Church* (Marian Press, 2004) and *The Virgin Mary and Theology of the Body* (Marian Press, 2005).

Father Calloway is the vicar provincial and vocation director for the Mother of Mercy Province.

To learn more about Marian vocations, visit
marian.org/vocations
or visit
Fr. Calloway's website,
fathercalloway.com

BRING HOME YOUR SPIRITUAL FATHER!

10" x 18" gallery-wrapped canvas prints.

Handmade at the National Shrine of The Divine Mercy

St. Joseph and the Child Jesus
Y87-JC10GW

St. Joseph Assumed into Heaven
Y87-JA10GW

St. Joseph, Patron of the Universal Church
Y87-PA10GW

Call 1-800-462-7426 or visit fathercalloway.com

Commissioned by Fr. Donald Calloway, MIC,
these newly created images are available for the first time!

The Immaculata and the Terror of Demons
Y87-IM10GW

St. Joseph, Terror of Demons
Y87-TE10GW

St. Joseph, Terror of Demons
Y87-DD10GW

Call 1-800-462-7426 or visit fathercalloway.com

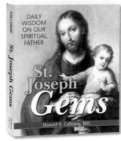

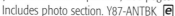
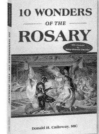
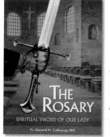

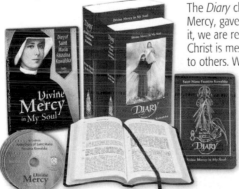